JOHNNY

FROM
PEANUTS
TO PLASMA

THE LIFE STORY OF
JOHNNY D. WILLS

outskirts
press

DEDICATION

This book is dedicated to my wife, Juanita Wills,
to my children, Harvey, Wendy Echo, Kelly Denise,
and to my three granddaughters and one grandson.
Their love and support have made this book a pleasure to write.

To: April,

Thanks so much! I hope you will enjoy my story. Wishing you the best always,

Johnny Wills

SPECIAL THANKS

My sincere thanks to Sherrie Farmer, a born-again Christian in Johnson City, Tennessee. Without her inspiring comments, this book would never have been written.

A very special thanks to my brother and my sister-in-law, Don and Carolyn Wills, of Fritch, Texas, for their many tireless hours spent on editing my story.

A special thanks to my daughter, Kelly Wills Sears, who has stood by me through the entire process of writing my book and has assisted in the title selection, writing the prologue, selecting and organizing the photos, and so much more.

And to Scott DeBoer, Cheryl Gable Marks, Misty Fowler Melton, and award-winning writer, John DeBoer, for their help in making my book become a reality.

My deepest appreciation to Edna Johnson, Jamie Johnson, Kelly Wills Sears, David S. Sears, Pam Wills Keller, Cheryl Gable Marks, Clyde Edwards, Scott DeBoer, Peggy Wills Freeman, David G. Sears, Jennifer Wills Bussey, Delores Rodriguez, Debbie Freeman, Larry Carmichael, Bobby Jenkins, Lori Anderson, and Richard Edwards for their generous financial contributions toward the publishing of my book.

Table of Contents

Prologue

IN WRITING THIS book, I have tried to be as honest and true to the stories as I remember them happening or as they were told to me. I have written this book with dialogue that was used in the Deep South with the hope that I do not offend anyone reading this text. The dialogue is not a reflection of how I speak today, nor is it a reflection of the way any of my family members speak in modern times. However, it is a true representation of how things were in the Deep South when I was growing up there.

In addition, I have used some profanity to show the raw emotion that some people expressed in the stories that I tell. I do not mean to offend any readers, but I am writing the truth as I heard it or as it was recited to me. Also, some names have been changed to protect those portrayed in a negative light, as I do not wish to cause any bad feelings with family members of those individuals.

I am not a perfect man, and I have never proclaimed to be one. I am telling my life story because I have often been told that my life could be portrayed on "the big screen." My life has been full of ups and downs, good and bad decisions, and happy and sad times. But through it all, I am still me, and I am proud of my accomplishments, my family, and my life. My mistakes have helped make me the man that I am today. I hope you will all understand that, respect that, and continue to love me for the man you have always known.

And now, I share my life story with you....

-Johnny

CHAPTER 1

In the Beginning

I WAS BORN Johnnie David Wills in Webster County Georgia on February 11, 1939. My parents were Bernard Sidney Wills and Johnnie Lee Chambers Wills. I was born at home as were all my siblings except my youngest brother, James Lewis (Jimmy), who was born in a hospital in Americus, Georgia. I weighed just over seven pounds and had dark brown hair and blue eyes. People would say to my mother, "Well, ain't she got pretty blue eyes." Mama would reply, "It's a boy." I was named after my mother, Johnnie Lee and my paternal grandfather, Dave Sidney Wills. Grandpa Dave died in 1941 at the age of 67. I have no recollection of him whatsoever.

In late 1941, my father purchased a farm adjacent to where we were living. The farm contained 256 acres and had a house and barn. It had woods, open fields, a pecan orchard, and on one side it was bordered by Bear Creek. The purchase price of the farm was $1,500.00. We moved into our new home in the fall of 1941. The distance we had to move was less than half a mile, and we moved everything by mule and wagon.

Although I have a few vague memories of things that happened at my birth home, my first vivid memory took place on December 7, 1941. My uncle, Lucius Black, stopped by the house that evening and told us the Japanese had attacked Pearl Harbor. That's when the United States got involved in World War II. I recall spending much time looking at all the pictures of damage and destruction that took place at Pearl Harbor in Life Magazines during the following weeks.

I had two brothers at that time: Gerald Gordon (Jerry), who was a little more than four years older than me, and Melvin Maurice who was more than ten years older. Jerry was mentally retarded, although my Mom used the word afflicted. It's not clear to me if he was born that way or if it resulted from an extremely high temperature that he had when he was a baby, that resulted in brain damage. I recall my parents taking him to a specialist in Atlanta to see if anything could be done for him. It could not. It was obvious that he was extremely near-sighted as he would get to within four to six inches of an object to see it. My parents took him for an eye exam and had glasses made, but he wouldn't wear them. If you tried to put the glasses on him, he would immediately jerk them off. Although Jerry was older than I, we were almost the same size, therefore we played well together; that is, for the most part. One of our favorite things to do was wrestle. We would get out in the sandy front yard and really go at it. We would throw each other to the ground and pile on top of each other. I don't think we ever got hurt.

Our house had four rooms with a hallway running through the center of the house. The dining area was at the end of the hall adjacent to the kitchen, and a sitting area was located at the other end of the hall. The other three rooms were bedrooms. Each room had a fireplace. We had no electricity, plumbing, running water, or telephone. The well was on the side of the house near a huge red oak tree. A large black oak was in the front yard, and there were also a pecan tree and a Chinaberry tree in the yard. The outhouse was located about seventy-five yards from the back of the house. A path led through the bushes to reach it.

The old barn stood on the other side of the dirt road. It had a hay loft, stalls for the farm animals such as horses, mules, or cattle and a shelter for a wagon or other farm equipment. My Dad was a farmer. We grew peanuts and corn. We had two cows, Dottie and Sukie, with Sukie being the first offspring of Dottie. The cows provided us with milk and butter. A new calf would be born every year, and any male calves would be slaughtered at about six months of age to provide us with beef. Female calves would be sold. We always had hogs which provided us with pork and lard for frying food. We had a hen house and a yard full of chickens; therefore, we had plenty of eggs. If Mama wanted to have fried chicken for dinner, she would go out and wring the neck of a young, frying sized chicken, scald it, pluck it, and fry it. I remember my brother Melvin always saying, "Fried chicken is my favorite vegetable!"

Speaking of vegetables, we had a large garden and grew a variety of veggies. The garden had a fence around it to keep the rabbits out and a scarecrow to keep away the birds. So, it's easy to see that we were pretty much self-sufficient. About the only thing we had to buy in the way of groceries were sugar and flour. We took corn to a grist mill to be ground into cornmeal.

Although my brother Jerry was afflicted, he was smart in certain ways. It was obvious that he could not attend public school, so Daddy went to Preston, the county seat of Webster County, to meet with the county school superintendent and was able to get some beginner books. I well remember that first-grade reading book, *Dick and Jane,* along with Baby Sally and the pets, Spot and Puff. It wasn't long until Jerry was reading the book very well. Then he started reading the Bible. I don't recall him reading anything other than those. It was amazing. He seemed to be able to pronounce every word, even proper names that my parents couldn't pronounce. Jerry had a puzzle map of the United States and he soon learned all the states and capitals. I learned them along with him, as we spent lots of time quizzing each other. Jerry also liked to play in the yard. He liked to make a road by pushing a brick through the sand in a snake-like manner for 50 to 75 feet until he decided to make a turn-around place. Sometimes he would drive that brick back and forth on his road for hours. I remember a few times I would deliberately mess up his road. I could be a little meanie if I wanted! He also liked to make mountains by taking a handful of sand and pouring it in a pile until it was 10 to 15 inches high. I also tore his mountains down a few times. Bad, bad, bad!

Our house was built on a brick foundation, and the house stood about two feet off the ground. One day Jerry and I were playing under the house. We had been playing for some time when Mama came out calling and looking for us. We wouldn't answer, so she started looking under the house. She walked all the way around the house, looking underneath on each side. We kept hiding behind the brick chimney. Then she began to panic, and I heard her say, "Oh my God, they've probably gone to that creek!" Bear Creek was almost a half mile down

the hill from the house, and she started running down the hill screaming for us. When she couldn't find us at the creek, she ran back up the
hill, completely exhausted. There we were, standing in the front yard
watching her. She probably wanted to tear our behinds up, but she was
so relieved to see us and that we were OK, that all we got was a tongue
lashing. We never did that again, or at least I didn't.

Jerry loved to get up early in the morning to watch the sun rise. To
him, the sun was simply rising from just beyond the open field he could
see on the horizon. One morning he decided to go over to that point
where he could see it better, so he started walking in that direction. A
few minutes later Mama and Daddy didn't see him in the yard, and they
started looking for him. Daddy saw his tracks where he had crossed the
dirt road and headed in the direction of the open field. Daddy tracked
him across the pasture, through a small patch of scrub oaks, and spotted
him almost across the open field and headed toward the deep woods. A
couple more minutes and he would have been in those woods and possibly not been found in time to save him. On another occasion, Mama
looked out and saw Jerry following something across the yard. He was
bending over to see it better. Mama went out to find that he was following a small rattlesnake!

In the winter of 1942-1943 I saw my first snow. It wasn't much, but
enough that Mama raked up enough to make us some snow cream. That
was a real treat!

The following spring, I remember Mama having a colored woman
come over to help her do some house cleaning. She brought her son
with her who was about the same age as me. Jerry had gotten a little red
wagon for Christmas, and the little colored boy and I were pulling each
other around the yard. Mama came out to let me know that I couldn't
be playing with him because white boys and colored boys didn't play
together. I didn't know why. Now I realize that was my first encounter
with prejudice and discrimination. It wouldn't be my last. A while later
Mama called me in for dinner, which is now what I call lunch. We were
sitting in the dining room eating when I noticed the colored woman and
her son eating in the kitchen. "Why are they eating in the kitchen?", I
asked. "Because colored people are not allowed to eat together with
white people," she replied.

Late one afternoon Jerry went to the outhouse to do his business. He had gotten in the habit of sometimes taking tiny steps when he was walking. These steps were no more than two or three inches long. He decided to take such steps on the way back from the outhouse, which meant it would take at least an hour to get back to the house, and it would be totally dark by then. Mama opened the door and yelled, "Hurry up, Jerry. The old bobcats will be coming out soon, and they might get you." Mischievous Little Johnnie got an idea. He would sneak out and pretend to be a bobcat! So, I went up the path without Jerry seeing me and hid behind a bush. Jerry was almost to my position when I heard him say, "I ain't scared of them old bobcats. I'll outrun them." I jumped from behind the bush and shouted, "You can't outrun this old bobcat!" Jerry screamed and took off running as fast as he could, screaming all the way to the house and nearly tore the screen door off trying to get inside. He was white as a sheet and absolutely terrified. I came in right behind him. "What is going on?", Mama asked. I told her, and she said, "Don't you ever do anything like that again. You could drive him into hysterics!" I never did it again, though that would probably not be my last mischievous act.

That fall, a tropical depression stalled over South Georgia, and it rained constantly for four or five days. All the streams were overflowing their banks, and then the worst happened. Earthen dams began breaking; almost every one of them in South Georgia. Heron's Mill Pond, located about five miles from us broke, sending water rushing down Bear Creek. Mama had gone outside about 8 PM when she heard a loud thud down toward the creek. Daddy went to investigate. He found the bridge intact, but the road was washed out on both ends of the bridge. A few minutes later a car came by and was headed down the hill toward the creek. The driver spotted the damage and was able to stop in time to avoid a disaster. It was weeks before the road was repaired and passable again. A flood like this wouldn't happen again in South Georgia for more than 40 years.

That open field that Jerry was crossing when he was looking for the sunrise was located on a slight rise and was very sandy. We had been told that it was likely the site of an Indian village. The ground was littered with arrowheads and many other pieces of flint rock. If the field was plowed and a hard rain came, you could walk around and find many nice arrowheads. On one occasion I found a perfect tomahawk. Instead of preserving it, I made a handle for it and used it as a toy, eventually causing damage to it. I also put a shaft on some of the arrowheads and shot them with my homemade bow.

Located out behind our house in a small open area was a perfect circle, maybe six or eight feet in diameter, where nothing grew. Mama and Daddy said it might be the burial site of an Indian. One day Jerry and I decided to dig it up. After digging for an hour or so and reaching a depth of about four feet, we began finding bones. We were so excited! We grabbed a handful of bones and ran to the house saying, "Look! We found that old Indian!" Daddy examined the bones and determined that they were dog bones. That was later confirmed by contacting Mr. Berry Ford, the gentleman who had lived there before us. He said one of his dogs had died many years earlier and had been buried at that location.

About once a year my paternal grandmother, Mattie Wills and her mother would come and live with us for about a month. After Grandpa Dave Wills died in 1941, Grandma Mattie stopped keeping house and began staying with her children. There were eight of them, and she would stay about a month and move on to the next one. Great Grandma Slocumb was always with her. She was the oldest person I had ever seen. In 1949 her youngest son, Ruric, hosted a 95th birthday party for her. They put 95 candles on her cake and lit them. What a sight to see! Grandma Slocumb loved to tell stories about the old days.

Our favorite was one from 1864 when she was 10 years old and in the fourth grade. She said that one day a group of soldiers came to her school, some walking and some on horseback. They were soldiers from Union General Sherman's Army as he marched through Georgia. She said they searched every room at the school, apparently looking for Confederate soldiers that might be hiding. After finding none, they asked for food and then went on their way.

I only remember having one pet in those early years. Mama and Daddy didn't believe in having animals in the house, so we had an outside dog whose name was "Sport". He was a medium-sized black dog with a curled-up tail. He was a good dog, but old. One day "Sport" died, and Mama had to bury him. It was a sad time, and we both cried for a while.

As I mentioned earlier, my Daddy was a farmer. We had two mules. I don't remember their names, but they were used to till the land, cultivate the crops, pull the wagon, and any other jobs we needed them to do. After the crops were harvested in the fall of 1943, Daddy sold the mules, and in December of that year, bought a brand-new Model B John Deere tractor. It was bright green, my favorite color, with yellow wheels. He had it parked under a shelter at the barn. I went out to see it, and Daddy let me sit on it. I remember very well that it was a cold and rainy December day. Mama came out and said, "Johnnie, you get back in this house. You'll catch your death of pneumonia out there in that weather." I pitched a pure fit but had to come back in the house anyway.

The following spring, Daddy let me ride on the tractor with him over to Grandpa Gordon Chambers' house to help him do some little job. Whatever it was, it didn't take long, and we were ready to go home. The tractor was backed up near a wooden fence, and Grandpa was standing behind the large, left rear wheel. They were chatting, the tractor engine was running, and I thought we were ready to go. I reached over and engaged the hand clutch. Instead of going forward, we shot backward. By the time Daddy could stop the tractor, we had pushed Grandpa back against the fence. The fence broke with him pinned between it and the tractor wheel. Thankfully, Grandpa was not seriously hurt, due to the fence giving way so easily.

One day in April 1945, Mom and Dad told me that I would be going over to Grandma Rushie Chambers' to spend a couple of days. I didn't know why I was going, and I didn't ask, but I didn't mind, because Grandma had promised to take me fishing the next time I came to see her. After lunch on my first day there, we went out to dig some worms for fish bait. We went to a place just outside the kitchen door where Grandma would throw out the dishwater after doing the dishes. A big pile of rocks was at that location so that the dirt wouldn't wash away when she poured out the dishwater. We moved a couple of big rocks and found an abundance of worms. Now we were on our way to the pond. It wasn't really a pond, but rather a site where a pond had once been. The dam had washed out years earlier due to a flood, but there was a stream and a large, deep hole of water next to the old dam.

That's where we fished. I was barely six years old and had never been fishing before. Grandma baited my hook and helped me throw it in the water. She told me to watch my cork and to jerk if it went under. It never moved the whole afternoon. Meanwhile, Grandma caught eight or nine hand-sized bream. She cleaned the fish when we got home and fried them for supper. That was the first time I had eaten bream, a thoroughly new experience for me. We went fishing again the following afternoon, and I caught my first fish, but only one. Grandma caught nothing. She said, "I guess we caught 'em all. "

After spending two days with Grandma, I was ready to go home and what a surprise I got. There in the bed with Mama was a tiny little baby. I said, "Who is that?" She said, "This is your new baby brother, Don Raymond." She had wanted to name him after her two brothers, Eldon and Raymond, but Eldon Raymond didn't sound right; neither did Raymond Eldon, so she took Don out of Eldon to give him his name, Don Raymond. My next question was, " Where did you get him?" I didn't get an answer to that, but I kept bugging her for about a week until one day she patted her tummy and said, "From right inside here." I asked, "How did he get in there, and how'd he get out?" I don't think she knew exactly how to answer that, but she finally replied, "God made it happen." I accepted that, at least for the time, and when Daddy came in from work that evening I said to Mama, "Why don't you get another baby out of your tummy for us?" She said, "You shut your mouth and don't ever say that again!" I don't think Daddy heard that, or if he did, he didn't say anything. I never brought it up again, ever! I think I was 15 before I finally got it all figured out.

A lot happened in 1945. World War II ended when Hitler was defeated in Germany, and the Japanese surrendered after the U.S. dropped two atomic bombs on them. Mama was so happy about the war ending, because her two brothers would soon be coming home. Her first cousin, also "Aunt" Gladys' brother, John Willard Laye, was not so fortunate. He was killed in 1944 when his tank was blown up in Germany. He had been a member of General George Patton's armored division.

My brother, Melvin, graduated from high school that year. At that time schools had only 11 grades, but a 12th would be added very soon. Since Melvin was more than ten years older than me, we didn't spend much time together. He mostly hung out with his older friends. That would soon change, and I would become his favorite brother. I do remember Melvin playing basketball in high school and sometimes coming home with his knees and elbows all skinned up. Apparently, Melvin was also a lady's man or at least thought he was. For a while he would come home almost daily with some girl's hair bow. All the teenage girls wore bows in their hair, and Melvin would swipe one every chance he got. Mama fussed at him for doing that but to no avail. He had a nice collection that was displayed on a board in his closet. I had a collection also but not hair bows. My collection consisted of Indian Head Cents, V-Nickels, and a few other coins.

We also got our first car in 1945. It was a 1935 Ford; black and powered by a flat-head V-8. There were no power brakes and the headlights were of poor quality as compared to today's standards. Melvin used to tell me in a jokingly way that if he wanted to stop, he would have to open the door and drag his foot. He said the lights were so dim, you had to strike a match to tell if they were on or not! Melvin was excited to have a car to drive, but he didn't drive it very long. It would be a total loss by the end of summer. One of the first things Melvin wanted to do was get a driver's license. It was easy to get a license in those days; very little in the way of questions, no road signs to learn, and no eye exam. So, Melvin went to Preston to get his license. A state trooper from the Americus office would come to Preston one afternoon per week to administer driver's license exams. The trooper gave Melvin a road test and everything went fine until they were returning to the exam station. The trooper yelled, "Slow down!" But Melvin couldn't slow down because the car had mechanical brakes, which meant the only power you had was what you could apply with your foot. They came into the station almost on two wheels and finally stopped before hitting anything. Melvin said it scared the crap out of the trooper and the trooper said, "I shouldn't even give you a license!" But he did and that might have been a mistake.

Mama also tried her hand at driving. Daddy let her drive to the mailbox one day, which was about half a mile away. On the way back, unable to slow down enough, she hit the gate post and put a nice dent in the right front fender. I remember her crying for hours. It would be 30 years before she would attempt to drive again.

Melvin was an accident waiting to happen and happen it did. First of all, he was near-sighted, not nearly as bad as Don and me, but bad enough that he should have been wearing corrective lenses. Like Jerry, he would not wear glasses, but for a different reason. Glasses were not hep, and the girls might not like him.

The first major accident happened one night when he was heading down GA Hwy 41 toward Preston. As he approached Kinchafoonee Creek, he spotted two mules pulling a wagon on the bridge, coming in his direction. He tried to stop but couldn't. This was a one lane bridge with no chance to pass. Not wanting to hit the mules head on and injuring them or possibly killing them, Melvin attempted to go between the wagon and the steel frame on the side of the bridge. There was not enough room. The left fender of the car took both wheels out from under the wagon, and the right front fender hit the end of the bridge, curling it back. When the car stopped it was hanging over the edge of the bridge, ready to drop into the creek some 20 feet below. Fortunately, no one was hurt, including the mules. Only cosmetic damage was done to the car, and Daddy was able to repair it somewhat with a ball peen hammer.

A relatively short time afterwards, Melvin left the house one Saturday evening to pick up some friends and go out on the town, the town being Dawson. Melvin didn't return home that night. The next morning, he still wasn't home. Then at about 8 or 9 AM a car pulled into our yard. Mama anxiously went out, fearing the worst. Mr. Monk West, an acquaintance of ours, got out of the car and asked in his slow southern drawl, "Is Bernard home?" Mama came back in the house crying and Daddy went out to get the news. Monk was one of the few people in the neighborhood who had a telephone. He had received a call from Daddy's brother, Cleo, that morning saying that Melvin had been in an accident but was OK. Melvin had refused to seek any medical attention, and instead, went to Uncle Cleo's home to spend the night.

It happened when Melvin and his friends were headed down the street toward The Green Top, a bar and grill, and a favorite hangout for young people. R.E. Jones the front seat passenger cried, "Watch out!" It was too late. Probably traveling too fast, they had come upon a slow-moving truck which Melvin didn't see, probably due to his poor vision and poor headlights. It was also questionable if the truck had tail lights. Melvin swerved left, and the right front of the car wedged itself under the truck, crushing the top of the car down into the passenger compartment. The right front seat was torn loose and thrown from the car along with passenger R.E. Jones. He was the most seriously injured with his leg shattered. It was said to have been broken in 16 places. The two passengers in the back seat, Earl Leverett and Earl Walker were unhurt. Melvin suffered cuts, bruises, and a possible fractured wrist. I remember his hand being swollen to the size of a baseball glove. It took a long time to heal.

They brought the wrecked car back home, and Daddy and Melvin removed the body of the car. The frame, along with the engine, transmission, and wheels were sold to Bill Cole who ran a garage in Parrott.

Our next car, which Daddy purchased shortly afterwards, was a 1937 Chevrolet. It was green and was shaped kind of like a box, not nearly as sporty as the old Ford had been. We had that car for a couple of years. Melvin never wrecked that one, instead, he would soon be using it to date his future wife!

CHAPTER 2

Little Johnnie Goes to School

ON THE FIRST day, Mama and Daddy drove me to school in the old Chevy. My school was in Weston, GA, a one-horse town located at the intersection of GA Highways 41 & 55, approximately 45 miles south of Columbus. There were three elementary schools and one high school in Webster County as well as several colored schools. Webster, being one of the smallest and least populated counties in Georgia, meant there were very few students, especially when dividing them between three schools.

Upon arriving at the school, Mama took me to my classroom and I was introduced to my teacher, Miss Pool. She was actually Mrs. Roberts but continued to use her maiden name as a teacher. Miss Pool had three grades in her room, 1st, 2nd, and 3rd. My only classmate was a very small boy named Buddy Jones. There were four students in the 2nd grade and seven in the 3rd. All the students in my room were boys. We didn't do much that first day except get our books and become familiar with where everything was, such as restrooms, lunch room, etc. We were dismissed after a couple of hours and went home.

On Tuesday morning, Mama made breakfast and got me ready for school. I would be riding the bus today for my first time. Daddy was already in the field working and Melvin and Jerry were still in bed. The old yellow school bus pulled into the yard, and Mama walked me out to it. The door opened, and Mama said, "Good Morning." The driver, Mr. Joe Peterson, whose face Mama described later as being unusually red, replied in a stern voice, "I'm running late!" The bus was very old, I'm guessing a model from the late 1930s, certainly different from any other bus I rode afterwards. It had a bench seat on each side running the full length of the bus, a row of seats down the center with an aisle on each side of those seats. There were eight or ten students already on the bus when I got on, and I was seated on the bench seat about half way down on the passenger side.

Since we were running late, I'm assuming we were speeding along much too fast and certainly much too fast for the sharp curve we were approaching. As we entered the curve, I was looking out the window and realized we were about to run in the ditch. My thoughts were; "We're going to run in the ditch, and my Daddy will have to come with the tractor and pull us out." Then it happened. The bus ran into the ditch and slammed against the hard, red dirt bank, coming to an abrupt stop. Then I was mingled in a pile of boys down in the steps of the bus. We were all covered with blood and fecal material. Kids were crying as we pulled ourselves out of the heap and began making our way toward the back of the bus. The driver had opened the back door and was helping kids to the ground. Blood was streaming down my face as he helped me out. He handed me his handkerchief and said, "Hold this on your head." The worst injury I remember seeing was on a high school student named Judson "Jughead" Leverett. He was sitting on the bench behind the driver, and a broken window had cut his lip from the corner of his mouth down to his chin. It was hanging open, showing his lower gum and teeth. Not a pretty sight.

Meanwhile, a colored woman who was living in the house where we had moved from several years earlier, was outside and heard the crash. She could also see the bus. She ran down the road to our house and yelled, "Lawd ma'am, dat school bus done wrecked!" Mama, in a panic, started running up the road toward the site which was no more than half a mile away. Brother Melvin was getting dressed at the time, so he jumped in the car and sped away as fast as he could go. By now, Mama was halfway to the bus. Melvin went right by her without stopping to pick her up. I saw the car coming around the curve and said, "Here comes my Daddy." Melvin said when he arrived at the scene, I was lying in the ditch. That I don't remember. I thought I was simply wandering around. Melvin picked me up, put me in the car along with two or three other injured boys, and headed to Parrott, the closest town with a doctor. Mama had still not arrived at the scene. Parrott was only about five miles away, so within minutes we were arriving at the office of Dr. Arnold. I remember being laid on a table and the doctor suturing two deep lacerations in my forehead. Back home, my parents put me in bed. A short time later a Georgia state trooper stopped by to talk with my parents and ask how I was. I stayed at home for the remainder of the week.

The following week, with no school bus, my father and Mr. Buren Jones, my classmate's father, volunteered to take the kids in our neighborhood to school. They drove on alternate days. Mr. Jones drove a Nash, probably the only one I ever rode in; its manufacturer having gone out of business many years ago. After about two weeks, the county had purchased a new bus and a meeting was held to determine if Mr. Peterson would continue to be the bus driver. The meeting was held in the auditorium at my school. My father, along with Mr. George Hardwick, whose daughter had also been in the accident, attended the meeting together. During the meeting, a county school commissioner posed the question, "Does anyone have any objection to Mr. Joe Peterson continuing to drive the bus?" My father stood up and said, "Hell yes, I've got an objection!" Mr. Hardwick, seated beside my dad said, "Sit down Bernard, you're gonna make 'em mad." My dad replied, "I don't give a damn if I do make 'em mad!" "What's your objection Mr. Wills?", asked the commissioner. "I don't want that SOB driving the bus again. If he does, my son won't be riding on it!" said my dad. Mr. Peterson never drove a school bus again.

In a way, school was fun. Learning came quickly and easily, with a minimum of effort. On the report card you got either a U or an S, with S meaning satisfactory. I never received a U on my report card. However, I did run into a problem with conduct a couple of times. Once, Miss Pool checked "whispers too much" and "rude and discourteous at times." I don't remember what I did, but it didn't sit well with my parents. It didn't happen again.

I was an extremely shy kid and that made me a perfect target for bullying. A second grader, Frank Rogers, was the worst, just plain mean. He picked on me constantly or instigated others to pick on me. Many days I came home crying.

Miss Courtney Edwards was the school principal and also taught the 4th and 6th grades. There was not a 5th grade class. Miss Edwards had about 12 students in her room, which meant there were about 25 students in the entire school. I did not like Miss Edwards. Once a month she held "court." She would assemble the entire school in her room and have the students tattle on each other. Then she would punish the guilty for their "crimes." I'm not saying that I was perfect, but more times than not, I was punished for things I didn't do.

The worst example of my being falsely accused was during one of Miss Edwards' court sessions. There were very few "innocent" students left and court was about to adjourn, when Frank Rogers said, "I saw Johnnie Wills throw a rock and break a window." A window had recently been broken, but I didn't do it. I have no idea who did, but in Miss Edwards' court, if you were accused, you were guilty. There was no defense. I was sentenced to write, "I will not throw a rock at a window again," 100 times on the blackboard. This had to be done during recess and the lunch break. I was in the 1st grade and had just learned to print, and I was very slow doing it. After five days of writing and still only a little more than half way finished, she decided I had been punished enough and I was excused from further writing. It was at this point that I really started hating this school.

One day we were told that a photographer was coming the following day. I had never heard that word before and had no idea what it was and was too shy to ask. Well, next day he was there. I asked another student what he was going to do, and he said, "He is going to shoot us." I thought he was joking, but when it was my turn to go in and see him, I quickly found out he was right. The man said, "Come over here and sit on this stool and I'll take a couple of shots." I can't begin to tell you what was going through my mind; things like, "I'm going to die!" and "I'll never see my Mama and Daddy again!" If you could see my 1st grade picture, you would see the sadness in my face. Needless to say, I survived!

The most embarrassing incident in my entire life was about to happen. One morning after class had begun, I began to feel the urge to pee. I was too shy to ask if I could go to the restroom, so I decided I'd just wait until recess. Unfortunately, I couldn't wait. I peed in my pants, and it puddled in my desk and ran all down the floor. Kids were snickering and saying, "Johnnie Wills wet his pants." Moments later the bell rang for recess. I went out in the sun and sat in a swing with hopes that my pants would dry. They didn't. For the remainder of the school year my teacher periodically asked if I needed to go to the restroom.

Toward the end of my first school year, we went on a school picnic. We went to some farm and drove along a dirt road beside some woods until we found what looked like a good place for a picnic. We got off the bus and as the teachers and a few parents were preparing everything for us to eat, some of us boys were walking around in the edge of the woods. One boy, whom I assumed was familiar with the area said, "There's a small creek just a little way from here." We started walking in that direction, deeper into the woods. After walking maybe 100 yards, no creek. I asked, "How much further?" He said, "We're almost there." We walked, and walked, and walked, but still no creek. By now, we must have been at least a quarter of a mile into the woods, and I was becoming frightened. So, I decided to turn around and go back. I began walking in the direction from which we came, but I wasn't getting out of the woods. Then I started to realize that I was lost and might not be going in the right direction. I panicked. I was afraid I wouldn't find my way out, so I began shouting, "Help!" After shouting several times and still not getting any answer, I began to see the open field ahead. I was so relieved. When I came out of the woods, the group was about 100 yards from me. A couple of the teachers came to me and asked where the others were, and I told them, "Deep in the woods." They said, "Take us to them." I said, "No! There's no way I'm going back into those woods!" A few minutes later the others made their way out. I suppose that was the most frightening incident of my life. To this day I still don't understand why no one answered me when I was calling for help.

I suppose the worst "crime" I committed while going to school at Weston was when I was in the second grade. I was chasing after two first grade girls. The final bell had rung at the end of the day, and the busses were being loaded. Anyway, I ran after the girls, and in order for them to get away from me, they ran into the girl's room. That didn't work. I went in right behind them. Then I realized I was in a place I shouldn't be. I ran out just as fast as I had run in. As I made my exit, I looked to my left and there at the end of the hall stood Miss Edwards, looking straight at me. I grabbed my books, headed out the back door, ran around the building, and got on the bus. I knew trouble was on the way. She came out to the bus and saw I was on it but left without saying a word.

The next day at recess she came for me. She sat me down and asked me why I went in the girl's room. I said, "I didn't go in the girl's room." She said, "Yes, you did. I distinctly saw the door open from the inside and saw you come out." I said, "Wasn't me. You must have seen someone else." We argued back and forth during the 15-minute recess, and it was then, that I made up my mind she was not going to make me confess. After all, I didn't like her. She had punished me several times the previous year for things I really didn't do. Finally, after several days of trying to get me to confess, she said, "If you will admit that you did it, I won't punish you." I said, "OK, I did it." Then she asked. "Why did you do it?" I answered, "I didn't do it." She shot back, "Why did you just say you did it?" My answer was, "Because you said if I would admit it, you wouldn't punish me." She simply shook her head, got up, and walked away. It was never brought up again. I can be a very stubborn person.

I might note that Miss Edwards was a relative, my first cousin once removed. Her mother, who was already deceased at that time, was my maternal grandfather's sister. I had no idea that we were related. She must have known it, but I doubt it would have made a difference one way or the other.

During my time at Weston School, I never wore shoes except when the weather was cold. I always got a new pair in the Fall and would wear them until the weather got warm enough to go bare-footed in the Spring. By the following Fall they would be too small or worn out.

All the floors at school were wooden, and one day as I was dragging my feet as I walked down the hallway, I jammed a splinter into the ball of my foot. Although not visible, I was sure the splinter had broken off in my foot. After walking around on my heel for about a week, Daddy took me so see Dr. Holt in Parrott. He examined me and said he didn't believe the splinter was still in my foot, but he prescribed a black salve that he said would draw it out if it was still in there. A few days later and still unable to walk, I felt the splinter with my fingers. It went all the way through the ball of my foot and moved up and down like a see-saw when I would press on it. Daddy had me lie on the bed, and with the help of his pocket knife, he was able to remove the splinter. It was the size of a large wooden match. It healed quickly, and I was soon back on my feet again.

Weston School wasn't all bad. My favorite event was Halloween night. A variety of stations were set up around the school auditorium such as apple bobbing, pin the tail on the donkey, and my favorite, the fish pond. There was a clothes pin on the end of the line and you threw it over the top of a curtain to fish. When you felt something jerk on the line, you would pull it in and there would be some little prize on your line. The fee was ten cents at each station.

In those days, religion existed in the schools. We said the Pledge of Allegiance and The Lord's Prayer each morning, and in December we would sing many Christmas carols. They were mostly religious carols except for maybe Jingle Bells.

I ate in the lunch room most of the time. On occasions, Mama would make an egg biscuit or a ham biscuit for my lunch when we couldn't afford the ten cents it cost to eat in the lunch room.

With the war being over, the government had lots of surplus food on hand. That food was distributed to schools all over the country. I remember boxes of raisins, probably 20 pounds or so, being set out on the steps at recess. That was a real treat, and many times I would fill my pockets and snack on them all day.

The boy's and girl's restrooms were on opposite sides of the school. I was amazed the first time I went in the boy's room. There were words, phrases, and sentences written all over the walls. I had never seen these words before and had no idea what they meant, but the older boys knew, so I learned quickly. I suppose that was the closest thing to sex education I ever had in school.

After my second year of school was over and I was out for the summer, I did many fun things. I saw my first movie. It was a western movie, and after it was over, country music star, Cowboy Copas, performed live on stage. He had a #4 hit at that time, "Filipino Baby."

One Saturday a colored couple, Clyde and Clara Hall, stopped by our house on their way to fish at Bear Creek. They invited me to go with them, and Mama let me go. Clyde and Clara were very nice people and were respected by everyone who knew them. We fished all day. They caught lots of fish, but I only caught a couple of minnows. When they took me home that afternoon, they gave me a mess of fish which Mama cooked for supper.

Daddy took me fishing twice that summer. He said that we would set out hooks. We left the house shortly after lunch to catch our bait, a bucket of minnows. Late that afternoon after catching plenty of bait, we began to set our hooks. The hooks were on a heavy line about three feet long and attached to a pole we cut from a small tree. After baiting the hook with a minnow, we would stick the pole in the creek bank with the bait dangling in the water. We would set out about 20 or so hooks about 25 feet apart as we made our way down the creek. Daddy said we would check the hooks after supper and again in the morning. I didn't get to go back that night. Daddy took a lantern, and Mama went with him to check the hooks. They returned with a blackfish, a jack, and several catfish. I went with Dad the following morning, and we had a few more catfish. We took the fish over to Grandma and Grandpa Chambers' that night for a fish fry. Mama's sisters, Goldie and Nell, along with their families were also invited. There was plenty of fish for all. Daddy took me fishing again a short time later, but we didn't have much luck that time.

As I mentioned earlier, we had no electricity, so lighting at night was by a kerosene lamp. Daddy loved to read western and detective magazines, but before he started reading his stories, he would read a story to Jerry and me from our Uncle Remus book. Daddy was excellent at reading the stories which were told in Negro dialect.

That summer Daddy bought his first truck, an army truck. There were thousands of military vehicles left over after the war, and they were distributed to dealerships in most of the larger cities throughout the country. That truck, however, was not very practical for the farm, so we only had it for about a year.

Melvin was now dating his wife to be, Faye Anderson. They had promised to take me to see a movie that summer, so one night we went to the theater in Dawson. It was so boring; black and white with the entire movie taking place in one room. As we were taking Faye home that night, Melvin suddenly stopped on a lonely stretch of dirt road. "Why are we stopping?" I asked. "To let the car cool down," Melvin replied. After a half hour or so the car was cool, and we were on our way again. Much later, I finally figured out that it wasn't the car that was hot!

During the war, no new cars were made. Ford, General Motors, and Chrysler all had government contracts and were working 24-7 manufacturing military vehicles. It was also virtually impossible to buy a bicycle during that period. Other items such as sugar and gasoline were also rationed. I remember having to have red or blue point tokens and stamps or coupons to purchase certain items. My brother, Melvin, had wanted a bicycle badly. In 1944, he found one at Cook Brothers store in Parrott. They had only one, and it was hidden in the attic, but they let Melvin purchase it. He rode it everywhere he went before we got that first car. It had no lights, and one dark night as he topped a hill, he saw a figure walking toward him in his lane. That figure was a colored woman who lived alone in the neighborhood, by the name of Roxie Laney. Roxie had also seen him, and they had both moved to the opposite lane to avoid each other. Then it happened. Melvin ran directly into her, knocking her down. She cried out, "Oh Lawd, I is kilt!" Melvin helped her up, and fortunately she was OK.

When I was seven years old and in the 2nd grade, I wanted to learn to ride that bicycle. It was a full sized 26-inch bike, but Melvin worked diligently with me, and soon I was riding. I recall Melvin telling me, "There are two things you can't forget once you learn them: how to ride a bike and how to swim." Later he would also teach me to swim. After I was riding well, Mama let me ride the bike to the mailbox, which was half a mile from home. On one such trip, I decided to see how fast I could go. The front wheel began vibrating, and I lost control and was thrown over the handlebars. I returned home all skinned up. I didn't try that again.

Back at school we began playing baseball. I loved it. We would choose sides, and I was usually the last to be chosen and also the last to bat. One day when it was my turn to bat, I hit a line drive that rolled all the way to the fence. I easily ran around the bases for a home run. The kids couldn't believe a 2nd grader could hit a ball that far. They even went back in the classroom telling the teacher about it. Then one Saturday when I was in the five and dime store, I bought a Jackie Robinson comic book. It told the story of the first Negro to break into the major leagues. I read it over and over again. I can still see some of the pictures in my mind, and I remember how he stole every base in that first game, including home.

My love for baseball continued. I had a ball and an old glove that Melvin had given me, but no bat. With no hope of getting a real bat, I began looking for something I could use as one. I had found something in the woods near an old sawmill site that resembled a baseball bat with a large, movable steel hook attached to it. Daddy said it was a tool used for rolling logs. Removing the hook from the handle, I had myself a bat. I would spend hours out in the cow pasture, throwing the ball in the air and hitting it. I played a game of trying to hit the ball further with each swing. I had a beautiful fossil rock that I would place at the point where the ball came to rest each time I would break the record. My rock probably weighed about a pound and had an absolutely perfect impression of a sea shell on it. There were many fossil rocks in the coastal plain region of Georgia, as it had been the floor of the Atlantic Ocean millions of years earlier. Anyway, by practicing hitting the ball, I developed great power in my swing. I also spent many hours learning to catch the ball by throwing it as high into the air as I could and then catching it. I would also throw the ball on top of the house to catch it as it rolled off. I would practice throwing the ball at a target to obtain accuracy. One day I was playing pitch with brother Melvin. I had the glove and he was catching bare-handed. I asked, "Can't you throw any harder than that?" He said, "You really want me to throw it hard?" When I said yes, he wound up and threw it directly at me as hard as he could. I saw a blur and raised the glove just in time to catch it in the pocket of the glove. I never asked him to do that again.

The second grade was not much different from the first, except Miss Edwards had discontinued her court sessions. The bullying continued, and I continued to dislike going to school there.

Many things happened in 1947. Melvin married Faye that year, and that pleased me because I liked her, and she was good to me. Also, for the first time in my life I had a sister, although she was really a sister-in-law.

I remember my Aunt Elva, wife of Uncle Raymond Chambers, giving them a wedding shower. They received lots of nice gifts, but the one I remember best was a picture of a lone, grey wolf with his head held high and howling. I was fascinated by that picture, which hung on their wall for many years.

Daddy sold the John Deere that year, and he let me go with him and Melvin to Sylvester, a town about 50 miles south of where we lived, to buy a new tractor. It was a Model M Farmall and Daddy taught me how to drive it. The following year, at age nine, I was pulling a harrow to till a small field.

We also sold our timber that year. I think it brought a little more money than Daddy had paid for the whole farm. The logging company had two or three trucks for hauling logs and a skidder for dragging the logs to the loading site. All the trucks were Army surplus vehicles and I was amazed at how powerful they were. If they needed a road through the woods, they would simply drive over trees, some of them up to five or six inches in diameter. It took quite some time for them to harvest the timber because all the cutting had to be done by two men using a cross-cut saw. The chain saw had been invented but was not widely used at that time.

Later that year, Daddy began having some serious, lower back problems. His back had been injured several years earlier in a run-a-way wagon pulled by mules. They had pulled the wagon across a terrace in the field, and Daddy was thrown from it, landing flat of his back on the terrace. He was now seeing a chiropractor regularly, but each visit seemed to make the condition worse. By the end of the year he could barely walk and couldn't sleep in a bed. He lay flat of his back on the floor most all the time. Then he was told by a medical doctor that he needed surgery, or he would soon be paralyzed permanently. A short time later an appointment was made, and Daddy was transported to Piedmont Hospital in Atlanta for surgery. A neuro-surgeon performed a lumbar laminectomy. He said that one of the vertebrae in the lumbar region was crushed, and after removing bone fragments, he fused the spine together. The operation was highly successful, and Daddy was able to be discharged in a few weeks. While he was in the hospital, Mama was able to visit him one weekend. On the following weekend,

Uncle Gene Wills, one of Daddy's five brothers made the trip also, and I was invited to go with him along with one of his sons, Dallas, and a cousin, Raymond Slocumb. It was a very enjoyable day. Daddy was in a ward with about five other patients. We were introduced to all of them. It seemed like one big happy family, the way they all talked and laughed together.

CHAPTER 3

Let's Make a Move

1948 WAS A year of moving and changes. For two years in a row, our crops were poor, so in 1948 Daddy made the decision to sell the 256-acre farm. The Cook Brothers in Parrott bought it for the sum of $2,500.00. We would continue to live in the house for the remainder of the year. In the meantime, Daddy had leased a 415-acre farm known as the Clark Place about seven or eight miles away in Centerpoint Community. It was a much nicer house, and the land was much better for farming. Melvin and Faye had been living with us since their marriage, but were eager to have their own place, so they immediately moved into the "Big House" at the Clark Place.

School was about ready to start up again, and the county allowed the bus from Centerpoint to drive the five miles out of the way to pick me up. That would only be necessary until Christmas, when we would be moving to the Clark Place.

Centerpoint School was laid out about the same as Weston, except it was constructed of wood instead of brick. There was also a gymnasium which was separated from the school. The school had three classrooms with two grades per room. My teacher was Miss Doris Heron, a young teacher who had probably been teaching only a year or so. She had the 3rd and 4th grades. Mrs. Stephens had the 1st and 2nd grades, and Mrs. Clark, the school principal, had the 5th and 6th grades.

Miss Doris would call the roll each morning: "Gerald, Jimmy, George, Johnny, and Margaret." Gerald Smith was one of my best friends, and we were classmates all the way through graduation. Jimmy Faust was a one-year classmate as his family moved away. George Alston was 13 years old, whereas the rest of us were nine. He had spent three years in the first-grade learning to talk, although he still had a speech impediment. He and I would be good friends for the next three or four years. Margaret was a great reader, the best I had ever heard, and she too was a one-year classmate.

Meanwhile, after having sold the farm, Daddy bought our first new vehicle, a 1948 Ford truck. It was red and had a 1 1/2-ton capacity. He also bought a new Model 8N Ford tractor. Since we would be moving to the Clark Place at the end of the year, and he and Melvin would be farming double the acreage, we would need the additional tractor, plus other equipment. By now, Daddy had fully recovered from his surgery, but his doctor warned him that he must "take it easy", so he had a back rest welded to the seat of the Ford tractor for added support.

That fall, I noticed that Mama and Faye seemed to be getting rather fat, but I had no idea why. Then in November, Mama was taken to the hospital in Americus and came home with my new baby brother, Jimmy. In December, Faye went to the same hospital and came home with my very first niece, Peggy Ann. This time I didn't ask where the babies came from, as I noticed that Mom and Faye seemed to have suddenly lost a lot of weight.

I loved my new school. I was no longer being bullied. The first four grades played on one side of the school, and the 5th and 6th grades played on the opposite side. Sometimes if the "big boys" needed an extra person to make up a baseball team, they would ask my teacher for permission for me to go and play with them. I remember on one such occasion when it was my turn to bat, I hit the ball over the shortstop's head into left center field. They couldn't believe the power I had!

That fall, we began practicing for a play that we would be doing in December. I had the lead role and played the part of a king. I remember one scene where I had to dump a bag of money on a table, pretend to count it, and put it back in the bag. For money, I had taken the pennies from Jerry's piggy bank. When I dumped them on the table they went everywhere. It took a while to pick them up. There were smiles and giggles coming from the audience.

During the Christmas holidays, we moved into our new home. The

25

house was quite impressive. It had four large rooms with a hallway and a front porch. On the back of the house was an open hallway with two adjoining rooms: the kitchen and dining room. A full porch was built on both sides of those rooms. The house was built somewhere around 1880 with the kitchen and dining room being added a few years later. The old house was white, but was in bad need of a paint job, though it never got one. There were green wooden shutters on all the windows, a fireplace in every room, and lightning rods on the roof. The ceilings were 16 feet high, constructed that way so the rooms would stay cooler in the summer. Brother Melvin used to joke about seeing clouds floating around in the top of the rooms because the ceilings were so high. He referred to the Clark Place as the "Old Plantation", and that it could have been. There were many out buildings including a large barn, corn crib, storage buildings, chicken house, smoke house, pump house, shelters, and most impressive of all, a blacksmith shop, complete with a forge, bellows, anvil, and many other tools. There were numerous pecan trees, a pear orchard, peach trees, grape vine, and scuppernong vine. There was also a quince tree, the only one I've ever seen. My friend George Alston called it a "consequence" tree. There were four very large blackjack oaks in the yard and two large red cedars at the end of the kitchen. There were two family size tenant houses on the property. My brother Melvin had moved into one of them, so we could move into the "Big House". The house had a party line telephone and some furniture including an organ and a roll-top desk.

When school started back after Christmas, I was the third person to get on the school bus as the driver lived near us. The ride to school took about an hour. 1949 brought a lot of new things and new looks. I think I was most impressed by the new Ford automobiles. They were a total remake from previous models. On Feb. 11th, I celebrated my 10th birthday. Mama gave me my very first birthday party. It was held in the conference room of the school on a Saturday afternoon. My closest relatives were there as well as a few friends. I received some gifts, and Mama had made me a caramel cake, my favorite. After having cake, we played some games. The game I remember most was a game called "animal". We were told to form a circle, and then someone came around and whispered in our ear a certain animal. At the count of three, we were told to shout out the sound of that animal as loud as we could. I had been assigned a tiger, and I was ready. At the count of three, I roared as loud as I could. To my surprise everyone else was silent and began laughing. They had all been told to remain silent. I thought, "What a dirty trick to play on the birthday boy!"

CHAPTER 4

Family, Friends, Acquaintances, and Stories

AT THIS POINT I would like to talk about my relatives on both sides of the family and some of the stories told by them or about them. I'll also be mentioning some of our neighbors and closest friends. Keep in mind that this book is written strictly from memory and from some things that were told to me by my parents. I have not researched family history, family tree, or had any conversations with anyone concerning the events in my book. Some of the dates I refer to may not be correct, but they will be very close.

As I mentioned earlier, my paternal Grandfather was Dave Sidney Wills and my Grandmother was Mattie Slocumb Wills. Grandpa Dave's father was Angier Wills, a veteran of the Civil War. He was wounded in one of his knees by a mini-ball, and when the knee healed it was turned at a 90-degree angle, facing away from his body. I believe Grandpa Angier was born in 1844 and died around 1915. My father was seven years old at the time, and he told me the casket was taken to the cemetery by a horse drawn carriage. He is buried at Macedonia Church Cemetery in Webster County. He was married twice, with Dave and Frank being two children from the first marriage. One night in the 1880s' Grandpa Angier heard what sounded like a freight train. He opened the door to look out, and that's when the storm hit. Unable to close the door, the tornado lifted him up, blew him over some trees and set him down in a field. He was unhurt. Meanwhile, Grandma was in bed with a new baby. As the log house was torn apart, logs were piled up around her bed. Dave and Frank, young boys at that time, were in their bed. The storm literally blew the bed from beneath them and left them lying on the floor holding onto the bedsheet.

My father had five brothers and two sisters with the two sisters being the oldest and the youngest. Aunt Annie Mae was born in 1899 and married Joe Ben West. They had several children, but I won't attempt to name them for fear I might miss one.

Uncle Ray was born in 1900 and was married to Aunt Blanche and they had three children. They were farmers in Webster County, and I might add that they were quite successful.

Uncle Guy was born in 1902 and was married to Aunt Lucy Belle. I believe they had four children. They Lived in Dothan, AL most of their married life, but later moved to Tallahassee, FL. I only remember visiting them once and that was in Tallahassee.

Uncle Cleo was born in 1904 and was married to Aunt Frances. They lived and worked in Dawson, GA their entire lives. Uncle Cleo owned and operated Wills Welding Shop, and Aunt Frances worked in a jewelry store. They had two daughters.

Uncle Eugene (Gene) was born in 1906 and was married to Aunt Lucille. They had four children.

My father was next in line and was born in 1908. Uncle Johnnie was born in 1910 and was married to Aunt Irene. They had three daughters. Uncle Johnnie worked at a shipyard in Charleston, SC during World War II but later moved back to Bronwood, GA where he farmed for a while. Uncle Johnnie was an excellent woodworker and furniture maker.

Aunt Olivia Eudora (Doddie), born in 1912, married Bill Taylor and they had six children. They lived in Perry, GA all the time I knew them, but had once lived in Webster County. I was told that Uncle Bill drove a school bus at Centerpoint School, probably in the late 1930s when they had a high school there. One night when he was driving the bus back from a basketball game, a car full of soldiers from Ft. Benning ran head-on into them, killing one student. I believe that all occupants of the car were killed. The engine of the bus caught fire and Uncle Bill, with a broken arm, still managed to put out the fire by throwing sand on it.

The following is what I believe to be the most horrific crime ever committed against anyone in our family. This tragedy occurred some-time during the 1930s' and was told to me by my parents. Grandma Mattie had a sister named Rena, and she was married to a gentleman named Levy Adams. He and Aunt Rena had gone to bed one night and were sound asleep, when sometime late that night, someone broke into the house, then picked up the fire poker and struck uncle Levy on the head, knocking him unconscious and then brutally raping Aunt Rena. Then the attacker, or some believe there were two involved, proceeded to strike both of them in the head, blow after blow, leaving their skulls crushed. Uncle Levy eventually regained consciousness, walked to the nearby home of a colored gentleman, and demanded to be taken to the nearest doctor's home. Returning, the doctor pronounced Aunt Rena dead at the scene. The news spread quickly, and the following morning many family members and friends were at the scene. It was horrific. The bed was soaked with blood and there was blood splattered on the walls, ceiling, and floor. Someome shouted, "This is the work of a nig-ger! This is the work of a nigger!" So, the sheriff went and arrested the same colored man who had taken Uncle Levy to get the doctor. The accused was quickly tried, found guilty, and sentenced to die in the electric chair. Some believed that the colored man had been falsely ac-cused, but there was little defense for a colored man. That's just the way it was in the Deep South in the 1930s'. Many speculated that the crime was committed by someone who was close to the family and had been in the house many times before. This was based on the fact that the fire poker had been stored in a crevice beside the fireplace. An unfamil-iar person would not have known where the poker was and certainly would not have found it in the darkness of the room. Some even specu-lated that they knew who had committed the crime, but by now it was too late to change what had already been done. A few years later Uncle Levy was found dead on the bank of a creek where he had gone fishing.

Grandpa Dave had several brothers and sisters, most of whom I nev-er knew. The two that I do remember were Great Uncle Floyd and Great Uncle Clifford (Cliff). About the only thing I remember about Uncle Cliff was that he was always smoking a pipe and drove a Model A Ford. I believe that was the only car he ever owned. I remember him coming to our house in the 1950s to have my dad help him with some repair job on the car. Daddy was an excellent mechanic, in fact, he built a garage around 1946 and did mechanic work on the side for a while.

Uncle Floyd was a farmer, a big-time farmer. He cultivated hundreds of acres of peanuts and corn. His wife was Aunt Daisy, and they had one son, Gartrell. Gartrell was the overseer of the farm in the later years. It seemed that Uncle Floyd had owned trucks and tractors since their invention. He had one of those old tractors with iron wheels, the only one I ever saw when I was growing up. He also owned a sawmill. He had four colored men, called "hands", that worked for him. There were Tom Hall, his son Coon, Dan Blue, and another known only as Justice. Justice had the reputation of being the bad one, as in the past he had been in a fight with Blue and shot him. Everyone in the neighborhood seemed to be afraid of Justice. The following is one of my favorite stories as told by Justice himself. This occurred in the 1930s.

Justice decided one day that he wanted to be a cowboy. So, he got on a freight train and hoboed his way out to Kansas. He hadn't had much to eat lately, but he had a few dollars in his pocket, so he got off the train and went into a little country store. "I'd like to buy some cheese and crackers", said Justice. "I ain't got no damn cheese and crackers", said the man behind the counter. "Yasser you is, I sees 'em up da on dat sheff", said Justice. The man replied, "Nigger, I told you I ain't got no damn cheese and crackers." Four dusty cowpokes were seated around a potbellied stove and had been watching. One of them said, "Nigger, can you dance?" " Naw suh, I can't dance a lick", replied Justice. "I think you can, boy", said the cowpoke. The cowpoke then pulled a six-shooter from its holster and fired a round on the floor at Justice's feet. Justice said he started dancing, and the cowpoke fired again, and he began dancing toward the door. When he got near the door, he ran out and continued running until he reached the railroad. He said he hid until the next train came by. He got on that train and headed back East. He worked with Uncle Floyd for the remainder of his life.

One day my mom was walking over to see Aunt Daisy, which was about a two-mile walk. As she walked around a curve and started down the hill toward Spring Hill Branch, she saw Justice standing in the road at the branch. She thought about turning around but thinking that might be worse, she continued toward the branch. There was no bridge, only a narrow foot bridge. She had to pass within about three feet of him. They both said, "Good morning" and Mom continued on her way. She said she had never been so scared in her life.

My maternal grandparents were John Brown Gordon Chambers and wife Rushie (pronounced Rooshie) Culpepper Chambers. My mother was the oldest of five children, followed by Goldie, Eldon, Raymond, and Nell

Aunt Goldie, born in 1912, was married to Hiram Hasty, who was killed in a tragic accident. She later married Max Dillard. They had one son.

Uncle Eldon, born in 1914, was a career soldier and airman. He went all the way through World War II and finally retired in the '60s with 30 years of service. Right after the war he and my brother Melvin, whom he called Bill, would run around together. One night they decided to go see the Thompson sisters who lived about three miles from us. The girls lived at the end of a narrow, red dirt road. It was raining that night, and when it rains that red dirt gets muddy and slick as a greasy meat skin. They started up the road and slipped in the ditch. Walking for about a mile, they got Cousin Gartrell Wills to come with the tractor and pull them out. Gartrell left and they proceeded up the road. Boom! Into the ditch they went again! They walked back and got Gartrell and he pulled them out again. By now it was too late, and they were too muddy to think about seeing any girls.

A short time later, Uncle Eldon finally got married. He and his wife Mattie had two children, a son and a daughter.

Uncle Raymond, born in 1919, was drafted into the Army around 1942. His wife, Elva, gave birth to their only child, in 1943. Their daughter was two years old before her father got to see her, as he served in the Army Air Corps until the end of the war. The Air Force was not a separate branch of the service at that time. During the later years of the war, he was stationed in Iceland. After returning home, he farmed for a year and then decided to further his education. He had dropped out of school in the 9th grade. Since he needed to finish high school, he enrolled at Parrott High and completed the last three grades in one year, then entering the University of Georgia at Athens, he received his degree in pharmacy in 1951.

Aunt Nell, born in 1921, married Lucius Black. He was a very successful Webster County farmer. He was also a State Representative and served in the Georgia Legislature for many years. They had two children, a son and a daughter.

My book wouldn't be complete without telling of an event that happened with my great, great grandparents, Grandma and Grandpa Cook. This story was told to me many times by my mother and is one of my favorites. I'm guessing that this took place in the 1840s or 1850s.

One afternoon at dusk, Grandpa walked down the hill to the spring to get a bucket of water. Returning, he set the water on the shelf and right away heard their dog barking. The little dog was on the porch, up against the house. He continued barking for some time, and Grandpa said, "What in the world is that dog barking at?" He opened the door and there standing next to the porch was a large black bear. The bear reared up on his hind legs and Grandpa quickly shut and bolted the door. The bear had likely followed him up from the spring. The dog finally stopped barking, the bear apparently having left. The next morning their nearest neighbor, Mr. Stokes, was having breakfast when he heard his baby pigs squealing. He thought that was unusual, so he walked out to the pig pen to find the old sow dead and partially eaten. The pigs were hungry and were rooting on their dead mother, unable to get something to eat. Then Mr. Stokes noticed what he believed to be bear tracks around the area. The next morning another neighbor found a dead calf in the pasture, partially eaten.

Grandpa and the neighbors decided that something had to be done, so they got their rifles and gathered the dogs together and headed to the place where the bear was last known to have been. The dogs picked up the scent and began tracking him. As they headed down a trail deep in the woods, the dogs began barking louder and running faster, indicating the bear was not too far ahead of them. For some unknown reason, another neighbor, Mark Moses, was walking the trail that day. He heard the commotion and hid behind a tree, then saw the bear coming his way. He took out a large knife, and as the bear passed his position, he reached out and sliced the bear's hind leg. The bear stopped, reared up, and made a swipe at him with his claws, ripping his shirt from his body, but not putting a scratch on him. The bear turned and continued to run but was unable to run fast because his heel string had been severed. The dogs quickly caught up and surrounded the bear. As the men got there, one of them took aim, fired, and brought the bear down. They hung the bear in a tree, skinned it, and divided the meat. The person who shot the bear got the hide and made a bearskin rug from it. I'm told that was one of the last bears to be seen in that part of Georgia.

The following story has been passed down from generation to generation. It is said to be a true story but does not involve any of my relatives. Nevertheless, it's a great story about a family who apparently lived on the early Western Frontier.

A man and his wife, along with their two small children, a boy and a girl, lived on a farm where they had settled and cleared the land for planting. The nearest store to them was more than 20 miles away, and it took a full day to get to the store and back by horse and wagon. They usually made the trip about once a month to pick up their essentials. On this particular day, the man was making the trip alone while his wife would take the children to the field to pick cotton. The husband reminded her to make sure she came back to the house before dark,

as it was not safe to be out then. She picked cotton all day while the children played. As the sun was about to go down that afternoon, she was on the last row. Wanting to please her husband by telling him she had finished picking the entire field, she decided to finish that last row. It would only take another 10 or 15 minutes. As dusk settled over the field, something caused her to look toward the woods. There at the tree line, stood a lone, grey wolf. She froze in her tracks for a moment and then remembered the children who were playing by a large pile of cotton where she had been emptying her sack. She looked back toward the woods. Now there were three wolves. As she watched, more wolves began coming out of the woods, maybe 10 or 15, an entire wolfpack! They began slowly making their way toward her. "Oh, God! What am I going to do?", she thought. Gathering her thoughts, she suddenly remembered that she had read somewhere that wild animals were afraid of fire. She reached in her pocket. There were two matches. She would set the cotton afire! She struck a match, but it flickered out before she could light the cotton. With only one match left she prayed, "God, please let this match work." It did. By now the wolves were surrounding them and were no more than 30 feet away. As the fire blazed up, they began to back away somewhat and then held their ground. As the blaze began to die down, she began pulling up cotton stalks and throwing them on the fire. She pulled stalks as far away as she dared to go, and the wolves were beginning to inch closer. As the fire died down to no more than a flicker, she thought, "This is the end." But wait! That sound! A wagon was coming! Her husband had gotten home and seeing that his family was not there, he grabbed his rifle and headed toward the field as fast as he could. Spotting the leader of the pack, he fired, and the big wolf went down. With their leader dead, the remainder of the pack quickly fled back into the woods, leaving a happy ending to what could have been a great tragedy.

Theron Helton was our mail carrier. He and his wife Lois had four children: Amelia, Charles, who was my age, Butch, and Winston. They had no family, at least anywhere nearby, so Grandma and Grandpa Chambers had taken them under their wings, and they had been like part of the family for many years. They were always there for Thanksgiving dinner, Christmas, and all other family gatherings. When Winston was about eight or nine years old, he got a .22 rifle with scope for Christmas. On the afternoon of Christmas day, he and some friends were out shooting. One of his friends was looking through the scope and taking aim at his target. He squeezed the trigger. He later said that as he squeezed the trigger, the scope went dark. Winston had walked in front of the rifle and had been struck in the head. Winston was dead.

Late one afternoon in 1946 brother Melvin was visiting with Grandpa Gordon Chambers. They were standing outside when they heard what sounded like gunshots coming from the direction of Mr. Ben West's store. There were maybe 15 or 20 shots fired. Ben West was not a relative of mine. My uncle was Joe Ben West, no relation. Ben West had a general store out on GA Hwy 55, just a couple miles away. He was a strange character to say the least. For example, he would run a special that went like this: "15 cents per lb. or 2 lbs. for 35 cents." Sounds like a real bargain doesn't it? Unknown to most, he had built a large room onto the rear of the store and turned it into a honky-tonk for colored people. The joint had a juke box, dance floor, and several slot machines. He also had boot-leg whiskey for sale, the whiskey and slot machines both being illegal. Apparently, someone had tipped the law about his operation, so the Sheriff of Webster Co. and a single Georgia state trooper had come to raid the place that afternoon. Instead of walking in and confronting Mr. Ben, they got out of their cars with weapons drawn. Mr. Ben didn't like what he saw, so he crouched down beneath a window and began firing. The lawmen jumped behind their cars and began firing back. The sheriff was hit in the shoulder. The trooper got him into the car and sped away to the hospital. Mr. Ben's operation was shut down, and he went to jail. He later said that he didn't mean to shoot the sheriff, because he was a friend. He said, "I meant to shoot the controlman."

CHAPTER 5

Back to the Farm

NOW THAT WE were all settled in our new home, it was time to get started with our first year of farming at the Clark Place. We had already begun tilling the fields for planting our crops. I had been doing some tilling, and I enjoyed that, because I got to drive one of the tractors. We would be planting some 45 acres of peanuts and an equal amount of corn, maybe more. Peanut acreage was tightly regulated by the Dept. of Agriculture, the purpose being that a set price could be guaranteed for your crop. The number of acres allowed was based on the size of the farm. A government agent would come to the farm in early summer to measure the acreage you had planted. If you had overplanted, he would see to it that those excess acres were destroyed by plowing them up.

The first crop to be planted was corn, which would begin in early March. With the equipment we had, we could plant two rows at the time with the rows being 36 inches apart and the corn 36 inches apart in the row. That's much different from the way corn is planted now, and today's crops will yield up to 10 times what they did in the 1950s. When the corn was a few inches high we would plow the field to get rid of as much grass and weeds as possible. No herbicides were used then. Plowing would continue until the stalks were too tall for the tractor and cultivator to pass over. Next, we would give the crop an application of sodium nitrate. This was done by taking a bucket of soda, as we called it, and walking the row, placing a small handful by each stalk. When the next rain would come, the corn would turn dark green and grow very fast. One thing I liked about growing corn was the fact that we didn't manually hoe it. There would be weeds and grass, but by now the corn was tall enough that it didn't matter. By early summer, the corn would be mature, and we would gather some while it was tender enough to eat. By now we had bought a chest type freezer and Mama would cut the corn off the cob and freeze it. Also, some would be eaten as corn on-the-cob. The crop would remain in the field until late fall when it would be picked and placed in the corn crib for feeding the hogs and chickens. Some would be sold or taken to the mill to be ground into cornmeal.

When April came around it was time to plant peanuts. There were two varieties which we planted, Spanish and Dixie Runners. The Spanish Peanut was a bunch type plant with all the nuts being in a single bunch beneath the plant. The runner was a vine type with its roots running several inches in all directions from the main plant. Peanuts would grow along all those runners. It was also a slightly larger peanut. Peanuts were planted much closer together than corn; I believe the rows were 24 inches apart, and nuts were planted about four inches apart in the row. Fertilizer was applied at the time of planting. Peanuts had to be plowed just as the corn did. Then came the part I disliked most, and that was hoeing them. That generally took place about the time school let out for the summer. I really hated those long days, from sunup till sundown with temperatures sometimes reaching 100 degrees. By the way, no one hoes peanuts anymore, thanks to the use of herbicides. We would usually be finished with hoeing by the end of June with nothing more to be done until harvest time, around the first of September. Peanuts were harvested by plowing them up and raking them into wind rows. This was all done mechanically with the tractor. Then the vines would be stacked on poles to dry. That meant that before the plants were plowed up, hundreds of stack poles would have to be put up in the field. Many days would be spent cutting poles from pine trees which were about four or five inches in diameter. They were cut in length to about eight feet. The poles would last for about two years before they began to rot, and new ones would have to be cut. Holes had to be dug manually with post hole diggers. Once the poles were in the ground, two slats, each about two feet long would have to be nailed in a cross position about a foot off the ground. Now it was time to stack the peanuts on the poles. So, with pitchforks we would begin stacking. That was the other job I disliked so much because it was so hot and dusty. They would dry for about two months, and then a peanut picker would be brought to the field. It was operated by a belt from the tractor. The stacks would be brought to the picker by a lifter attached to the back of a tractor. That was usually my job, and I enjoyed that. Now that the picking was completed it was time to take them to the market. At the market, the peanuts would first have to be graded. Then they would be unloaded, and the weight would be calculated. Then you would go to the office, and a check would be cut for you. A ton of peanuts would bring from $180.00 to $220.00 depending on the grade.

Since it cost about $50 per acre to produce the peanuts, you would have to harvest at least 1/4 ton per acre to break even. Most of our crops produced from 1/3 to 1/2 ton per acre. Hopefully, after you sold the crop you would have enough money to pay off your farming loan. Then it was time to get a new loan and start all over again. More than once I remember saying, "When I get grown, I will not be a farmer!"

Living on the farm required much more than just working in the fields. There were cows, hogs, and chickens to care for. My daily chores included bringing the cow from the pasture to the barn for milking. As hard as I tried, I could never milk a cow. Daddy usually took care of that. I had to shuck corn for the hogs and shuck and shell corn for the chickens. Thankfully, we had a mechanical corn sheller whereas we had to shell it by hand when we lived at Bear Creek.

We had a fireplace in every room except in Mama and Daddy's bedroom. They had a heater that would burn either wood or coal. We mostly burned wood but when Daddy could afford it, he would buy a ton of coal which would last a few weeks. After the crops were gathered, we would go in the woods and cut down some oak trees to be cut into firewood. We would also gather some pine knots from fallen trees, called lightwood, and cut these into splinters to help start a fire. It was my duty every afternoon to bring in enough wood to last through the evening and to build a fire the following morning. I remember one time when we were cutting trees deep in the woods near a stream, we came across a moonshine still. It was not active, and we had no idea who had built it. I only know that no one ever returned to use it again.

In September 1949, I started the fifth grade. My teacher was Mrs. Roma Clark, a middle-age woman, who was married to one of the relatives whose ancestors had owned and lived at the Clark Place. Mrs. Clark taught both the fifth and sixth grades. She was a good teacher, but strict, and no doubt the most religious teacher I ever had. She was always assigning us Bible verses, and sometimes full chapters to memorize. I probably learned more about the Bible from her than any other person in my life, except maybe from my parents. We had two new students to join us in the fifth grade, Jerry Kirksey and Tomas Kimbrell. They had previously attended Parrott School, but that school had burned to the ground that summer. It would be several years before Parrott school re-opened.

I should note here that by now I had begun spelling my name Johnny instead of Johnnie. The reason being that someone, I don't remember who, told me that Johnnie was the spelling used by girls, and I didn't like that. I now know that to be untrue. Anyway, I changed the spelling to Johnny and have used that spelling since. Although my birth certificate reads Johnnie, no one has ever questioned the spelling, including, the military, Board of Registration, or Social Security Service.

I was a straight "A" student in the fifth grade as I had always been and the only one in my class. Mrs. Clark came to me one day and said, "Johnny, we have some important visitors coming for a meeting and visit to our school next month. They are from the County School Board and I want you to memorize a chapter in the Bible to recite at that meeting." I said, " OK", thinking it would be something short and easy like the 23rd Psalm. But no, she wanted me to learn the entire 12th chapter of Romans. That's not a short chapter. It's 21 verses long and takes up almost a full column on a Bible page. Well, I got busy, working on it every night, and by the time the meeting came around I could recite it without a single hesitation. I think our visitors were impressed, and I know Mrs. Clark was proud. I later learned that Centerpoint School did not have a good reputation for sending quality students to Preston for the 7th grade. I never forgot that chapter and can still recite it today.

My favorite hobby was coin collecting. Almost every night my Dad would let me look through his pocket change for rare coins. They weren't really rare, but I was able to find some Barber coins and V-nickels. One morning Mrs. Clark was taking up our lunch money. By now, the price of lunch had gone from 10 cents a day to 25 cents per day. As my classmate Gerald Smith paid for his lunch, he said, "This quarter was made in 1899." It was worn slick, but everything was readable, and I wanted that Barber Quarter for my collection. The next day I brought a quarter to school and asked Mrs. Clark if she still had it. She did, and I was able to obtain it. I still have that quarter today.

In early 1950, my Great Grandmother, Georgia Slocumb, the one who remembered the Civil War, became deathly ill, and a few days later, passed at the age of 96.

The county agent came to our school during my 5th year, and we formed a chapter of the 4-H Club. If I remember correctly, our pledge was:

I pledge my head to clearer thinking,
My heart to greater loyalty,
My hands to larger service, and
My health to better living,
For My Club, My Community, and My Country.

I was elected president for our club. That summer of 1950 I got to go to the 4-H Club Camp. The site was Camp Fulton in Atlanta. There were clubs from several other schools, mostly from around South Georgia. The swimming pool was the biggest attraction there. They even gave swimming lessons, but I didn't learn to swim. We also competed against each other in things like softball. I pitched for our team and struck out several players. I always liked to start out with a fastball down the center, come back with a change-up, and finish them off with a high inside fastball. We didn't win any games because we didn't have enough good players to put together a competitive team; however, I did make the all-star team.

Faye gave birth to their 2nd child in January of 1950, a daughter, Diane. I spent lots of time visiting with Melvin and Faye. Melvin always had something interesting to talk about. That summer he was telling me about the Confederate Soldiers Convention in Atlanta. There were only 24 of them left that year whereas there had been over 50 the previous year. In a couple of years, they would all be gone. I remember that their ages ranged from 102 to 121, and they all held the honorary rank of General.

My brother Jerry now had an imaginary friend by the name of Murph, whom you could hear him talking to quite a lot. He had also taken an interest in country music. He especially liked to listen to the Grand Old Opry every Saturday night. Mama ordered Jerry a record player from Sears, Roebuck & Co., but we never received it. Finally, after Mama wrote them several letters they sent a replacement. He also got three 78 RPM records: one by Hank Williams, one by Hank Snow, and one by Roy Acuff. He would play those records over and over, day and night. I heard them so much that it wasn't long until I knew the words to all the songs.

In the summer of 1950, our family hosted the Wills Family Reunion. That was an annual event that had been going on as long as I could remember. On a Saturday afternoon, we would kill a hog and prepare it for barbecuing. This was done by digging a pit in the ground, building a fire from green hickory wood, adding hot coals to the pit, and placing the hog over the pit using steel rods to support it. More coals would be added as needed to keep it hot. The hog would be placed over the pit late in the afternoon and would cook all night long. Several men would sit up all night to tend to it. Sometime around midnight the hog would be turned over to cook on the other side. I wanted to sit up all night with the men, because I loved listening to the stories they told. However, I was only 11 years old, and at midnight Mama made me come in and go to bed. Next morning the hog would be done, and it would be taken up, chopped up, and sauce added. Some of the women would make Brunswick stew. At around 10 AM, the families would be arriving, and all would bring a covered dish. I always enjoyed the reunions because that would be the only time of the year that I got to see some of my relatives.

Mama and Daddy had been going to church as far back as I could remember. They were members of the Turkey Creek Primitive Baptist Church there in Webster County. Church was only held there every 4th weekend, Saturday and Sunday. There were four churches in the association and only one pastor to serve all four, so each church held service once a month. The other churches were Beulah in Parrott, Liberty near Americus, and Bethel in Phoenix City, AL. My parents would attend service at these churches as often as possible. I didn't like going to church, especially when I was very young, because it was boring, and the Primitive Baptist preachers tended to preach very long sermons. We would rarely get out of church before 1 PM. Our preacher was Elder B.F. House. He lived in Columbus, GA which was some 50 miles away, so he would usually spend the night with us on Saturday. On Sunday morning I would usually wake to his singing "Amazing Grace" or some other gospel song. As I grew older, I enjoyed going to church. Elder House built a fish pond on the property of one of the church members, and many times we would spend Sunday afternoon fishing.

After a decent year of farming in 1949, Daddy told me I could have an acre of peanuts in 1950. He said that whatever profit we made on that acre would be mine. My hopes were that it would be enough to buy a new bicycle. My hopes turned into reality. After the crop was sold that fall, Daddy said it was time to go shopping for that bike. We went to Dawson and checked out all the stores that carried bicycles. I found one that was OK but not exactly what I wanted. At the last store, I found it; exactly what I was looking for. It was a Schwinn, two toned black and white and loaded. It had a tank with built in horn, headlight, rear reflector, and luggage rack. The price was $56.00 which was a big price for a bicycle at that time. Daddy reminded me that we could get the other one for only $39.00, but I didn't want any part of that. So, the Schwinn it was. I had the nicest bike in the neighborhood, and I rode it for many years. I was very proud of that bike. I never left it out in the weather, always keeping it parked on the back porch.

I was in the 6th grade that fall, which would be my last year at Centerpoint School. My favorite subject was science. When we got to the chapter on the planets, I fell in love with it. Right away, I said that when I grew up I wanted to be an astronomer. Of course, that never happened, although I have always maintained an interest in it.

On February 10, 1951, the day before my birthday, I was awakened at 3 AM by my brother Melvin climbing in bed with me. "We've got a new baby, this time a son.", he said proudly. Instead of congratulating him, I simply said, "Why do you want so many little babies?" I don't think he ever forgot that.

I was still president of the 4-H Club and was looking forward to go-ing to summer camp again. After school turned out for the summer, I was notified that there would be a meeting of the 4-H Club in Preston, and I was supposed to attend. I would be getting all the info about sum-mer camp. With my dad working and my mom unable to drive, I had no way to get there except on my bike. It was seven miles to Preston, but Mama agreed to let me ride my bike. It took me about 45 minutes to get there, and I had no trouble at all. There was one long hill, more than a half mile long with part of it being very steep. It was fun coasting down that hill, but coming back I would have to push the bike. Everything went fine until I was about two miles from home, and then my side be-gan hurting. The pain grew worse, and by the time I got home, it was se-vere. Mama made me go to bed, and after a couple of hours, I was OK.

The meeting had gone fine, and I learned that we would be going to Camp Wahsega in the mountains of North Georgia. That was especially exciting because I had never seen a mountain before.

Around the middle of June, it was time to leave for camp. We all gathered at the high school in Preston early that morning, boarded the school bus, and were on our way. There were 10 or 15 of us in the group. Marvin Herrington, the agriculture teacher was in charge. He and the bus driver were the only adults making the trip. It would take some five hours to reach the camp. We stopped at Eatonton for a short break and to grab a drink and snack. When I paid for my purchase and looked at my change, I couldn't believe my eyes. There in my hand was a 1912 Liberty Nickel! I needed that one for my collection, but I was thinking, "Why couldn't it have been a 1913." B. Max Mehl, a coin dealer in Ft. Worth, TX had recently been advertising that he would pay $500.00 for one. That was nothing more than a publicity stunt, because he knew well that only five of those coins were made, and they were all accounted for. Today that coin is worth millions. We continued toward the mountains. I don't believe many, if any, on the bus had ever seen the mountains, because people kept asking Mr. Herrington if that were the mountains that we could see in the distance. He kept answering, "No, that's only the foothills." We finally reached the mountains and what an awesome sight! Camp Wahsega, located near Dahlonega, GA was nestled in a valley surrounded by high mountains on all sides. It had been an Army training camp during the war. After the war ended, it was no longer needed and was now used as a summer came for various clubs and organizations. There was a little creek running through the center of the camp, and the swimming pool was a natural lake, less than an acre in size. Our sleeping quarters were a military barracks that was lined with bunk beds and wall lockers. As we were getting settled in, another group arrived. They were from somewhere in Texas, and they all wore western garb: boots, jeans, hat, etc. One of the boys opened his suitcase, and as we all gathered around, he took out a big stack of comic books. "Anyone wanna buy these?", he asked. "How much?", asked one of our guys. "Four bits", replied the Texan. Our guy quickly handed over a half dollar. Another Texan opened his suitcase. When he laid the lid back, everything became deathly silent as we gazed in absolute amazement at what we saw. There on top of his clothes was a gun belt with two pearl-handle revolvers in their holsters. I think we all just walked away, completely stunned. I've often wondered if those guns were real. If they weren't, they sure looked to be. Can you imagine what would happen if someone showed up at camp today with two six-shooters in his possession? The second day at camp my friend Gerald Smith and I decided to go to the lake for a dip. I don't think either of us could swim, but we both said we could swim a little. One end of the lake was shallow, so we started playing around in that end. After a while, we started wading out into the lake until the water was up to our shoulders. Then we climbed out of the pool and started jumping into the water at that point. We kept moving a little further out until the water was up to our necks. Then I moved out a little too far. When I jumped in the water, it was well over my head, maybe seven feet deep. Well, then it was obvious I couldn't swim. I went under and my feet touched the rocky bottom. I shoved myself back to the surface and took in a breath of air. Now I was panicking and fighting the water. I realized that unless I got help, I was going to drown, because I couldn't get out of the water. The second time my head came up I was facing toward the lifeguard who was sitting in his chair on the platform. I went under again, and when I surfaced again, I yelled, "Help!", then went under again. Next time I surfaced, he was standing up watching me. Later he said he thought I was playing. After a couple more times of going under and coming up yelling for help, I saw him getting off the platform and swimming toward me. When he reached me, he calmly said, "just take it easy, I've got you." I was able to remain calm, and he swam, carrying me back to the platform and telling me to sit in his chair for a while. By now, all activity at the pool had stopped, and everyone was looking at me. I was embarrassed but most grateful to that lifeguard who had just saved my life. Apparently, I was holding my breath when I went under and taking in a breath of air when I would surface, because I never got strangled or coughed. I believe that was the only rescue the lifeguard made that week. I don't recall going back in the lake the remainder of the week.

When I got home from camp and told my family what had happened, my brother Melvin said, "You will learn to swim before the summer is over." He wasn't joking. He started taking me swimming every chance he got. There in our community, everyone went swimming in Bill Fussell's pond which had recently been designated as the Community Club Pond. The pond was a little more than an acre in size, and at one corner, it was shallow with a sandy bottom. There was a diving board, and at the center was a platform that we called the float. Beyond that were lots of stumps, and it was also infested with snakes. I never heard of anyone being bitten, because they pretty much stayed away from where the people were.

Melvin worked very hard with me, and finally I began making some progress. I could actually swim a little. Melvin said, "It's time for the big test." He swam out to the float and told me to wade out toward him as far as I could. I did and was still 10 or 12 feet from him. He said, "Shove off with your feet and swim to me." I was scared, but I did what he said, and I made it. I was so happy. Then he told me to swim back. That's when I was really scared but he told me to put my feet against the float and shove off as hard as I could toward the shallow water. He assured me that he was there to help If I couldn't make it. But I did make it, to a point where I could stand up. We practiced that exercise over and over until I was comfortable with it. From there, my swimming continued to improve. I now consider myself an excellent swimmer, and I played a large part in teaching my daughter Kelly to swim.

Late in the summer of 1951 my brother Don, who was now six, and I were out walking in the woods when we came upon a snake skin. As snakes grow, they shed their skin periodically. This skin was about two feet long, and it appeared to come from a snake that was about one inch, or a little more, in diameter. I have no idea what kind it was, but I don't think it was from a poisonous snake. I said to Don, "Wanna have some fun with this snake skin?" He said he did, and I told him my plan. We would take it to the house and without being seen, we would place it on Mama and Daddy's bed. Later that evening Mama went in the bedroom and spotted it. She said in a low voice to Daddy, "Bernard, there's a snake in our bed!" Well, they began stripping the covers off the bed, piece by piece. Then the mattress came off and they were down to the slats, but no snake. Mama said, "He's in this room somewhere." They searched the entire room, but still no snake. "Where could he be?", said Mama. Then it hit her. "The closet! He's got to be in the closet!" There was just enough space under the door that a snake could slither under. They started taking things out of the closet, examining them thoroughly. It was amazing how much stuff came out of that closet, but still no snake. Meanwhile, Don and I had been watching and smiling at each other. Mama said, "Where in the world is that snake?" Then I spoke up, "There is no snake." "What do you mean?", Mama asked. I told her that Don and I had put it there as a joke. They didn't believe us at first, and they certainly didn't think it was funny. That was another occasion when she should have tanned my hide, but she was so relieved that there was no snake, that I didn't receive any punishment. We never pulled another stunt like that.

CHAPTER 6

Heading to High School

THE THIRD AND final school I attended was Webster County High in Preston. Although I still had two years to go until I would actually be in high school, it was big time moving up to the 7th grade. In order to get to school, I had to ride the bus to Centerpoint School, then change busses to get to Preston.

When I walked into my classroom, all the desks up front had been taken, so I had to take one in the back of the room. Taking my seat, I looked around the room and counted about 15 students. Wow! That was the largest class by far that I had ever been in. Then to my horror, I spotted him. It was my old arch enemy, none other than Frank Rogers. Somewhere along the way he had failed a grade and was now in my class. What luck!

My teacher was Miss Agnes Agerton, a middle-aged woman with jet black hair with every hair in place. I never saw her any other way. She had been teaching for a long, long time and had been one of my brother Melvin's teachers in high school. She was an excellent teacher, and I respected and liked her a lot. She later told someone that I was by far the best student to ever come from Centerpoint School. I continued to be a straight "A" student and was in the top two or three in the class. My favorite subject that year was Georgia History. By the end of the year, I knew all 159 counties in Georgia along with the county seats and where they were located in the state. Georgia has more counties than any other state in the union, except Texas, which has more than 200. Our project that year was to make a scrapbook on Georgia, and I had the best one in the class. I received an "A+" on that project. The following year Miss Agnes asked me to put my scrapbook on display for her new class. I did, but later wished I hadn't. The kids destroyed my book.

I got along well with all my classmates that year, and surprisingly, didn't have much trouble from Frank Rogers. There were enough of us boys that we could play a little football and baseball. One day we were playing baseball, and I was the last to bat, as usual, and finally got a turn just before the bell rang, ending recess. I got an inside fastball and hit a grounder out toward 2nd base, which I beat out for a single. The way the bat cracked when I hit the ball, I was pretty sure that I had broken it. The bat belonged to one of my classmates, and after examining it, found that indeed it was broken. I had hit the ball up on the handle of the bat. That will break a wooden bat almost every time if you hit with decent power.

I think I grew faster between the ages of 12 and 13 than at any other time in my life. When I was 13, I weighed 130 lbs. and was 5' 10" in height.

During my 7th year of school, I was introduced to the game of basketball. I had seen a basketball, but I had never seen a game or had any idea how it was played. That was all about to change. One day we were in the gym shooting some goals when someone said, "Let's play a game." We chose sides and began playing. Someone shot the ball, missed and the ball rebounded my way. An eleventh grader, Rainey Davis, went up for the ball, but I out-jumped him and got the rebound. I immediately started running for the goal, but someone yelled, " traveling!" I had no idea what that meant, but they explained that you have to dribble the ball when walking or running. I had seen people dribbling but didn't know that was part of the game. I simply thought they were just showing off.

My dad was a very hard worker, but he never worked on Sunday. That was a day of rest. If Melvin wasn't busy with something, he and I would go fishing on Sunday afternoon. We rarely caught anything larger than your three fingers. We would usually end up with 20 or 25 small bream. He never took any of the fish home with him. I was always stuck with the fish and the chore of cleaning them. I recall one time when we went fishing on Saturday and after catching a few little fish, we headed home. It was late afternoon, probably close to 8 PM, when he decided to stop at Major's Place. That was a bar and pool room on GA Hwy. 55 about half way home. Melvin told me to wait in the car, that he was going in to have a cold beer and would be right back. Well, at 10 PM he had had a few more than a single beer and still wasn't back. About that time, I saw our truck drive up with Melvin's wife, Faye, driving and Mama with her. Faye knew exactly where Melvin was, and she marched right in and told him, "Get your butt out of here and get home!" Mama made me get in the truck with her and Faye, and we followed him. He was able to keep the car between the ditches, but that's about all you could say. We did a lot more fishing over the years but nothing like that ever happened again.

We had two large mulberry trees across the road, in the edge of the pasture. Every year they were loaded with berries. I would climb the trees, sit on a limb, and eat mulberries. One morning I was out there in one of the trees when I heard our dog barking a short distance away. I figured he had probably treed a squirrel. I went back to the house and told Daddy that the dog had something up a tree, so he grabbed the shotgun, a single shot 20-gauge, full choke. He also grabbed a few shells with #6 shot. We headed out to the pasture and spotted the dog barking up a tall pine, maybe eight inches in diameter and 60 to 70 feet tall. Then we spotted something that I had never seen before and have not seen since. A grey fox was clinging to the tree with all four legs wrapped around it. He was about 30 feet off the ground. I had no idea that a fox could climb a tree but have since learned that in fact, they do. Daddy took aim from about 25 to 30 yards away and brought him down. We cut off his ears, because the county would pay $2 per head for any fox killed.

Late one morning, Melvin and I were standing outside talking, when we noticed a column of smoke rising above the trees. "That looks like it could be a house or some building burning", said Melvin. As we were watching it, Mr. Theo Alston, the father of my friend George, came walking by on his way home from the store. Mr. Alston had not seen the smoke and Melvin said as he pointed it out to him, "That's in the direction of your house. Let's get in the car and go take a look." As we drove toward the smoke, it became obvious that it was further away than it appeared. As we neared Mr. Alston's home, he became very concerned. It was, in fact, his home that was burning. As we arrived on the scene, the house was a massive inferno. George was outside along with a neighbor, Bill. We were standing at least 200 feet from the house, and the heat was intense. Bill pointed out that he had been able to remove all the furniture from one room of the house. However, he hadn't moved it far enough away, because suddenly every item that he had removed, burst into flames. I then noticed a pen full of chickens, some 75 feet from the house. Chickens were running around like crazy, trying to escape the heat. They couldn't, and in an instant, I saw every chicken fall dead, simultaneously. Bill told Mr. Alston that George had started the fire by trying to burn a wasp nest. As George stood there with tears in his eyes, Mr. Alston said, " Damn it George, I told you about burning those wasp nests!"

When Miss Agnes would give us an exam, she would write the questions on the blackboard. We would have to write the question and the answer on our paper. Since my desk was in the back of the room, it was very difficult for me to read the questions, especially some of the words. I didn't want to get up and walk to the front of the room and stare at the blackboard, so I would get up and go to the pencil sharpener near the front and pretend to sharpen my pencil as I read the questions. This would happen several times during an exam.

Then one day a man came to our school to do an eye exam on the students. A few days later when we got the report, it said that I needed glasses and that in the meantime, I should be sitting in the front of the room. Miss Agnes moved me to the front right away, and Daddy took me to an eye doctor in Albany, GA. When the doctor asked me to read the letters on the eye chart, I could only see the big "E" at the top of the chart. He said my vision was 20/200, but corrective lenses would easily solve the problem. A couple of days later we went back, and I got my glasses. They had plastic frames, and they cost $15.00. I was amazed at how well I could see. It was a whole new world out there. I stared out the window of the truck all the way home. I could see individual leaves on trees, I could see tiny twigs, and I could see birds sitting on limbs. Back at school, I could see the blackboard from anywhere in the room. I was very careful with my glasses, because I knew if I broke them my parents might not be able to afford another pair right away. So, when I played baseball or basketball, I would always take them off, but that put me with a distinct handicap which I would later learn.

There had not been a girl in my class since the 4th grade, but now there were two: Joanne, a brunette, and Betty, a blonde. I liked looking at the pretty girls, but I was far too shy to dare talk to them. Besides that, I was not a very popular person. I suppose I was considered a loner, a bookworm, or maybe even a nerd. I worried about ever having a girl-friend or ever getting married. My Dad used to grin and tell me, "Aw, some little ole puddin' faced girl will have you." How right he was!

In 1952, Daddy decided to add cotton to our crop list, so we plant-ed a few acres. Cotton required a lot of work as peanuts did. One day while Daddy and I were hoeing cotton, a neighbor of ours, Bobby Alston, dropped by to chat with us for a few minutes. As we stood there in the field talking, Bobby spotted something partially buried in the soil. He picked it up and handed it to my Dad. It was a dime, an 1882 Liberty Seated Dime in excellent condition. It was likely lost around the time the old house was built. Dad handed it to me and said, "This is yours." I still have that dime today. At the time it was found, it was valued at around $3.00. Today it's worth $30 - $40.

That fall, I picked cotton for the first time in my life. That was a back-breaking job. Pickers were paid about two or three cents a pound for what they picked in a day. A good picker could pick up to 200 lbs. in a day. The most I ever picked was 98 lbs. in a day. My brother Jerry wanted to pick some cotton, so Mama let him go out to the field to pick. He was very slow. I think he crawled down the row instead of bending over. He seemed to have enjoyed it, but he got badly sunburned. Jerry had skin like mine. It wouldn't tan in the sun, just turn red and blister. That was the only year Daddy ever planted cotton. Thank goodness!

The fall of the year was also the time to harvest the pecan crop. They had to be picked up off the ground by hand. We had many trees and would harvest several hundred pounds each year. That would provide a little extra money for Christmas. There were several varieties, but the most valuable was the Schley (pronounced sly}, or paper shell variety. We always saved some of those for our personal use. We had one tree that produced a strange looking nut. It was flat on two sides. I would often keep some of those in my pocket as they were easy to shell and made an excellent snack. I never saw another tree like that.

Brother Melvin was a great fan of the University of Georgia Bulldog Football team. So, he sat me down one day just before the football season started in 1952 and proceeded to teach me all about football. I caught on quickly, and it wasn't long until I became a lifelong Dawg fan. I learned the names of all the players on both offense and defense. But I didn't stop there. I also knew the weight and hometown of all the players. I found it strange that hardly any of the players were from Georgia. Most were from the Northeast with more from Pennsylvania than any other state.

Georgia opened the season that year against Vanderbilt University and won 19 - 7 and ended the season with a 7 - 4 win/loss record. I listened to all the games on the radio except for the Georgia-Auburn game in November. Uncle Max Dillard and Melvin had been going to that game for years, so they invited me to go with them. The game was played at Memorial Stadium in Columbus, GA. I was thrilled, especially since we won the game. I went to several more Georgia-Auburn games before they discontinued playing the game in Columbus, due to the small 8,000 seat capacity of the stadium.

I started the 8th grade that fall. My home room was in the high school building, and we changed rooms and teachers for all our classes. We started practicing basketball almost immediately and would be playing a few J.V. games. I didn't have a pair of tennis shoes, because my parents couldn't afford them. My cousin, Sanford Wills, an eleventh grader, gave me his old pair. They were black where all the other kids had white shoes. They were also a half size too small, and my little toe stuck through a hole in the side of the shoe. Nevertheless, they served the purpose, and I was thankful to have them. I was the starting center for our first game, and we won 23 - 20. I scored 8 points in that game and my teammate, Alfred Hudson, scored 11. Before the next game, I received a badly sprained ankle when I went for a rebound in practice and came down on someone's foot. It took several weeks for my ankle to heal, so I missed all the remaining games.

For Christmas that year Daddy gave me $20 and told me to buy whatever I wanted. I bought an electric football game which gave me much enjoyment, mostly playing against my brother Melvin. My younger brothers, Don and Jimmy, each got a bicycle for Christmas.

On January 1, 1953 we got the sad news that Hank Williams was dead at the age of 29. In my opinion, he was the greatest song writer and country music singer that ever lived. Many of his songs are still very popular and being played today. Later that year, my Dad's brother, Cleo died of a massive heart attack. He was only 49. I remember how devastating it was for my Dad.

So far, I hadn't had much trouble from Frank Rogers. Then one morning during study hall, I was working hard to prepare for an exam. Several others including Frank Rogers, were congregated at a nearby table. I saw Frank look my way and say something to Eugene Hancock. Then Eugene got up and walked by me, bumping my chair to disturb me. Then he sat back down, and Frank whispers something to him. Then Eugene walks by and bumps me again. Frank was really enjoying this, and I was getting madder by the minute. So, I decided that if he bumped me one more time, I was going into action. Well, here he came again, bumping me. I jumped up and began to pound him in the face with my fists as fast and hard as I could. He was startled at first but then tried to fight back. Miss Bearden, the librarian and first year teacher, was yelling for us to stop. We did and then she marched us down to see Mr. McDuffie, the principal. Mr. Mac asked what the problem was, and I told him. He said that regardless, he couldn't tolerate that kind of behavior and would have to punish us. He opened a drawer and came out with a paddle about two feet long with three holes drilled in it. Since we were in the 8th grade, he would give each of us eight whacks while the other waited in the hall. Mr. Mac was a frail looking man, and he hit with all his might. I think he was exhausted when it was over. Eugene and I shook hands and agreed that we would be friends from that point on, and we were. Once again, I regretted that it wasn't Frank I beat up on. When I went home and told my Dad what had happened, he let me know that if I got another paddling at school, I would get another when I got home. I didn't like that, but anyway, I never got into another fight or got another paddling.

After the crops were gathered that year, Melvin and his family moved away from the Clark Place. Now they had four children. Sharon had been born in February of that year. They moved into the house with Faye's mother and would farm the 300-acre Anderson Place the following year. Meanwhile, new tenants, Bill and Mary, were moving into the house that Melvin and family had just vacated. Bill would help us farm the following year.

Daddy came in one evening and asked me if I would like to go fishing. I was always ready to go fishing, so I said, "When? Where?". He said, "This weekend, in Florida." I got all excited. I had only been to Florida once, and that was on a Sunday drive with Melvin and Faye, and we had barely even crossed the state line. Dad said we would be going to the Gulf Coast to a little town called St. Marks, southwest of Tallahassee. Then it hit me. I was going to see the ocean for the first time! Dad said that we wouldn't be fishing with a cane pole, which was all I had ever fished with, but instead, with a rod and reel. I had no idea how to use a rod and reel, but Daddy said he would teach me. The next day we went out in the yard, and he drew a circle on the ground about six feet in diameter. He said, "This is our target and we'll try to cast into the circle from about 20 yards away." He removed the hook from the line and replaced it with a small weight. He then showed me the technique of how to cast, and he demonstrated it for me. He was pretty good at hitting the target. Then it was my turn. On my first try, the weight only went about five feet, but after many attempts, I finally got the hang of it and began to hit the target or at least close to it. Dad said, "Looks like you're ready."

We left on our trip on Friday afternoon, right after lunch and after a 3-hour drive, arrived at Crumb's Fishing Camp. The camp was located on the St. Marks River a few miles from the open sea. Paul Black, my Uncle Lucius' brother, and his father were also with us. After checking into our cottage, we rented a boat, a rod and reel for me, bought some mullet to be used for bait, then headed down the river. Our boat was made of heavy wood and was 16 feet long. The outboard motor would move us along at about 25 miles per hour. We also had paddles and life preservers on board. On the way down the river, one of the men was cutting the mullet into small pieces for baiting our hooks. When we got to the open sea, I was fascinated. I had never seen so much water in my life! We continued to go about two miles out to a place they called the "flats". The water was not that deep, maybe 10 feet and there was tall grass growing on the bottom. They said that was the ideal place to catch speckled trout. Paul threw out and caught the first fish, about a two pounder. We all caught a few fish and then headed back in for the night.

Sometime late that night, I was awakened by a severe thunderstorm, but it passed quickly, and the sun was shining brightly the following morning. As we were preparing to move out, Paul's father, Mr. Liston, said, " Must have come a hell of a rain last night. The river is up two or three feet!" No one said anything. We just grinned at each other, knowing we were at high tide. Fishing in the same general area, we caught quite a few speckled trout that morning and after a lunch of saltines, sardines, and potted meat, we caught a few more before going in. I caught a small shark, maybe 18 inches long. Boy, did he pull good. They told me not to try to get the hook out of his mouth, so I just cut the line and tied on a new hook. A drove of sea gulls were constantly hovering over the boat and would try to grab the bait each time we would cast. I thought to myself, "I can catch one of those birds by casing by bait high in the air." On the second try, my line wrapped around a wing of one of the gulls. He couldn't' get loose and I reeled him in. The others had never seen that before.

On Sunday morning, we fished in closer to the shore where the water was deeper, and the bottom was sandy. There we caught white trout and sand mullet. Suddenly a large shark showed up and began biting our fish as we would reel them in. Many times, we would reel in half a fish. More sharks began coming, and soon there were a dozen large shark, five and six feet long, swarming around our boat. We began to get uneasy as they could have easily capsized the boat. We pulled in our anchor and called it quits for the weekend. We had a large cooler full of fish. We divided them when we got home, dressed them, and put them in the freezer. My first fishing trip to Florida had been a most enjoyable one.

When school started up in September, I was a high school freshman. One of my courses that year was agriculture, and I would be joining the FFA (Future Farmers of America). Joining the FFA required an initiation which was promptly set up. This initiation was conducted by those who were already members and supervised by the Agriculture teacher, Mr. Marvin Herrington. The initiation took place on a Friday night, and afterwards we would have a chicken barbecue across the street at a little park. When we arrived that evening, we were taken to the shop and blindfolded.

The first stop was the electric chair. I was strapped in a high-back, wooden chair and electrodes were attached to my arms and legs. The electricity was generated by turning a crank on some device, perhaps an old type telephone. Whatever it was, it gave a pretty good jolt. Next came the slop jar. They told me the slop jar was filled with urine and had turds floating around in it. I would have to reach in, grab a turd and eat it. That did not seem very appetizing to me, but I reached in and grabbed one. It turned out to be pieces of a Baby Ruth candy bar floating in Coca-Cola. Not so bad after all. Then I was taken outside to the gallows. I had to stand on a platform, and a noose was placed around my neck. Then the platform was raised until I felt my head touching the leaves of the tall oak tree we were under. I was told to jump off the platform. I hesitated but jumped anyway. To my surprise I was only a foot or two off the ground. There were a few more events to endure, but the worst was yet to come. My blindfold was removed, and we walked across the street to the park. There were two rows of boys facing each other, with about five feet between the two rows. Each boy had taken off his belt and held it in his hand. This was the dreaded beltline I had heard so much about. I would have to run uphill through this beltline which was about 50 yards long. I made it through OK but took a pretty good beating. I had some nasty looking red welts on my back and legs. Afterwards, we each roasted a half chicken over an open fire. Thank God that was over!

We were already practicing basketball as the season would be beginning soon. The school had purchased new uniforms a couple of years prior to that, which were black with red numerals on the jerseys. When the uniforms were issued, there were not enough of the new ones to go around, so most of us freshmen got an old uniform which was red with black numerals. I sat on the bench all that season, maybe getting in a few games with less than two minutes to go and our team behind by 20 points or more.

That spring of 1954, we were told that we would be going a big FFA rally at Abraham Baldwin College in Tifton, GA. There would be many competitive events to participate in, and we would be having some try-outs to see who would represent our school. There would be events such as throwing a baseball and a basketball for distance, base running, and a 75-yard dash to name a few. I knew I could run fast, so I figured the 75-yard dash would be my best event. The coach marked off 75 yards, and we had about 20 or so that wanted to run. We all lined up at the starting line and at the gun, I got off to a great start and began pulling away from the pack. I looked over and saw a senior, Sam Jones, running neck and neck with me. As we hit the finish line, I thought it was a tie, but the coach said that Sam had won by half a step. and he would represent us in that event. I didn't try out for anything else because I knew there were others who were better than me. As it turned out, Sam injured his foot and was unable to run, so I took his place.

When we got to the event, I was ready, or at least I thought I was. When it was my turn to run, I got off to a bad start. I was a step behind the leader and was unable to make it up, so I lost by that step. I enjoyed watching the other events, and little did I know that one of them was going to change my life forever. That event was the string band contest. I simply fell in love with the idea of playing one of those instruments. I made up my mind right then and there, that I was going to learn to play the guitar.

Upon returning home, I pulled my grandfather's old guitar out of the closet. He had given it to my brother Melvin years earlier. He had fooled around with it some but was not interested enough or dedicated enough to learn to play it. The old guitar had only three or four strings on it, so I bought a set of Black Diamond strings and Daddy put them on the guitar. I knew that he had played in his younger days, but I had never heard him play. He tuned up that old guitar, and wow! I couldn't believe how good he sounded as he began running through some chords. I thought he was good enough to be on the Grand Old Opry! Now it was my turn. Daddy showed me the chords he knew, and I began to practice them. It did not come easy.

I spent a minimum of two hours per day practicing those chords. Finally, I could run through the exercises that Daddy had shown me. I had learned five chords, but I couldn't put them to use in a song. My ear just wouldn't tell me when to change chords or what chord to change to. Then one day after about six months of practicing, it finally came to me. Now I was able to sing a song and get the chords in the right place. I only sang country songs, and most of them were three chord songs.

One day a friend of mine, Lawrence Hudson, invited me to go fishing with him. We put some hooks out in Bear Creek. After checking the hooks that night, to my surprise, he brought out a guitar. I didn't even know he could play, but actually he was pretty good. I learned three or four new chords that night and now I would be able to play in about five different keys, A, C. D, E, & G. whereas with the chords that Daddy taught me, I could only play in C & G. Lawrence also gave me my first lesson in playing lead. That was so exciting to me, and I continued to work on it.

During the 9th grade, I was invited to join the Beta Club. The Beta Club was, and maybe still is, an elite club for students who carry an 85 or better grade average in all subjects. One of the privileges of being a Beta Club member was that we got to take turns being secretary to the principal. I'll never forget the first time I had that duty. I even hesitate to put this in my book because people will think that I was the dumbest or most naive person that ever lived. Maybe I was, if not I was close. Anyway, it seemed that Mr. McDuffie was always out of the office, and I was there alone. I had absolutely no knowledge of the telephone or how to answer one. I had never been in a home that had a phone, and no one had ever taught me anything about one. So, when the phone would ring, I would simply pick it up, hold it to my ear, and say nothing. Sometimes after a long hesitation, they would say, "Hello?", and sometimes they would just hang up. The next time I worked in the office, I knew how to answer a phone.

Toward the end of the school year, we held the final meeting of the Beta Club. The main order of business at that meeting was to elect officers for the coming year. Someone nominated me for the office of president. I immediately declined, saying that I didn't feel I was qualified for the job. The president, Sanford Wills, also my first cousin, asked this question, "Johnny, who do you think is more qualified?" I thought for a minute, looked around the room and said, " OK, I'll take it." And so it was, I would be president for the next three years.

Since Melvin was now farming the Anderson Place, Daddy had hired a guy named Bill to help us that year. Bill and his wife Mary lived in the house where Melvin and his family had lived. Early one morning Mary walked up to our house. When Mama saw her, she said, "Oh, my God! What happened to you?" It was quite obvious that she had been severely beaten. She had two black eyes, and her face and neck were badly bruised. If there was one thing my daddy absolutely couldn't tolerate, it was a man hitting a woman. Daddy walked down to the house they were renting from us and confronted Bill. When Daddy was mad, he spoke with authority. He told Bill in no uncertain terms, "It's a low-down man that hits a woman. I want you out of this house before the sun goes down!" We never saw Bill again. Mary asked Daddy if he would move her and her household goods to Newnan, GA, which was roughly a hundred miles away. I don't know what her connection was to Newnan, but that Saturday, Daddy and I loaded up the truck and made the trip. That was also the last time I saw Mary.

Daddy was beginning to have problems with his back again. His doctor advised him to stop farming and to find some other way to make a living. Daddy agreed. After the crops were gathered that fall, Daddy began classes in upholstery and wood re-finishing at the South Georgia Trade and Vocational School in Americus.

During the latter part of June 1954, I began feeling bad. I was having abdominal cramps and pain. I felt tired all the time. Mama looked at me one day and said, "Your eyes are yellow. I think you've got yellow jaundice." Then my skin also started to look yellow. It took the best part of summer to get over it. I now know that what I had was Hepatitis "A" or Infectious Hepatitis. That's a serious disease that's transmitted by contaminated food or drink. It varies in severity from being so mild that you don't know you have it, to even death. I can't be 100 percent sure where I got it, but I've always believed it came from swimming in Bill Fussell's pond. The pond could have been contaminated with the hepatitis "A" virus. With no chlorine in the water, all one would need to do was accidentally consume a small amount of the water to become infected. Four years later when I was in medical laboratory school, I learned that my liver function tests were slightly elevated, indicating that I had suffered some slight liver damage. The test results have remained slightly elevated throughout my life.

When school started back that September, I was in terrible physical condition, but after about a month I was back in shape and ready to play basketball. I got a black uniform that year. My jersey was #5, the same one that my cousin Sanford had worn the previous year. Mama had ordered me a new pair of tennis shoes just before school started back. They were not the same brand as the other boys had, but they were white, and I was so proud to have them. We played Lumpkin High at home on the opening night of the season. Mr. McDuffie, the principal, was also our coach. He told us that he would be starting all seniors for that first game. We were losing the game early and Mr. Mac put one of my classmates, Bud Bone, in the game. Shortly afterwards, he looked at me and said, "Johnny, go in at center." I was really nervous but was ready. We were playing a zone defense, and I could tell they wanted to get the ball to their big center. I was guarding just to his right and slightly behind him. As the ball came to him, I was able to get a hand in and deflect it out of bounds. On their next attempt to pass to him, I intercepted the ball and began dribbling down the court. As I got to the top of the circle, I heard someone say, " shoot", so I shot. I had a very high arch on the ball, and for a second, I thought it was going over the backboard. Instead, it banked off the backboard right into the net for my first ever basket as a varsity player. Next time we came down the court, I fired a long shot from the left side of the court, which would easily have been a 3-point shot in today's game and hit nothing but net. We had the lead by the end of the first quarter and never trailed again. That big Lumpkin center tried to intimidate me by saying things like, "I'm gonna scratch your eyeballs out", but that didn't work. My playing had earned me a spot on the starting line-up, and I played virtually every minute of every game for the remainder of the season. I didn't score a lot of points in my sophomore year, 10 was my high for the season, but I was an excellent guard and rebounder.

Since Daddy was in school that fall, I would usually go to Melvin's on Saturday and help him however I could. On Saturday afternoon, we would listen to Georgia play football, and then at night we would play a card came called "set-back." We would usually play until the wee hours of morning, and once I remember playing all night. Faye would usually fix us a pitcher of ice water, or sometimes iced tea to drink while we played.

One day I was helping Melvin bale some hay, and we also had a colored boy, about 15 or 16 years old, helping us. Those old hay balers had some giant cog wheels on them, and somehow that boy laid his hand on a wheel, and it pulled his hand between the wheels, mangling his fingers. I heard him scream and turned around and saw what had happened. I ran to Melvin and told him. He took the boy on the tractor and headed to the house as fast as he could. I took a shortcut through the pasture and got there before they did. Melvin put a clean handkerchief over the boy's hand, so he wouldn't be looking at it. We put him in the car and headed toward town as fast as we could. The colored boy sat between us, and I put my arm around him and tried to comfort him as much as possible. I felt so bad for him because he was in so much pain. He cried and prayed all the way to the doctor's office. I was hoping they would give him something for pain right away, but instead, the nurse started asking a bunch of questions, like, "What did you have for breakfast?" I guess they had a reason for those questions, but I was thinking, "What the heck difference does it make about what he ate for breakfast?" The kid ended up losing his entire index finger, his middle finger and ring finger at the second joint and his thumb at the first joint.

Early in 1955, Daddy began to do some upholstery work. He had gotten some kind of assistance from the state to go to school, and they also provided him with the necessary tools to start his business. At first, he was working out of one of the rooms at home, but as business began to pick up, he opened a shop in Preston. I worked with him, doing whatever I could and at the same time learning as much as possible.

By now, I was doing pretty well with the guitar. Mama had said that when I learned to play, she would buy me a new one. Well, she stuck to her word and for my 16th birthday, she ordered me a new Silvertone from the Sears catalog. I think it cost about $15.00. It was so much nicer than the one I had been playing. I remember writing "1955" inside the guitar.

Since we weren't farming the Clark Place anymore, we had to move. So, we moved back into our old house at Bear Creek. That April, my brother Don was ten years old. We spent as much time as we could, fishing at the creek. We even built a trap from a nail keg to catch cray-fish. We would kill a bird for bait, put our trap in the creek overnight and catch 20 or 30 crayfish. We had no idea of how to cook them, so we would break off the tail and peel off the shell. Mama didn't much like doing it, but she would fry them for us. It was something like eating popcorn shrimp. That fall Don & I took care of cutting the firewood we would need for the winter and what a winter we had. We had about a 3-inch snowfall, the first in years, and it stayed on the ground for about a week.

In September, I started my Junior year of high school and was look-ing forward to a great year of basketball. I now weighed 155 pounds, and they measured me at 6 feet tall. Our entire team was made up from the junior class. Only Bud Bone and I had been starters the previous year. We started out kind of slow but improved dramatically throughout the season. I scored in double digits in quite a few games and had some very memorable moments. In a game at Lumpkin, the score was tied with 25 seconds to go. I had an open shot from 20 feet away, took the shot and it went in. They got off one last, long shot that missed. I got the rebound and dribbled out the clock. Some of our fans took up a collec-tion and gave me five dollars. That was a lot of money to me. In another game, I hit 6 out of 6 long shots in the first half. I went on to score 16 points, which would end up being my career high.

The tournament was played that year on our home court in Preston, and we drew a bye in the first round. We were playing Shellman High, a team that had beaten us twice in the regular season. We surprised them by beating them by 20 points. Now we were in the championship game against Ft. Gaines High. They were highly favored, but we kept the game close. In the fourth quarter with about two minutes to go in the game, we were down by three points when I hit a jump shot from the top of the circle. I was fouled on the play and made my free throw to tie the game. I believe that was the only three point play I ever made. After a couple more baskets by each team, the game ended in a tie, 55-55. In the two-minute overtime, each team scored four points to keep it tied. The referees then called for a sudden death overtime; the first team to score two points would be declared the winner. Ft. Gaines had the ball, and suddenly it was loose on the floor. One of their men dove for the ball and our center, Big George Hancock, also went for it. A foul was called on Big George and their star player, Jerry Hart, sank both free throws to win the game 61-59.

Since I was now 16 years old, I wanted to get my driver's license. An examiner came to Dawson once a week to give the exams. I did fine on the written exam, but when I got under the wheel of the pick-up truck, I blew it. First, I ran a stop sign and then cut a corner poorly. He asked, "Why did you run that stop sign with me in the vehicle with you?" I said, "Because nothing was coming, sir." He just shook his head and said, "Doesn't matter. You still have to come to a complete stop at stop signs." We went back inside, and he said, "Boy, I can't give you a driver's license. You go home and practice some more. Come back in two weeks and try again." When I returned two weeks later, I was scared to death that I would fail again. Instead, he handed my license to me and said, "Have a nice day and be safe." I was so happy and relieved.

I had my first date ever toward the end of the school year when I got up the courage to invite Martha Jean Bridges to the junior-senior prom. My classmate Thomas Kimbrel invited Jackie Hudson, and the four of us sat together that night. We all had a good time.

We made two big moves in early 1956. First, Daddy moved his upholstery shop from Preston to Dawson. Dawson was a much larger town, and he would be able to generate a lot more work. Then we left Bear Creek and moved to the Chambless place. The Chambless Place was located on GA Hwy 55 about 12 miles north of Dawson. It was also in Terrell County which meant I could now transfer to Terrell County High School for my senior year. But I didn't want to do that. I wanted to finish at Webster County High. Since we were only about a quarter mile from Webster County, I could walk over to the county line and catch the school bus there. The Chambless house was a much nicer house than we had at Bear Creek. It even had an indoor bathroom, although it was not usable. We still had an outhouse, which was all I ever had when I was growing up. The place contained more than 600 acres, and my Uncle Lucius Black had it leased for farming. He eventually purchased the place. The railroad track ran through the place with a freight train passing within a hundred yards of our house twice a day.

I was still working very hard with my guitar and was actually getting pretty good with it. My brother Don was learning to play the mando-lin and Jimmy, now seven, was playing the ukulele. I began taking my guitar to school almost every day. While on the bus, I would play, and several of the kids would sing along with me. We had a couple of pretty good musicians at school, all with the name of Blankenship. Aaron was an excellent harmonica player. By the way, he was the same guy that punched me in the nose for throwing his cap on the rooftop at school. Richard had been playing and singing for years, and Buddy, a new-comer at playing, was getting better by the day. We formed a little band and began playing quite often for a teen dance at the community center at Dumas, GA. One large family would come to our house on Saturday nights to hear me and my brothers play and sing. I suppose that was their big family night out.

One day our agriculture teacher asked us boys in the band if we would like to be on TV. It seemed that he had been invited to be the guest on a farm program at WRBL-TV in Columbus, GA. I chose a song I wanted to sing, and we began practicing. The song I chose to sing was "Why Don't You Haul off and Love Me" by Wayne Rainey and Lonnie Glosson. The song featured a harmonica, and since Aaron would be playing lead, it would be a perfect song. When the big day came around, everyone said we did very well, but nobody offered us a recording contract.

Back at school, girls were getting interested in my playing. They would come and sit by me and sing. Sometimes I would let then strum while I played the chords with my left hand. They loved that.

Then it happened. I got invited out by a girl! Wow! She asked me to come and go skating with her on Saturday night. I told her I couldn't skate, but she said, "That's OK, I'll teach you." Her name was Brenda Jo Thurmond. She was two grades behind me. I had first seen her when she was in the first grade at Weston School, but hadn't seen much of her since then. Weston School was now closed, and the auditorium was being used as a skating rink every Saturday night. Brenda's mother, Mrs. Lois Thurmond, was the person in charge of running it.

Saturday rolled around, and I was pretty excited about going, but I knew I would be falling on my butt and that would be embarrassing. When I arrived, she met me with a big smile and "hello". I rented some

65

skates and put them on. I couldn't even stand up, but she held my arm and kept me from falling. She held on to me for the entire evening as we slowly made our way around the rink. The evening went quickly, and I actually had a good time. She asked if I would come back next Saturday for lesson number two. I told her I would love to, and we said good-night, and I went home.

I could hardly wait for the next Saturday night to roll around. I had spoken to her briefly at school that week and told her I would be there. I met her as before and put my skates on. This time I was able to keep my balance a little better. However, she was there if I needed her. Brenda was an excellent skater. She could skate backwards as well as she could forward. There were only two others who could match her performance, and they were the McNeil kids, a brother and sister from Parrott. They would dance together most of the evening. I was definitely making some progress. I could go around the rink without falling, although slowly. Then Brenda said, "Take my hands." I did, and around the rink we went with her going backwards. We danced away the evening like that, and again time went by very fast. I asked her if I could drive her home that night. The Thurmonds lived on Hwy 55, only a mile north of Weston. They had a nice brick home; far nicer than any place I had ever lived, and they also had a little country store near the house. We went to her mother and asked if I could take her home, and her Mom gave permission. After driving her home, we said good-night as before, and I was on my way. At that time Brenda was two months shy of her 15th birthday, which would be coming up on July 7th. Sometime during the following week, she said, "Why don't you come by and pick me up to go skating this Saturday?" She said she would be at the store. I reluctantly said I would. I knew I would have to meet her father, Mr. Claude Thurmond, and that made me uncomfortable. I had never met him before but had heard that he was a pretty rough character.

When I walked into the store the following Saturday, Brenda again met me at the door with that big smile. I said hello to her mother, who was always very nice, and then she took me over to meet her father, who was seated in a big chair at the end of the store watching TV. I was so scared I was shaking in my shoes. We shook hands, but he didn't speak, just stared at me. I was glad to get out of there and be on the way to the skating rink. She said he would be different once he got to know me. I wasn't so sure about that.

School was finally out for the summer. I went to work almost every day with my Dad to help in the shop. I would strip the old covers off of sofas and chairs that he was re-upholstering and would remove all the old tacks and staples. I enjoyed removing those covers because you never knew what you would find. There would almost always be a few coins in every sofa or chair. Then I learned how to cut the material and would assist Dad in tacking or stapling on the new covers. About the only thing I never learned to do well, was sew on the heavy-duty sewing machine. On Friday afternoon, Daddy would always give me a $10 bill. I had never made over $2 per day on the farm, however, Uncle Lucius had begun to pay $3 per day when I would help him that summer.

I continued to go skating with Brenda every Saturday night that summer and became a pretty good skater, although I never learned to skate backwards. I asked Brenda if she would like to go to a movie with me sometime, maybe the following Friday night. She said she would, so we approached her mom for permission. She gave the OK, but said she wanted Brenda home by 11:00 PM. That Friday night we went to Americus, which was 27 miles away, for a movie. On the way home that night, we had a little extra time, so we pulled off the road very near the place where my school bus had wrecked on my first day to ride the bus. We sat there and talked for a little while, and then she said, "Say terrify." I had no idea what she was getting at, but I said it. Then she said, "Say tissue." I did and then she said, "Say both words together, fast." So, I said, "Terrify tissue." She responded by saying, "No, go right ahead." It took a moment to realize that what I said sounded like, "Care if I kiss you?" I was stunned. I had never kissed a girl in my life and didn't even know how. Neither did she, but we both had our first lesson in kissing that night. We began dating regularly after that, and I began to have a special feeling for her. I was falling in love. So was she. Later that summer I gave her my class ring, and she gave me her gold watch.

Since my camping trip to the North Georgia Mountains in 1951 and the following year my brother Melvin telling me about Sir Edmond Hillary climbing Mt. Everest, the world's highest mountain, I had become fascinated with mountains. I had learned that Mt. Enota or

Brasstown Bald was Georgia's highest mountain at 4,768 ft. I wanted so much to go up on top of it. So, one Saturday, in the summer of 1956, Daddy agreed to let Mama and me take the pick-up and drive up there. We left early on a Saturday morning and arrived on top of the mountain around 11:00 AM. I felt like I was on top of the world. We had packed a picnic lunch, so we ate and then began our trip back. The road was very steep on the mountain side, and I didn't put the truck into a lower gear. Instead, I was holding it back with the brakes. Next thing I knew the brake pedal was on the floorboard. The brakes were smoking hot. I finally got the truck stopped and figured out that I needed to put it in a lower gear. Anyway, we made it down the mountain safely and was on our way home. About halfway home, the truck began to make a terrible squealing noise. I had no idea what it was but slowed down and it stopped. When I would get above 25 mph, it would start squealing again. At that point, we were 100 miles from home, so we continued to drive home at 25 mph. Daddy was expecting us home at around 8:00 PM, but we finally pulled in at around 10:00 PM. Daddy was standing outside, worried sick and looking for us. We told him what the truck was doing. He raised the hood and determined that the problem was only a loose belt. He tightened the belt, and the problem was solved.

School started back in September, and I was now a senior. I was really involved with Brenda by now, and we were passing love notes back and forth. While the rest of the boys in my class spent their recesses and lunch break in the smoking area, I was sitting on the steps with Brenda. I didn't smoke, and I had no desire to. I had tried a cigar when I was 15. It made me deathly sick. I lay on the porch for an hour with my head hanging over the side.

Early in my senior year, we learned that our principal and coach, Mr. McDuffie, would be retiring at the end of 1956. He was going to be replaced by Robert Pinkston. We heard that Mr. Pinkston had had a lot of experience coaching basketball, and that he would be a great asset to our team. We were heavily favored to win the conference championship and go to the state tournament. We lost one game that fall to Plains, and we had received an invitation to play in a Christmas Tournament in Cuthbert, GA during the holidays. Mr. Pinkston would take over the coaching duties for that tournament. We were playing

Cuthbert High, a class "B" school in the first round. We were a Class "C" school. He started the usual line-up with me at one of the guard positions, but middle way the first quarter he pulled me out of the game. I will never understand why he pulled me out. I had been a starter since the first game of my sophomore year, and now he's replaced me with someone with zero experience. We went on to lose that game by 10 points. I never started another game, and I only got to play a couple of minutes, usually in the second half of the remaining games. Our team went 20-3 for the season, losing two more games to Vienna, who was in a different conference.

Brenda and I continued to date hot and heavy during my senior year, in fact I think we were known as the "love birds" of the school. Brenda also played basketball but was not a starter. At that time the girls played a six-girl team, three guards and three forwards. Brenda was a guard. Fans loved to see her in a game because she was rough on the opposing players. Because of that, she was called for lots of fouls.

By now, I think I was well accepted by both of Brenda's parents. Her mom wanted me to call her "Trapie", and her dad told me to call him "C.P.". They would often take us places with them and would always pay for our meals if we went out to eat. It was almost like I was part of the family.

At some point during my senior year, I was listening to some country music on the radio when I heard an announcement that Jim & Jessie, The Virginia Boys were going to be appearing in Shellman for a concert, but what really got my attention was when they announced that they would also be holding a talent contest. I began to consider entering the contest. I finally decided that my brother Don and I would enter together. I would play my guitar and Don the mandolin. I decided on a song by the Louvin Brothers. They were a duo that also played guitar and mandolin. The song I chose was "I Don't Believe You've Met My Baby", which was a big hit at the time. We began practicing, and by the time the contest got there, we were able to play it note for note without any mistakes. Don was especially impressive on his mandolin. He was only 11 years old at the time. Daddy drove us to Shellman that night. As we waited backstage, Don would play some tunes on his mandolin, so we would stay warmed up. There was a Blue Grass Band back there watching us, and I overheard one of them tell his mandolin player, "That little boy can play a mandolin better than you." There were four entries in the contest, the Blue Grass Band, a guy singing an Elvis song, another singer, and us. We performed our song flawlessly, but we didn't stand much of a chance to win. The winner was determined by the amount of applause from the audience. The Blue Grass Band won; I think because they were a local group, and they brought a lot of fans with them. We came in third. In all fairness, I think the Elvis singer should have won. He sang "Baby, Let's Play House", and boy did he nail it! Although we didn't win, we had fun, and it was a great experience. Had Don pursued it, he could have been a great mandolin player, but unfortunately, after I graduated and left home, he gave it up. I suppose he just didn't have the interest to keep going after losing his guitar partner.

The basketball tournament was being held in Lumpkin. After getting a bye in the first round, we were playing Shellman High in the second round. We had easily beaten them twice in the regular season. At half-time, we had jumped out to a 20-point lead. They began to make a comeback in the 3rd quarter. When one of our starters fouled out late in the 3rd quarter, I was sure the coach would put me in the game. Instead, he put in an inexperienced player, and by the end of the quarter, the lead was at 10 points. The final quarter did not start well as they got a quick basket to cut the lead to eight. Midway the quarter, the lead was at five, and then we lose another starter to fouls. The fans were now shouting, "Put Johnny in! Put Johnny in!" Mr. Pinkston walked down in front of the bench and picked out a sophomore who had hardly ever been in a varsity game. We were getting beat because Shellman had been applying full court pressure, and our guards couldn't get the ball up the court. Now with two inexperienced players trying to bring the ball up the court, it was a disaster. And there I was, probably the best ball handler on the team and no doubt the best rebounder, sitting on the bench, frustrated. They took a two-point lead in the final minute and then our star player, Bud Bone, hit a shot from the top of the circle to tie the game. In overtime, it was all Shellman as we suffered a humiliating defeat. Everyone was stunned. I was not only stunned, but mad. In fact, I was so mad I didn't even go to the consolation game the following night, a game which meant absolutely nothing anyway. I will never understand what Mr. Pinkston's way of thinking was. Apparently, he didn't like me for some reason. I'll never know what that reason was, I can only speculate.

When baseball got underway, it would be more of the same. I wasn't a superstar, but I understood the game and was one of the better power hitters. When the uniforms were issued to the starting lineup, Mr. Pinkston, also the baseball manager, made it known that he didn't want me on the team by not giving me a uniform. He said that more uniforms would be issued later, but I wasn't about to sit on the bench all season with very little chance of getting to play. So, I dropped off the team and used the activity period for another study hall.

Graduation would be coming up soon and we would be going on a class trip. We had been raising money for that trip by running the concession stand during basketball games. Most of the class was on the ball team, so we received lots of help from some of the teachers and parents. We decided on a trip to Florida. The trip would last for a week. We made all the necessary reservations so that we would be ready to go the week after graduation.

I was sure that Joanne Williams would be the valedictorian of our class, but she wasn't as sure. She and I had been running neck and neck with our grades throughout high school, but I had unfortunately made a couple of "C's" in the 11th grade, and I knew that was going to pull me down. She and I went to the office one day to check our records. As it turned out, she had a 92.2 average for the final four years, and I had a 90.8, so I would be the salutatorian.

We graduated nine boys and two girls. The only change during high school was that Betty had dropped out of school during the 11th grade to get married, but we picked up another student, Vickie, to keep the class at eleven.

During our senior year, Frank Rogers, my arch-enemy had actually started acting decent toward me. He even invited me to go with him to parties a few times. He always wanted me to bring my guitar so that he could impress the girls.

Graduation went smoothly, and I made my salutatorian speech without a flaw. I was glad to finally be out of school, but it was also sad in a way because I knew I wouldn't be seeing much of my classmates again. I received lots of nice gifts after graduation, including some monetary gifts. I could use that on the class trip.

The money that was left after we paid the lodging bills and transportation costs was divided among the students. We all had something over a hundred dollars each.

We headed off to Florida on a Monday morning. Our first stop was St. Augustine, the nation's oldest city. There we took in all the sights including the Fountain of Youth, which I drank from, but apparently it didn't help me. We spent our first night at the Holiday Motel, and the next morning we headed out to Marineland, a few miles to the south. We all enjoyed the dolphin and whale show at the aquarium. From there, we went to the Ocala area where we went to Silver Springs and to a reptile farm. There were a lot of orange groves in that area, and I remember the bus stopping at one point, so we could jump off the bus to steal a few oranges from the trees. Then we stopped at a little fruit stand, and my friend Jerry Kirksey and I spotted a sign that read, "All the orange juice you can drink for 10 cents." We walked in and said, "Is that sign true?" The man stared at us without cracking a smile and said, "Yeah, well, up to a point." I think he knew exactly what we were up to. We laid our dimes on the counter, and he brought out a quart container of juice which we promptly consumed and then asked for more. He brought out another quart, and we drank that one. We told him we would like one more. The third one was watered down so much, it was barely orange colored. We got up and walked out without saying a word.

Leaving Ocala, we made our way over to the Florida panhandle for a stop at Panama City. The beach was beautiful but crowded. Gerald Smith and I headed out for a swim. He was the same friend I was with back in 1951 when I almost drowned at summer camp. Undoubtedly, we were at low tide and we couldn't get over how far we could wade out from shore. We were only in waist deep water when the life guard began blowing his whistle and motioning for us to come back toward the shore. We didn't think we were in any danger, but I guess he thought otherwise. Now I realize he was probably right.

After spending Friday night at the beach, we got up early and began our four-hour trip home. By now, most of the class was flat broke, but being a conservative person, I still had $65.00 in my pocket. It had been a fun week, and it went by quickly. However, I was ready to go home, because I hadn't seen Brenda for a week. I picked her up that evening, and we went skating and then to the Dairy Cream in Richland for a milk shake.

I still had one more graduation present coming. Mr. J.P. Kinney, our chemistry teacher, had given all the boys in the class a fishing trip to Lake Blackshear. Mr. Kinney owned a cabin on the lake which was located on the Flint River near Cordele, GA. He would entertain two boys per trip. Gerald Smith and I went together. We arrived at the cabin on Friday evening, and Mr. Kinney was preparing dinner for us. After a good night's sleep, we got up early, had breakfast, packed a lunch and some drinks, then headed out on the lake. We caught lots of fish, but they were all small: bream and channel catfish. We returned to the cabin late that afternoon, thanked Mr. Kinney for an enjoyable time, and headed home.

Now that I had been around Brenda's father for a while, I had grown to like him, and we became close friends. One day he asked if I'd like to go fishing with him. I said, "Sure, I'm always ready to go fishing." He was a member of a club which had a nice pond that was well stocked and well maintained. C.P. had his own boat, a small two-man wooden boat which he kept at the pond. We would be fishing for bream this day, so we got two cane poles and a box of worms and headed out. He very gently paddled the boat to a spot among some dead trees and threw out the anchor. He said that this was a good place for bream. He was right. He baited his hook, threw in, and something grabbed it right away. I could tell that he was really enjoying this, because he began talking to the fish while he played it in. He pulled in a bream that was bigger than any I had caught in my entire life. It had beautiful shades of red, orange, and yellow on its breast. He said, "This one's got on a suit and tie." He explained that when you hang a nice one like that you have to just keep the line tight and let him fight until he's worn out. Then you pull him in. I caught on quickly and caught several nice fish. By the time we quit, we had 20 or more nice bream. Back at the store, we cleaned them, and Trapie fried them for us. She also made a big pot of grits. It just doesn't get any better than that. Brenda's aunt and uncle were also there to enjoy the meal with us. There was more than enough for all. C.P. told me that next time we went fishing, he would teach me how to fish for bass.

I couldn't wait!

I don't know why, but one day a man from the voter registration office came to the store and told me he would like to register me, so I could vote in the next election. He said it was just a matter of filling out a form and taking a little exam. I didn't see where that would be a problem, because I had just finished a course in government my senior year. He handed me the exam and scanning over it, I saw that the questions were pretty basic. Then he handed me another sheet of paper numbered 1-20 and I asked, "What's this?" He said it was the answer sheet and told me to deliberately miss one or two questions, so it wouldn't look suspicious. Heck, I knew the answers to all the questions without looking at the answer sheet. I told him I didn't need the answer sheet. He said, "Yeah, but most people do." Then he explained that when colored people try to register, they don't get the answer sheet. I didn't say anything, but I was thinking, "Something's not right here."

Brenda and I were deeply in love, and we began talking about getting married. I really wanted her for my wife. I guess she was that little puddin' faced girl my dad had talked about. One day I sat down and wrote her a little poem, which is also a song that I still sing occasionally. It's entitled, "You're the one for me".

> Every time I see you smile at me,
> And think of what it does to me,
> I know that I want you to be,
> The only one for me.
>
> Darling, when I hold your hand,
> Everything, it seems so grand,
> It's almost more than I can stand,
> Cause you're the one for me.
>
> When you and I go out at night,
> The stars above us shine so bright,
> And everything we do is right,
> Cause you're the one for me.

If everything will go my way,
And if I can get you to say,
That you'll be my own someday,
Cause you're the one for me.

I love you my dear you know,
What else can I do to show,
You how much I love you so,
Cause you're the one for me.

I began to see a problem, and that concerned me. I didn't have a job. I was helping my dad almost every day, but business wasn't good enough for him to pay me a salary. He gave me $10 per week so I would have a little pocket change, but that certainly wouldn't support a household. And besides, where would we live? We could probably stay with our parents for a while, but eventually we would want our own place to live.

We talked this over with Trapie, Brenda's mom, and she agreed that she would allow us to get married, but I would have to agree and encourage Brenda to finish high school. I had no problem with that.

Trapie had a brother, Millard Johns, and a sister, Elna, who was married to J.B. Budjinski. Both Millard and J.B. were career soldiers and had been in the Army for about 15 years. When they got the word that Brenda and I were planning to get married, they began talking to me about going into the military. I think the whole family, including Trapie, thought it was a good idea. C.P. never commented one way or the other. I believe my parents thought they might be pushing me into something I really didn't want.

CHAPTER 7

U.S. Army, Here I Come

I WANTED TO get more information about the Army, so I decided to go and talk with a recruiter. I learned that an Army recruiter from the Albany, GA recruiting station came to Dawson one afternoon per week, so I paid him a visit. He explained that by enlisting, as opposed to waiting to be drafted, I could choose almost any field I wanted to go into, and I would be sent to school to learn that job or profession. He also explained that I would go in as a Private E-1, with a starting pay of $78 per month. First, I would have to go through eight weeks of basic military training. I would then automatically be promoted to Private E-2 with a salary of $85.80 and would then attend the school I had signed up for. After that, I would be given a permanent assignment, and after I had been in for eight months, I would be eligible for promotion to Private First Class (PFC) and would then be paid $99.37 per month. I told him about my plans to marry and asked what, if any, benefits we might receive. He told me that once I got out of basic training, I would be eligible to live off post with my wife, and she would receive a check for $91.00 per month for housing allowance. I would also be able to draw about $30 per month for separate rations, in place of eating in the mess hall, and would also get a small clothing allowance. I certainly wasn't ready to decide that day, so I thanked him for his time and left.

A few days later, C.P. and I went bass fishing. We still used our cane poles but put on a larger hook. We had a bucket of live minnows for bait. C.P. paddled the boat out in the open water with no trees around. We adjusted the cork float so that we would be fishing at a depth of about two feet. He told me it would be a little slower than catching the bream. For me, it was a lot slower. I didn't get a bite all morning. He caught one that weighed about two pounds. We left at noon, and he said we'd try again another day. I didn't enjoy the fishing, but C.P. entertained me with some stories. He told me about a friend he once had, a fellow by the name of "Shorty." He said Shorty was a pool shark, and they would go around to pool halls and hustle people. It seems they would go to a town where no one knew them and would find a pool hall. They would enter the hall separately so that no one would know they were together. People were always betting on the players. Shorty would get in a game, and C.P. would place a small bet on him, maybe $5. Shorty would lose big time. Then C.P. would raise the bet to maybe $20, and Shorty would win, but he could make it look like he was just having a lot of luck with his shots. Then someone would want to bet C.P. maybe $50 or $100 that Shorty couldn't win again. C.P. would reluctantly take him up on the bet. If Shorty broke, he would run the table and if the other guy broke, he better not miss, or he wouldn't get another shot. If it looked like someone was catching on to their scheme, they would leave, but not together. Then it was on to the next town and next pool hall. C.P. also told me that he loved to play poker. He said that he had lost a thousand dollars more than once in a poker game, but overall, he thought he was about even.

I kept thinking about going in the Army. If I went in, what did I want to do? I started thinking about my relatives and what they did. Most of them were farmers, and that had been out of the question for a very long time. And besides, the Army didn't do any farming. Then I remembered my Uncle Raymond Chambers. He had gone to school to be a pharmacist, and now he was working in a drug-store, filling prescriptions. I thought that sounded like a neat job. Uncle Raymond had studied pharmacy at the University of Georgia. I knew my parents couldn't afford to send me there or to any other college for that matter. Brother Melvin suggested that I might be able to get some kind of assistance from the state or federal government.

I spoke to Uncle Lucius Black who was a representative in the Georgia Legislature. He said my best bet was to prove some kind of disability. I really didn't think I was disabled, but I had been having some problem with my upper back, so I decided to give it a try. I filled out an application and a few days later, I was notified that they had set me up an appointment with an orthopedic doctor to see if I would qualify. After my exam, the doctor said that he could not declare me disabled. Now I was back to square one. It looked like my only hope of becoming a pharmacist was to have the Army train me. So, back to the recruiter I went. I told him I was ready to enlist if he could get me into pharmacy school. He was excited to have a new recruit, but when he started checking on the school, he found that it had been closed. The Army was drafting all the pharmacists they needed as they graduated from college. Then he started telling me which schools were available in the medical field. These included X-Ray, Physical Therapy, and Medical Laboratory. I asked him what I would be doing in Medical Laboratory, and he started reading a description of what I would learn. In hematology, I would be counting red blood cells and white blood cells under a microscope. I would also learn chemistry, bacteriology, parasitology, serology, and blood banking. I told him that sounded interesting and for him to give me a guarantee that I would be going to that school. He said it wouldn't be a problem, that I would have it in writing and would be going to the induction station in Atlanta toward the end of September. He said he would be in touch with me.

Well, a few days later, he called and said I would be leaving for Atlanta on September 26. I asked if he had my letter of confirmation to go to Medical Laboratory School. He said he had not received it yet. I said, "Well, forget it. I'm not going in without it." He went into a panic and said, "Oh, no, don't back out. I'll work something out and call you back in a little while." An hour later he called back and said he had received my confirmation by telegram. I said, "OK, see you Tuesday."

I spent most of the weekend with Brenda, and we made tentative plans for our wedding on Sunday, December 22, 1957. I figured that even If I didn't get to go home for the holidays until the 21st, I could get a flight and still make the wedding. I knew I would be at Ft. Sam Houston in San Antonio, Texas for Medical Lab School. I kissed Brenda good-bye on Sunday night and spent Monday with my parents and brothers. Mama had tears in her eyes as I told her good-bye on Tuesday morning, then Daddy and I left for Albany. When we arrived at the recruiting station,

I told Daddy to go in with me, that I wanted to see that telegram. The recruiter opened my file and produced the telegram. It said something like I was enlisting with the understanding that I would be attending the Army Medical Laboratory School at Ft. Sam Houston, Texas. I told Daddy good-bye, and I was alone and on my own. The recruiter handed me a large manila envelope along with my ticket to Atlanta, then drove me to the bus station. It was more than an hour before my bus would be leaving. While I waited, a boy approached me, also with the same type manila envelope. He had spotted mine and said, "You goin' in?" I looked up and said, "Yep, I am." Now I wasn't alone anymore. We sat together and talked as we made the trip to Atlanta. We were met at the bus station by an Army guy in uniform who took us to the induction station. When I walked into the station, I spotted a familiar looking person sitting there. He saw me as I walked over to him, and he asked, "What are you doing here?" I replied, "I was about to ask you the same thing." It was my first cousin, Dallas Wills. He said, "I was drafted." And I said, "I enlisted." Now I was with both friend and family. Maybe it wouldn't be so bad after all. There were probably 15 or 20 recruits, and they took us into a large room full of cots. They told us to pick a cot and to come to the mess hall for dinner in 20 minutes. I was about to get my first big shock. I took a seat at the long table, and two colored boys sat down directly across from me. I had never eaten at a table with colored people, and I was not brought up that way, but I knew it was something I would have to get used to if I was going into the army.

We were up early the next morning, had breakfast, and then went through an extensive physical examination. Then we took some written exams, signed a lot of papers, and went before an officer to be sworn in. Before being sworn in, he said that if any of us who volunteered wanted to drop out, this was the last chance. Once sworn in, we were in for three years. After everyone was sworn in, we got on a bus and headed out for Ft. Jackson, SC for basic training. That evening, we were assigned to a barracks and retired for the night. We had double bunks, and I was sleeping on top.

At 5 AM, a speaker directly above me blared out, "Get out of that bed! Hit the floor! You've got ten minutes to be in formation at the orderly room!" I jumped out of bed, ran to the latrine (bathroom), shaved, got dressed as quickly as I could, and was out the door. It wasn't a formation, but a crowd gathered around the orderly room. We all got assigned service numbers that morning. If you enlisted, your number was "RA" followed by eight digits. If you were drafted, your number was "US" followed by eight digits. Then we went to the quartermaster. They gave us one set of fatigues, a pair of boots, and a cap and told us to put them on. Up until then, we had all been in our street clothes. They told us we would get our full clothing allowance the following day. That first set of fatigues was about two sizes too large. I had my picture made in them and sent it to my parents. Mama told me later that she felt so sorry for me. That night it started raining and turned off cold. Another boy and I were put on duty to keep the furnace going that night. We sat up all night and kept adding coal as necessary to keep the fire going. By morning, the temperature must have been in the high 30s. Anyway, we got our full issue of clothing that day. They said it would be a few days before we could start basic training, and in the meantime, we would pull whatever details that were necessary. We had not yet had a class in military courtesy but had been told to salute officers. Well, that evening, I was walking toward a building with a buddy, when a lieutenant walked out. We didn't salute. He turned around and really chewed us out. Next day as we walked along the sidewalk, we were meeting a sergeant. I asked my friend, "Do we salute him?" He said, "I'm not sure. We better salute. We can't go wrong." Boy was that a mistake! That sergeant turned us every way but loose. He told us not to ever salute a sergeant again. You can bet, we didn't!

By now, we had been at Ft. Jackson for a week and still didn't know when we would start basic training. Then one morning we were told that we wouldn't be able to start training for quite some time and that we would be transferred to Ft. Gordon, GA. That suited me fine, because I would be closer to home. The following morning, they loaded us on busses, and we began to make the 80-mile trip. As it was at Ft. Jackson, the post was filled with many wooden buildings that had been hastily built during World War II. We were assigned to one of the two-story wooden barracks. We were introduced to our platoon sergeant, and he informed us that training would begin the following day.

First, we learned to march and learned all the military commands.

Then we were issued an M-1 Rifle. We learned to assemble and disassemble the weapon and how to keep it cleaned and oiled. That rifle would be our best friend if we ever had to go into combat. The rifles were locked in a gun rack in the aisle of the barracks except when we went to the range. Ammunition was issued to us only when we were on the firing line. And there was one thing you better not do and that was to call your rifle a gun. The drill sergeant considered your private part your gun. And if he caught you calling your rifle your gun, he would make you hold your rifle over your head and hold your "gun" in your other hand and run around the platoon 10 times shouting, "This is my rifle, and this is my gun. This is for fighting and this is for fun." I never called my rifle a gun.

I enjoyed going to the rifle range except for one thing. The noise was hurting my ears. When some of us complained, our instructor simply said, "Get used to it. When you go into combat, you won't have any ear protection." I was at a point that I couldn't stand it anymore, so I took my scissors and cut some small pieces of material from my mattress and made some ear plugs. I packed them deeply into my ears, and no one ever noticed them. They worked fine. We practiced firing the M-1 from 100, 200, and 300 yards. After we finished the rifle range training, we had to take a qualification test by firing a certain number of rounds from each distance. You had to score at least 160 out of a possible 240 points to qualify. There were three levels of qualification: marksman, sharpshooter, and expert. A score of 160 to 179 qualified you as a marksman, 180 to 211 a sharpshooter, and 212 and above, an expert. A few days after qualification we got a sheet with everyone's score. I was thrilled when I scanned down the list to find a 212 by my name. I was awarded the Expert Rifleman's Badge to wear on my class "A" uniform.

We went through many different types of training. The training sites were scattered all over the post. We marched everywhere we went. To break the monotony, we would sing little songs as we marched. The drill sergeant would lead, and we would repeat after him, songs such as, "G.I. beans and G.I. gravy, gee it almost drives me crazy." Then he'd say, "Sound off". We'd say, "One, two", then he'd say, "Sound off", we'd say, "Three, four." He'd say, "Sing it on down". We'd say, "One, two, three, four, one, two (pause) three-four." There were many little songs like this that we sang.

One night we had to get up at midnight to go on a 14-mile walk, reaching our destination just before dawn. It was freezing cold that morning, and I remember us gathering twigs and making a fire in a 55-gallon drum, then hovering around it to stay warm.

The hand grenade course was one of my favorites. We would try to toss practice hand grenades into a ten-foot circle, some 30 yards away. I was really good at that, maybe from throwing a baseball so much when I was a kid. Some of the guys would tell me, "If we ever go to combat, I hope I'm with you." At the end of the course, we got to throw one live grenade. One by one we stood in a little cubicle with a three-foot log partition on each side. With the instructor beside us, we would toss the grenade over an eight-foot log wall. If for any reason we dropped the grenade, or if it didn't go over the wall, we were to dive over the partition and hit the dirt. Under no circumstance were we to pick it up and throw it again. We never had an accident in our platoon.

All of our drill sergeants and instructors were war hardened veterans who had fought through two wars: World War II and the Korean Conflict. Discipline and following orders were of utmost importance. They absolutely did not tolerate anyone getting out of line or back-talking. I don't know exactly what happened, but one morning while we were eating breakfast, one of the guys picked up a knife and threatened a drill sergeant. That was a mistake. I'm sure that sergeant had been trained in hand-to-hand combat. He stood right up to the guy and said, "Soldier, drop that knife or I'll break your arm!" After a slight hesitation, the knife fell on the table.

The confidence course was a lot of fun except for one exercise, and it was scary and downright dangerous. There was a pole about 60 feet tall, maybe a little more, with a large rope attached to the top. The other end of the rope was anchored to the ground about 100 feet away. You had to climb a ladder to reach the top, then wrapping your legs over the rope and hanging on with your hands, work your way to the ground. It made me a little nervous, but I was in great shape and had no problem with it, same with most of the other guys. When it was my cousin Dallas Wills' turn, I became worried. Dallas was a big man. He always had the tendency to be somewhat overweight. When he got to the top of the pole, he was shaking. I was very concerned that he couldn't hold on and would fall, and there was no net below, just the hard ground. Nothing good could come from a fall from 60 feet up. I watched as the instructor very patiently talked Dallas into first wrapping his legs over the rope and holding on with every ounce of strength he had, slowly work his way to the ground. I was so relieved to see him make it down safely.

I called Brenda once from Ft. Jackson but had not been able to call from Ft. Gordon, however, we wrote to each other often. It was always so exciting to go to mail call and receive a letter. There was another guy in our platoon named Johnny Wills. He was from Commerce, GA or somewhere around that area. As far as I know, we were not related, but they had trouble during mail call or when we were being put on some kind of detail. They would call Johnny Wills, and we would always say, "Which one?"

My best friend during basic training was a boy from Asheville, NC by the name of Bill Creasman. He had never had a girlfriend, so one day I suggested he write to one of Brenda's classmates, Sharleene Dunlap. Sharleene was Brenda's best friend in school. She was a redhead with a great smile and personality. I told Bill to write her a letter, but he had no idea what to say, so he asked me to write it for him. That was a little awkward, but I did it, and he copied the letter. He eventually made a trip to meet her in Preston, but their relationship never made it very far. A few years later, Sharleene married my cousin, Dallas.

We had been told that we would get a weekend pass midway through basic. The end of the fourth week rolled around, and we were dismissed on Friday at noon and given our pass. Dallas and I took the military bus to nearby Augusta, where we bought a ticket and took the Trailways Bus to Americus. Someone from the family met us there and took us home. It was great to see my family again. Brenda was also at my parents' home, and she had come prepared to spend the night. That way I got to spend more time with both her and my family. The weekend went by in a hurry, and on Sunday afternoon, Dallas and I took the bus back to Augusta.

The second four weeks went by smoothly, and then it was the big finale, the dreaded infiltration course, which we had to go through at night. That would determine if we passed basic training successfully. The infiltration course was a field about 100 yards wide and at the far end of the field was a ditch or trench about five feet deep. Just beyond the ditch were two machine guns which would sporadically fire over the field at a height of four feet. The barrels of the guns rested on a stationary steel bar that would not allow them to fire any lower. The field was filled with mines and several rows of barbed wire and concertina wire. Our assignment was to crawl across the field, go under the wire and into the ditch, then run to safety. I did the low crawl with my M-1 Rifle across my forearms. When I would get to the barbed wire, I would lie on my back with my weapon over my face and body for protection from the wire, pushing my way along with my feet. The machine guns were firing tracer rounds, and you could see the red streaks flying overhead. Meanwhile, explosions were going off all around me. I don't know how long it took, maybe 15 minutes, but it seemed like an eternity. I had made it through basic training, and now I could move on to my advanced training, which is what I signed up for.

I got my orders the following day for my assignment at Ft. Sam Houston, TX. That afternoon, all of us who were going into the medical field were transported to the Army Airfield, and we boarded a C-47 military transport plane. The C-47 is a relatively small, twin engine plane that was used extensively during World War II. This would be my very first time to fly. I was excited!

After taking off, the pilot banked hard right as we headed west and was gaining altitude. I began feeling a little queasy, but once we leveled off, I was fine. I had a window seat, and I think I gazed out that window the entire trip. The pilot would often tell what city we were flying over. It was a fascinating experience for me. We had left Ft. Gordon in late afternoon, and darkness had engulfed us about halfway through our trip. When we flew over Houston, TX, I was amazed at how spread out the city was. After landing at Lackland Air Force Base in San Antonio, we were bussed over to Ft. Sam Houston and were assigned quarters for the night.

Next morning, we were taken to a large meeting room, and a sergeant began calling names and separating us into groups depending on what school we would be attending. When he began calling the names of those going to Medical Laboratory School, I was anxiously waiting to hear my name. Finally, he announced, "That's it guys. That's everyone who will be going to a specialty school. The remainder of you will be trained as combat medics." I can't begin to tell you how I felt. I felt sick, I felt deceived, and I was downright mad. I jumped up and ran up to the desk and said, "I enlisted to go to Med Lab School, and there's a telegram in my file that guarantees me that school." Without saying anything, he began looking in my file, and he finally said, "OK, go over to that group." He could have been arrogant and told me to sit down but thank goodness he had the decency to look in my file.

Those of us going to lab school were taken over to that area and assigned to our barracks. Then we went to another meeting and were told that we wouldn't begin our classes until the first of the year. We were only in the first week of December, so it would still be three weeks before the Christmas break. They told us that during those three weeks we would be receiving field medic training. During that time, we learned procedures for stopping bleeding, making and applying splints, carrying stretchers, mouth to mouth resuscitation, and more.

We had learned that we would be able to sign out on the evening of December 20 for Christmas. That was less than two days before my wedding, which was planned for 2 PM on the 22nd. I called immediately to book a flight to Atlanta but was told there was nothing available. I was in a panic, but then I heard someone talking about renting a car and driving to Atlanta. I asked if there was any chance I could ride with him. He said there was room for one more. So, four of us rented a car and was ready to go as soon as we signed out that Friday evening. Two of the guys shared the driving duties, and at sun-up, we were reaching the Texas-Louisiana state line. We drove all day, and late that afternoon we were in Birmingham, Alabama. I made the decision to get off there and catch a bus to Columbus, GA, so they dropped me off at the Trailways Bus Station. To my disappointment, the next bus to Columbus would not leave until 3 AM. That was an eight hour wait, but I had no other choice. I called my father and asked if he would meet me In Columbus at 7 AM. He said he would be there. We got home a little after 9 AM. It was only five hours before the wedding.

We were married at the Baptist Church in Weston, GA. The church was packed, and most of the guests were unsure I was even there until I walked in for the ceremony. It was a beautiful wedding, and everything went as planned. After it was over, Trapie handed me the keys to her 1956 Chevrolet Bel Air, and we drove away. We didn't have a lot of money, so we checked in at a motel in Dawson for the night. Next morning, Brenda and I had a late breakfast at one of the restaurants there in town, then returned to spend some time with our families.

Brenda and I made the decision that she would not join me until I had finished Lab School and gotten a permanent assignment. In the meantime, I would apply for her allotment check. My Lab School was a four-month course with three months in the classroom at Ft. Sam and one month of OJT (on the job training) at a hospital. From there, I would go to my permanent assignment. That week with my new wife was wonderful, but it went by much too fast, and on January 2nd, I was on a bus headed back to Texas.

CHAPTER 8

Army Medical Laboratory School

BACK AT FT. Sam, we began classes right away. One of the first things we learned was phlebotomy, the art of drawing blood. We teamed up with a buddy, and every morning we would take a sample of blood from each other. That was how we got our initial practice. Both my partner and I had good veins, so we never had much of a problem. I remember that one guy in our class had very poor veins, and it was nearly impossible to get his blood. After being probed numerous times daily for about a week, he dropped out of school. We used our blood samples each day to perform the various procedures we were learning. In hematology, we learned to count red and white blood cells under the microscope. We also performed many other procedures such as differentiating between the different kinds of white cells. Chemistry was a lot of fun. Those procedures were performed using serum. Serum is the part of blood that contains no cells or the protein fibrinogen. To perform these tests, we might have to add certain chemical solutions or acids and boil the test tubes or place them in an ice bath. We had a procedure book to follow. It was just like following the recipes in a cook book. That's a far cry from the way things are done in chemistry and hematology today, where everything is done by automated machines. In bacteriology, we learned to culture specimens for bacteria, identify that bacteria, and determine what antibiotics it would be sensitive to. Parasitology was very interesting as I learned to identify all the human parasites from around the world. In blood banking, we learned to type and cross-match blood. That's when I learned that my blood type was

O negative. That's a relatively rare type that is found in only 6.2% of the population. Both my parents and all my brothers are O positive, the most common blood type. I learned that there was only a 25% chance that my parents would have a child with O negative blood. O negative is the most important blood type because it is the universal donor, that is, it can be given to patients with all the other blood types.

Toward the end of January, I received a letter from Brenda. I was always happy to hear from her, but this one really surprised me. The letter read something like this, "I'll be arriving by bus on Saturday. Have us a place to live when I get there." Sure, I would be glad to see her, but I had less than $20 in my pocket. I panicked. What was I going to do? I pulled myself together and started thinking. I had to have money, so I began explaining my situation to my classmates and asked for any amount of money they could loan me. A couple of the guys let me have $10, and several loaned me $5. After talking with all the guys, I had about $75. Next, I had to find a place within that price range, but it had to be close enough to post that I could walk to work. I thought, "This is not going to be easy", because it was almost two miles to the rear entrance. I started looking in the newspaper's classified ads for "Houses and apartments for rent." Luck was on my side. There it was, "Apartments for rent, near Ft. Sam Houston's back gate, $50 per month. Apply at address." I began walking. It took an hour to get there, but I found the place and knocked on the door of the duplex apartment. A Mexican-American lady came to the door. She showed me the apartment. It was fully furnished except for cookware. I paid her the $50 and left, a very happy man.

I met Brenda at the Trailways Bus Station that Saturday, and we took a post bus back to Ft. Sam and exited the bus near the back gate. We walked the short distance to the apartment. She was pleased. Later that evening, we found a store nearby, and with the remaining $25 I had, bought some cookware and some groceries.

Payday was only a few days away, and I repaid all the guys who had so generously loaned me money, without them having to ask for it. A short time later, we received a letter from Trapie, and inside was Brenda's first allotment check for $91. I guess we thought we were rich, because we went downtown shopping and spent half of it on things we really didn't need. I bought a cowboy shirt, pants, and belt, and Brenda bought a Mexican skirt with sequins to sew on it.

Brenda was a big hit with all my friends because of her friendly personality. My best friend was a guy named Kenneth from Marietta, Ohio. Brenda, Ken, and I spent a lot of time together walking around San Antonio and visiting such places as the Alamo. One night as we walked along the street, with Brenda between us, holding hands, we met two Mexican looking dudes. As they passed, one of them said to Brenda, "Two timing!" Without thinking, I said, "Kiss my ass!" They turned and said something in Spanish that I didn't understand. Ken said, "Be careful what you say! Those guys might put a knife in your back!"

Brenda found a high school and enrolled there to continue her education as we had promised her mother.

As we neared the end of March, we were told of the places we could go for our four weeks of OJT, and we were asked if we had any preference. When I learned that Ft. Benning, Georgia was one of the sites, I applied for it right away and got it.

I had noticed my clothes were getting a little tight, so I stepped on the scales one day and, "Oh, my God!" I weighed 186 lbs. I had been at 155 when I arrived at Ft. Sam. I had been gaining two pounds per week. The mess hall was a lot different from what it was in basic training. At Ft. Sam you could go back for seconds and even thirds if you wanted to, and they had milk machines, so you could drink all the cold milk you desired. I would never see 155 again. in fact, I stayed around 186 for the next ten years.

Brenda and I were not allowed to travel back to Ft. Benning together, so she left a couple of days ahead of me. She would be staying at home with her mother while I was at Ft. Benning. It was only 50 miles away, so we could see each other every weekend.

The hospital at Ft. Benning was spread out into a lot of the wooden buildings from World War II, with covered walkways between them. I would start each day by taking my blood collecting tray and going to the various wards to collect blood from the patients. There were four of us students at Ft. Benning for our final four weeks of training. We each spent a week in hematology, chemistry, bacteriology, and the blood bank.

While at Ft. Benning, I took a bus on two occasions to see the minor league Columbus Foxes play baseball. On another occasion, my cousin Gladys Laye, whom I called "Aunt Gladys", because she was my mother's age, picked me up one evening and took me to her home in Columbus where she prepared a very enjoyable dinner for us.

At the beginning of our final week of training, we were about to learn where the permanent assignments would be. I told the sergeant in charge that if there was an assignment in Georgia, I would like to have that one. Two of the students wanted to stay together if there were two assignments in the same place. As it turned out, there were two assignments at Ft. McPherson, Georgia, one at Ft. Jackson, South Carolina, and one I don't recall. The Sergeant honored my request, and I was assigned to Ft. McPherson along with Marty Collingsworth of Arcadia, Florida. One of the guys was from Los Angeles, and he wanted Ft. McPherson because it was in Atlanta, and he wanted to go to a big city. He ended up with the spot at Ft. Jackson near Columbia, South Carolina.

CHAPTER 9

My First Permanent Assignment

MY VERY FIRST time to ride a train was the trip from Ft. Benning, Georgia to Ft. McPherson in Atlanta, Georgia for my first permanent assignment after graduating from Medical Laboratory School. The train made a stop directly across the street from the post. With our duffel bag over our shoulder, Marty and I made our way across the street and onto post. Ft McPherson was a very small post but was the headquarters of the Third United States Army. After being assigned to our quarters, we were taken to the lab and introduced to the staff. The supervisor was a Specialist-5 Waddell. There were two females there also, Pam and Claudia. They were the only two WACs that I would work with during my 10 years of service. We received our white uniforms and were told to report for duty the following day.

The first Saturday I was there, Brenda came up, and we began looking for a place to live. We found a nice apartment about a mile from post, rented it, and moved in. We located a grocery store about half a mile away and bought what we thought would be a month's supply. We each carried two large bags as we made our way home.

I enjoyed working in the laboratory. Most all the procedures were done the same as I had learned at Ft. Sam, but there were also new things to learn. The lab was responsible for doing all the EKGs, and we also had to assist the pathologist with autopsies. I had witnessed one autopsy at school but never assisted in one. That was probably my least favorite duty. I remember my first time to assist the doctor. It was on a baby, and that bothered me even more. The pathologist told me to put some formalin in a container for the tissue samples. I sat it on the table and he said, "That stuff is strong. It's burning my eyes. Where did you get it?" I showed him, and he said, "That's not formalin. That's formaldehyde. No wonder my eyes are burning. It has to be diluted." Formalin is only a small percent formaldehyde, which I don't recall, but he didn't worry about the percentage; he just started adding water to the container, and said, "That's better." I never made that mistake again.

A couple of weeks later, Brenda and I were visiting with our folks when my father-in-law, C.P., said, "Y'all need a car. Come on, let's go car shopping." We headed to Americus and went to the Chevrolet dealership. That's where he and Trapie always bought their cars. We began looking at the used cars and spotted a black 1950 Ford Coupe. "How do you like this one", he asked. "Yeah, looks fine", I said. Of course, I would have been happy with anything. "Let's try it out", he said. He fired it up, and we laid down a black streak of rubber as we left the lot. "This is a good one. It'll do it!", he said. So, he signed for me, and I had my first car. I believe the cost was $350.

Not long after that, I was called to go and see my commanding officer. I couldn't imagine what he wanted, except, well, I thought just maybe I was being promoted to PFC. After all, I had been in the Army the required time of eight months. I stood at attention, saluted and said, "Private Wills reporting as directed, sir." He told me to stand at ease and said he had been notified by the Red Cross that my father had had a massive heart attack and was in critical condition at the hospital. I was granted a one-week emergency leave, and Brenda and I headed south. Arriving at the hospital in Dawson, GA, we found Daddy in bed with a heart monitor going. A nurse was trying to start an I.V. but was having trouble hitting a vein. Daddy said, "I'll bet Johnny can hit the vein." The nurse stared at me, and I told her I was a lab tech and that I had trained in phlebotomy. She asked me if I would like to try. I declined because I didn't want to hurt Daddy, and besides, what if I missed? That would make both of us look foolish in the eyes of the nurse. I think Daddy was a little disappointed in me, but I think it was the right decision. Daddy stayed in the hospital for a few days, then returned home where he made a full recovery.

There was a lot to do around Atlanta, and now that we had a car, it was easy to get around and do things. During that summer of '58, my brother Don who was now 13 came up and spent a week. Among other things, we visited Stone Mountain. Stone Mountain was a dome-shaped rock of granite which sets all alone and rises 600 feet from ground level. It was located 20 miles east of Atlanta. There were two ways to reach the summit: climb it or take the cable car. We did both. One side of the mountain was a steep slope, but easily climbable if one was in decent physical condition. The other side was almost vertical. On the face of the steep side, is a large carving of the Confederate heroes, Robert E. Lee and Stonewall Jackson. The carving was begun in the 1920s but would not be completed until 1972. We also visited the zoo and the Cyclorama at Grant Park. The Cyclorama depicts the Civil War Battle of Atlanta and is the second largest painting in the world.

One weekend, my friend Marty Collingsworth asked Brenda and me if we would like to go out to a pizza parlor and have a pizza. Neither of us had ever had pizza, so we were anxious to go. It was quite an experience. We both enjoyed it tremendously. It wouldn't be our last pizza, by any means.

When I lived in the barracks, there was several things that were required: "lights out" at 10 PM, "bed check" at midnight to make sure everyone was in by the 2400-hour curfew, "G.I. party" Friday evening, and a personal and barracks inspection on Saturday morning. After the inspection, we were on our own time for the remainder of the weekend. One nice thing about living off post was that you got away from all that except for the personal inspection on Saturday morning. To pass that inspection, you needed a fresh haircut, clean shave, fresh, clean uniform, shined boots or shoes, and polished brass.

I didn't want to have a G.I. party at home on Friday evening, but I did believe in keeping the house clean. That's when I first discovered that Brenda didn't like housework. In fact, she hated it, and wouldn't do it unless I pushed her. As I left for work one Friday morning, she told me she would like to go out that evening. The house was a mess, and the sink and counter were full of dirty dishes. I told her if she would clean the house that day, we could go, and she agreed. Well, when I returned home after work, the house looked pretty good, and the dirty dishes were gone. As I was changing clothes, I reached under the bed for my shoes, and instead of pulling out a pair of shoes, I pulled out a dirty frying pan. I thought, "What the heck is this?" I looked under the bed, and there were all the dirty dishes. So, I said, "Hey baby, what's with the dishes under the bed?" Her answer was, "I didn't have time to do them, so I hid them and would do them later." I said, "No, we do them now." So, we did, and I don't remember where we went afterwards, if any place at all.

On one of our trips to visit our parents, we brought back a big box full of corn, freshly pulled from the field. We had a screened-in back porch that we shared with the landlady. We put the box of corn on the porch. I told her about it and told her she was welcome to help herself to it if she liked corn. I don't remember exactly how it came about, but about a week later she pitched a fit about that corn on the porch. She said it was rotten and full of maggots. Then she started complaining about Brenda and what a bad housekeeper she was. We had suspected she had been coming into the apartment when we were not at home. Now she had confirmed it. I was mad. We got in the car and went looking for another place to live, and we found it, just two blocks from post. We rented it that evening and began packing up to move. When the landlady realized we were moving, she called her son who was in the National Guard. He came over wearing his 2nd Lieutenant uniform, which I'm sure was to intimidate us. It didn't work. We let him know what we thought of his mother and told him we were leaving. He told us he would report us to the authorities on post for breach of contract. We said, "Do what you have to do." We finished moving that evening and never heard a word from anyone.

Around the end of August 1958, I was finally promoted to PFC. I was so proud to get my first stripe, and it also meant a whopping $14 per month pay raise. My base pay was now $99.37 per month! Wow! Everything was going smoothly. I was enjoying my work at the lab, and Brenda and I had a happy life together, but all that was about to change. In mid-November I got the news that I would be going to Germany toward the end of December. I didn't want to go. I was happy right where I was. My friend Marty told me that he would love to go, so we decided to see if he could go instead of me. Our request was denied because Marty had been drafted and had only about nine months left to serve.

They told me the tour of duty would be 24 months, and I couldn't take my wife because I was only a PFC. I said, "Hey, I've only got 21 months to go." They told me I would stay only until my normal ETS (estimated time of separation), which was September 26, 1960. I received my orders and would have about two weeks of leave time before I had to report to Brooklyn, NY where I would be boarding the Naval Transport Ship, The U.S.N.S. Geiger, on December 14.

My orders said I was being assigned to the 536th General Dispensary in Ansbach, Germany. That sounded like a small medical facility, but Ansbach didn't mean anything to me, because I didn't know anything about Germany except what I'd heard about Hitler and World War II.

While I was gone, Brenda now 17, would finish high school and possibly take up nursing. It would be a long time before I saw my wife again. That was not good.

CHAPTER 10

Germany, Here I Come!

THE GEIGER SET sail from New York Harbor just before dusk on Sunday, December 14, 1958. I was standing on the deck watching the New York City skyline and the Statue of Liberty disappear from the horizon as darkness fell over us. The sea was calm, and I thought, "This is going to be a very pleasant cruise."

The sleeping quarters were different from anything I had ever seen. The cots were only a metal frame with canvas stretched tightly between, with a two-inch pad for a mattress. The cots were stacked six high with only about 18 inches between cots. My cot was the top one, about eight feet off the floor.

I had retired for the night. Sometime during the early hours of morning, I was awakened by creaking and cracking of the ship as it was being tossed about by the sea. As soon as my feet hit the floor that morning, I was deathly sea-sick. I climbed on my cot and felt fine while I was lying down. People were throwing up everywhere. The whole place was a stinking mess. Then we were told that we had to go up on deck, so the place could be cleaned up. I made my way up to the deck, sick as a dog. When I looked out on deck, what a sight! The sea was wild! The waves must have been 20 feet or more, and they were washing over the deck. The ship was being tossed around like a toy. The crew had put a rope along the deck, about 10 feet from the railing. We were told not to go beyond the rope. We were called to go to breakfast, but when you're sick, food is the farthest thing from your mind. Once seated at the long table, unless you held onto your tray, it would go sliding from one end to the other. Is this what I would have to endure for the next week? I hoped not! But it was. Day after day, whenever I was out of bed, I was sea-sick. The ship was rolling so badly that whenever I was out on deck, one minute all I could see was water, and the next minute all I could see was the sky.

Finally, after what seemed an eternity, I awoke one morning, got out of bed and suddenly realized that I didn't feel sick. Had we docked? I quickly dressed and made my way up to the deck, on the port side of the ship. The sea was calm, and as I gazed toward the horizon, I could see land. Wow! We were passing through the English Channel! This was the seventh day of our voyage, and it was so good to see land again. I stood on the deck most of the day staring, as we passed by the White Cliffs of Dover. I couldn't help but think of D-Day, June 6, 1944 when tens of thousands of Allied Troops passed across this channel to invade the Nazis on mainland Europe.

I went to bed that night, happy to know that we would be reaching our destination tomorrow. When I arose the next morning, we had docked in Bremerhaven, West Germany. Then I remembered. This is December 22, the 1st anniversary of my wedding. I thought, "What a way to spend your 1st anniversary." Late that afternoon I boarded a train for my final destination, Ansbach. I was told that it would be an all-night trip. The trip was pleasant and after a good night's sleep, we reached Ansbach at around 9 AM. There were about half a dozen of us soldiers to get off in Ansbach, but I was the only one going to the 536th General Dispensary. The others were assigned to the 75th Field Artillery Unit. A military vehicle from the 75th was waiting outside, and all the guys except me climbed aboard. The driver asked me where I was going, and I told him. He said, "Climb in, the dispensary is on the same post as the 75th. Ten minutes later we passed through the gate of the Hindenburg Kaserne (German word for Fort or Post). The driver dropped me off at the door of a large, red, three-story brick building. A sign over the entrance read, 536th General Dispensary. I thought, "Well, here's my home for the next 21 months." Carrying my duffle bag in one hand and my military records in the other, I walked in and made my way to the office of the NCOIC (non-commissioned officer in charge). His name was Master Sergeant Ripley. The first thing he said was, "I sent someone to the train station to pick you up. Didn't you see him?" I said, "No, I didn't. I only saw the truck from the 75th Artillery, and I was offered a ride." He began looking into my records and said, "I see you are a lab tech. I don't have an opening for you now. We have a lab tech already, and he won't be leaving for another six months, but we'll find something for you." I didn't say anything, but I was thinking, "Why did they send me here if I wasn't needed?" Then he had someone take me over to the barracks and told me to get squared away, and he would see me tomorrow. The Hindenburg Kaserne was small as were all the Army Posts in Germany, but there were many of them, probably hundreds. Being small was great in a way, with everything so convenient. My barracks was only about 150 yards from the dispensary. The Kaserne was square shaped, about 1000 feet down each side. It was surrounded by a two-meter-high iron fence with spear-like spikes on top, and there was only one gate, which was manned by military police. There was a commissary, P.X., movie theater, service club, enlisted men's club, barber shop, bowling alley, post office, and more. And there were two more kasernes across town that were very much the same, except we were the only one with a medical facility.

After unpacking my duffle bag and arranging everything properly in my wall locker and foot locker, I walked over to the barber shop. There in the chair was Sgt. Ripley. We said hello, and then he asked, "Do you have enough money to pay for my haircut? I forgot to bring any money. I'll pay you back tomorrow." I thought it strange for a master sergeant not to have 50 cents for a haircut, but I said, "Yeah, sure, I'll take care of it." He did pay me back the following day but fussed a little because I didn't tip the barber a quarter.

I sat on my bunk that evening writing letters to Brenda and my parents. Tomorrow was Christmas Eve. I was feeling a bit sad and lonely when a heavy-set gentleman walked up to me and said, "Hello, I'm Ronald Weld, the clerk typist at the dispensary." I told him who I was, and he said, "I'm on my way downtown to the Methodist Church. They're having a Christmas party. Would you like to come with me?" I said, "Yeah, sure, thanks for asking me." Ron had just bought a new Volkswagen that he would be taking back to the states in a few months. He told me he was a school teacher from White Bear Lake, Minnesota and had been drafted in the Army. We arrived at the church and I was introduced to the minister, Reverend Autenwreith. He spoke very good English. Then I met his wife and children, a boy and a girl, both teen-agers. Neither of them spoke English, and of course I didn't know a word of German. I saw something that night that I had heard about but had never seen and have not seen since. There was a large Christmas tree with literally hundreds of burning candles. That was a sight to see. They sung lots of Christmas carols that evening, only one of which I recognized and that was Silent Night. I recognized the tune, but not the words. The family made me feel welcome, and before leaving, Frau Autenwreith gave me a present. Back at the barracks, I opened my gift and found two links of bratwurst (smoked sausage). It made a great snack later.

The next day I was given a tour of the dispensary and was introduced to all the personnel. In the basement was supply, motor pool office, and linen room. On the first floor was the reception area, emergency room, X-ray, and pharmacy. On the second floor was the dental clinic, labora-tory, doctor's office, and administrative offices. On the third floor was the ward, nurse's station, kitchen, wash room, and break room. There was a German civilian counterpart working in every department except X-ray and pharmacy. Everyone was friendly, and I felt that I would fit in well with the group, which I did. At age 19, I was the youngest in the unit, and most all the others were draftees and were 22-24 years old. Then I got the news I'd been waiting to hear. I would be in charge of the linen room, and that would be my job for the next six months until the other lab tech left. My job in the linen room meant that I would be taking in all the dirty items: sheets, towels, white uniforms, etc. and is-suing clean ones. Once a week I would load all the dirty clothes in a deuce and a half (2 1/2-ton truck), drive the 43 Kilometers (25 miles) to the cleaning facility in Nurnberg and pick up the clean linens and clothes and return. Then I would neatly stack everything on shelves, so they would be ready to issue again. The first thing I had to do was get a driver's license for military vehicles. Besides the deuce and a half, we had a jeep, a "cracker box" ambulance, that's the field ambulance with the big red cross on the sides and top, an Opel ambulance, and a 1957 Chevrolet staff car. I got a license for all of them. I didn't like it, but I worked hard and did a good job. I thought my six months would never end.

But it did end, and finally I went to work in the lab. Also, at about that same time I was promoted to Specialist-4 (E-4). My German counterpart in the lab was Else Preuss, a very nice middle-aged lady. Everyone called her Miss Price, although I'm not sure why. Our lab was a single room, and we performed most of the procedures a larger hospital lab would perform.

Every night there were two people on duty, a C.Q. (charge of quarters) and a driver. I was always on the C.Q. roster, but I also did my share of driving the ambulance. I had studied a map of the area and had familiarized myself with the surrounding towns and roads. I recall one night when a lady brought her son to the dispensary. He had been bitten by a dog. I wasn't on duty that night, but I was called out of the barracks to drive them home, pick up the dog, and take her and the dog to a quarantine facility at U. S. Army Hospital Nurnberg and then take the lady home. After driving 225 miles that night, I finally got back to the barracks at 6 AM, time to get ready for work again.

Back at Ft. McPherson, I had played my guitar regularly and was making progress. Since I was unable to bring my guitar to Germany, the only access I had to one was at the service club. They only had one electric guitar, and sometimes it would be in use when I would ask for it. One Saturday afternoon I walked downtown, and as I passed a music store, I spotted some great looking guitars, so I walked in to take a closer look. The one that really stood out was a Framus Guitar priced at around DM 200. That was $50 in U.S. currency. I asked the merchant if I could make payments on it, and he said I could. I picked out a small amplifier, and I purchased both for around a hundred dollars. I paid it off in about five or six months. Now I could play all I wanted to.

Since I was going to be in Germany for 21 months, I wanted to see as much of the country as I could. My first trip was a weekend trip to Munich. It was in the spring of 1959. There was some kind of celebration going on, so my friend Ron and I headed to Munich on a Saturday morning. There was a big parade with thousands of people lining the streets. Some girl dressed as a baby, and even wearing a diaper, ran up to me and stuck a baby bottle in my mouth. That was so unsanitary, but fortunately, I didn't get sick. We also visited the world famous Hofbrahaus, one of Munich's main attractions. It's a very old and very large restaurant/bar with hundreds of people sitting at wooden tables enjoying their food and very large steins of beer. They whoop it up to the live music which is always playing. Quite a sight to see.

The 1958 World's Fair had been held in Brussels, Belgium. Ron and I took a couple of days off to drive up and take a look at what was left. The main attraction was the atomium, an atom shaped structure that I believe was 166 billion times the actual size of an atom. It was so neat to walk all over it. Those were the only trips Ron and I made. He left shortly afterwards for Minnesota. He invited me to come to White Bear Lake, but it never happened, however, I would see him again.

Ron wasn't my only good friend at the dispensary. Jerry Bullock was our X-Ray technician, and he hailed from Walla Walla, Washington. Jerry was a camera bug. He was constantly taking pictures with his 35 mm camera. I learned a lot about cameras and photography from him, and I even bought a 35 mm camera for myself, complete with close up and telephoto lenses. Jerry and I went on three trips together, the first being to Interlaken, Switzerland. Interlaken is a tourist attraction and ski resort, which lies in the heart of the Alps Mountains. The village is over-looked by the Jungfrau, a majestic, snow-covered peak which towers more than 13,600 feet above the village and is one of the main summits of the Swiss Alps. We started out walking to see the town, but happened by a place that rented bicycles, so we each rented a bike to continue our tour. After we left Interlaken, we stopped by beautiful Lake Lucerne and the city of Zurich. One thing that stood out about Switzerland, to me, was their coins. They were beautiful, and being a collector, I was amazed at the number of coins I received in change that were dated from the 1800s. I brought quite a few back with me.

Our next trip was to Konstanz, a city in southern Germany which lies on the Swiss border. It is also on the Bodensee (Lake Konstanz). That's the starting point of the Rhine River which flows out of the lake and splits the city in half as it winds its way northward.

Our final trip was one to Strasburg, France. I think we mainly went there to say we had been to France, but it was an interesting city. It was my understanding that over the past several hundred years that there had been a border dispute between Germany and France as to whether Strasburg was in Germany or France. The city had been in both countries from time to time. With the dispute finally settled, most of Strasburg is in France. The city is also famous for storks, the large, long-legged, long-beaked bird that delivers babies all over the world. It was a common sight to see their nests on chimneys and rooftops. Maybe this is not a fair assumption, but I didn't find the French people to be nearly as friendly as were the Germans.

Ronald Weld's replacement as clerk typist was a young PFC named Kevin Gram. Kevin was from Jasper, Tennessee a small town just north of Chattanooga. He would end up being my best friend during my tour of duty in Germany. Kevin's office was located across the hall from the lab. One day a soldier from another kaserne was in his office, when he glanced over and saw me. He asked Kevin, "Who is that across the hall. I think I know him." A few minutes later he walked over. I couldn't believe my eyes. There was G.W. Blankenship! He had been in Brenda's class in high school. I said. "Hi, what are you doing here?" He answered, "It's not just me. Buddy is also here." Buddy Blankenship was G.W.'s cousin, and he had recently married my first cousin, Linda Black. Buddy was also in our high school band. They had enlisted in the Army under the Buddy System, which meant they had been guaranteed to spend their time in service together.

The three of us got together very soon at the service club and began to do a little guitar picking. I learned that G.W. was now playing drums. My friend Kevin had wanted to learn to play guitar, so he purchased a Framus, like mine. I had worked hard with him, and he was doing quite well. It wasn't long before the four of us formed a band. I believe we had played once at a private party at some officer's home.

I learned there was an All Army Talent Contest that would be held in Nurnberg, and I wanted to enter. I talked the others into it, and we were on. We began practicing. I would sing a song, and we would do an instrumental. I knew we didn't have much of a chance to win because the Army had the draft, and they were drafting all kinds of professional entertainers and musicians. After all, Elvis was over there with us, but he had decided not to entertain while in service. I admired the fact that he wanted to be a regular soldier in his armored unit and didn't want any preferential treatment.

I had assumed that we would take the train to Nurnberg for the contest, but when it was time to go, my boss, MSG Ripley called me in and handed me the keys to the staff car, the '57 Chevy and said, "Have fun and best of luck." I'm pretty sure he wouldn't have done that for many others in the unit.

We arrived in Nurnberg on a Friday morning. This would be a day of practice, and the talent contest would be the next day. There were many contestants. We were seated in a large auditorium watching the contestants run through their songs, acts, or whatever, as we waited our turn. Then a young man walked onto the stage with a very large amplifier and as he placed it down, I said to the others, " Oh my God, we're in the wrong place." Written across the front of the amp was "Paul Yandel, Grand Old Opry, Nashville, Tennessee." I knew that he was the lead guitar player for the star country duo, The Louvin Brothers. I had one of their albums back at the barracks and had been listening to his playing. What I didn't know was that he had been drafted in the Army. We watched in awe as he played one of the most difficult songs to play, "Malaguena".

When it was our turn, I almost hated to go on stage, but we did fine, and we weren't the only amateurs there by any means. Later that day, I introduced myself to Paul. He was very nice and friendly. I talked with him for a little while and then asked if he would show me how he made a certain run in one of the Louvin Brothers songs. He said, "Sure", and took my guitar and made it sound better than it had ever sounded before or would ever sound again. I still remember what he showed me, but I still can't do it the way he did. Paul finished 2nd in the talent contest, but in my opinion, he should have won. When Paul left the service, he joined my idol, the great Chet Atkins and toured with him for 10 years.

Shortly after the talent contest, Buddy and G.W. were transferred to Karlsruhe, and I never saw them again while in Germany. Then I was told one day that I was going on TDY (temporary duty) to the U.S. Army Hospital in Nurnberg for two months to work in the lab. That was OK with me. It was the largest lab I had ever seen, and I got some great experience and learned a lot.

One day while at Nurnberg, a convoy of ambulances with sirens blaring came roaring up to the emergency department. I walked out to take a look at what was going on. The sight was horrific. They began unloading blood-soaked soldiers with terrible wounds, some with arms and legs missing. There had been a terrible accident at a large training area near the Czechoslovakian border, east of Nurnberg. Someone had added too large a charge to an artillery piece, and the round had overshot the target and landed in a company formation. Several were killed and more than 20 wounded.

About two weeks before I would be finishing my TDY in Nurnberg, I met Bob Bone. Bob was a sergeant who worked there in the hospital, I don't recall where, but he was an excellent guitar player. He lived in military housing with his family. He invited me over for a visit and to do a little guitar picking. His Gretsch Guitar was in a stand in the living room, where he said he always kept it. That way it would be ready to play anytime. He picked up the guitar and began playing like Chet Atkins. I couldn't believe it. I visited Bob several times during that final two weeks and probably learned as much from him as I had from any other one person in my life. I never saw Bob again after I returned to Ansbach.

One night while on CQ I got a call that a possible DOA was on the way in. I really didn't know what a DOA was, so I calmly said, "OK, I'll be waiting." I soon learned what it was, but this was not a "possible", it was a sure thing. They brought in a soldier who looked to be about 40 years of age. He apparently had died of a massive heart attack. This was my first DOA, but not my last. One night a soldier over at the 75th Field Artillery climbed to the roof of his three-floor barracks and jumped to his death. It was an ugly sight when they brought him in. Bones were sticking out of both legs, and his head was caved in.

One of our ambulance drivers was returning to the dispensary one afternoon when he spotted a young boy riding a bicycle toward the road. The boy stopped at the road, apparently to let the ambulance pass, but as the driver approached, the boy suddenly stood up on the pedals and rode right into the path of the ambulance. There was no way to avoid hitting him, but the driver stopped as quickly as possible, picked up the boy, and sped to the dispensary as fast as he could. The doctor pronounced him dead on arrival. Since the kid was a German civilian, the place was soon swarming with German Police and other authorities.

We received a call one day that a car load of G.I.s' had rolled their car in a field about 20 miles out of Ansbach. There were injuries, and I was called upon to take the ambulance out to pick them up. I took the "cracker box", because I could bring more casualties back in it. When I arrived at the site, there were four men sitting beside the road with their overturned car in the field. Only one of them was slightly injured. On the way back to the dispensary, all they could think about was being hungry. They wanted me to stop so they could get something to eat, but I wouldn't do it. I told them, "I'm not running a taxi service. I was told to pick you up and bring you to the dispensary, and that's exactly what I'm doing. You can get something to eat when we get back." I think that was the most useless ambulance run I ever made.

World War II had only been over for 12 years when I arrived in Germany, and there were still plenty of signs left of the war. There were bombed out buildings, depressions in concrete structures where bullets had hit, and the fields were littered with bunkers that the Nazis used in their lines of defense. Most of the bunkers were damaged or destroyed. My lab partner, Frau Preuss, told me of the day the American Forces rolled into town. She said the tanks come over the hill and down her street. Everyone headed for the basement. There were only women and young children because Hitler had ordered old men and boys 12 and older to fight, even though some of them were armed only with sticks. She said as the tanks moved slowly down the street, machine guns on top of the tanks were firing just beneath the windows of every house. Following the tanks were foot soldiers, and they came in groups of four or five into every house and checked every room, probably looking for hiding German soldiers. One of the men that came to her basement was a black man, the first one she had seen in her entire life. She said she had heard of black men and had been told that they were very bad, but that wasn't true with this one at all. He was respectful to them, and the men asked if they had food. She said they gave them what they had, and the soldiers left.

Of our three nurses, Elizabeth Ruedel was my favorite. She had been a nurse at the local hospital during the war and told me that the hospital had been hit twice by bombs. During air raids she said every-one, including patients, would head for the basement. She also told of the SS troopers killing a man downtown and hanging his body in the town square, as an example of what they could do to anyone that might speak out against Hitler. The body hung there for a week. Elizabeth liked to hear me play my guitar and sing. One Saturday night she in-vited me to her home for dinner and asked that I bring my guitar. She made a wonderful dinner, and later we sat on her bed and looked at some of her photo albums. I didn't realize it at the time, but I think she was trying to seduce me. Even if I had realized it, the interest wasn't there. After all, I was 20 years old. She was in her mid to late 40s. That was my mother's age.

I won't ever forget one weirdo patient we had. I don't recall why he was admitted, but he would go into the kitchen and get a cup of boiling hot water and call it coffee. He would drink it and say, "This is prima coffee. You boys better have some." Prima was his favorite word. He would stand and stare out the window at the snow and say, "It's prima cold out there." His favorite food was whole kernel corn. In the mess hall he would fill his tray with a huge mound of corn and say, "prima corn." He was finally evaluated by a psychiatrist and was discharged from the Army. I have often wondered if he was crazy or if that was his way of getting out of the service.

In February of 1960, I turned 21 years of age. Some of the guys took me to a bar to celebrate. They tried to buy me beer or cognac and coke. I was not a drinker, and I didn't like that stuff. So, they bought a bottle of some kind of sweet, cordial drink, it was thick and creamy, and they poured me a glass. I took a sip and said, "Hey, this is pretty good." As I was drinking, I suddenly noticed that for some reason my glass was staying full. Then I realized they had been adding to my glass when I wasn't looking. I glanced at the bottle, and it was empty. I was having a good time, but I began feeling like I had never felt before. I was los-ing control, and I said, "I've got to go." It was just a short walk back to the barracks, and all I had to do was cross an open field to reach the front gate. Halfway across the field was a little stream. As I approached the bridge, suddenly I saw two bridges. I thought, "This isn't right. I'm sure there's only one bridge." So, I cautiously walked between the two bridges and somehow made it to the other side. Back at the barracks, I got in bed, and I had the sensation that my bed was turning over. I had to hold onto the sides of the bed to keep from being dumped to the floor. I began thinking, "This is not for me! It's not going to happen again!"

Two new movies came to the theater each week. I didn't miss seeing many of them. That was a big night out; movie, drink, and popcorn, all for about a dollar.

Then one night a friend and I decided to go down to the "Black Bear." That was the number one place in Ansbach for G.I.s to hang out. They had a good country music band playing every night, the band being made up from military personnel from the area. Then something happened that shouldn't have happened, and something I would come to regret. As we passed through the gate, I noticed two girls standing there as if waiting for someone. One was wearing a bright yellow dress. As we passed by them, we said hello, and they asked if they could walk with us to town. We said, "Yeah, sure." We introduced ourselves, and they told us their names. The one in the yellow dress was Elizabeth. Reaching the "Black Bear", the four of us sat at a table and ordered something to drink. The band was playing, and the dance floor was full, but we didn't dance. I struck up a conversation with Elizabeth, and we sat there and talked for a couple of hours. She could speak pretty good English, but her grammar was not good. She told me that she had a month-old daughter named Monika, and that the baby was being cared for by a local family. I asked her about the baby's father. She told me that she had been dating a Mexican-American from Texas. He had been with the 75th Field Artillery. She had become pregnant, and he had promised to marry her and take her back to Texas. Every afternoon she would walk to the gate of Hindenberg Kaserne to meet him. Then one day when she was seven months pregnant, she stood at the gate as always. He wasn't on time, so she began asking people if they knew him and if they knew where he was. Finally, a soldier told her, "Oh, he left to go back to the States this morning." She was devastated. She never heard from him again.

Then it dawned on me. This woman is looking for a serious relationship. I said to her, "Elizabeth, I have to tell you something. I am a married man. I have a loving wife back home, and I am not available for a relationship with you. She answered, "I no want relationship. We be friends. OK? You be my friend?" I stared at her for a moment. I really felt bad for this girl. I had missed my first two anniversaries and had not seen my wife in over 15 months. I guess I was a little lonely too. So, I said, "yes, I'm your friend." I had enjoyed meeting and talking with Elizabeth and as I got up to make my departure, she said, "When I can see you again?" I said, "Would you like to go to the movies tomorrow evening?" Her face lit up with a big smile, and she said, "Yes, I would." And so, we became very close friends, a friendship that would last for six months, when I would be leaving Germany.

At the end of March 1960, I was promoted to Specialist-5. That was quite an honor for me. Very few soldiers made E-5 in their first three years. Being an E-5 also gave me some additional benefits. Now I had my own private room in the barracks, which was great, and now I could go to the NCO Club if I desired. Extra responsibilities also came with my promotion.

One of the biggest advantages of working in a small unit like the dispensary was that you knew everyone. I also learned to work in every department of the dispensary: the emergency room, on the ward, X-Ray, and Pharmacy. I only messed up once in the X-Ray dept. and once in the Pharmacy. One night I was X-Raying a possible fractured wrist. It came out terribly overexposed. I repeated it using a shorter exposure time, and it was better but still overexposed. I couldn't understand what I was doing wrong. The doctor was able to read the second one, which pleased me, but I was not happy. The next day the X-Ray technician told me what the problem was. I had used a cassette instead of cardboard. The cassette allows for a very short exposure time. I never made that mistake again. In the pharmacy, I once filled a prescription with the wrong medication, a sulfa drug. As soon as I caught my error, I went to the doctor and explained what I had done. He told me not to worry about it because the drug I used was also a sulfa drug and was almost identical to the one he had prescribed. I also never made another mistake in the Pharmacy. The doctors liked it when I was on C.Q. because I was the only one who could work in all departments.

Elizabeth Koch was 26 years of age. She was not beautiful, and I wouldn't even say she was pretty, but she was clean, neat, trim, and had a good personality. As far as I know, she didn't have any family, or at least none that she ever spoke of. I asked her why she wanted to date Americans, and she told me that when she was a teenager, she had a German boyfriend who was several years older than her. They had gone on a camping trip, and he had raped her in the tent at a campsite. She said she would always hate German men because of that.

As I was nearing the end of my enlistment, I was beginning to think about what choice I would make. Would I get out of the Army or would I re-enlist? I didn't know. Then I remembered that the Army had an Advanced Medical Laboratory School that lasted for 52 weeks. I loved Ft. Sam Houston, Texas, and I thought it would be great to spend a year there. So, I applied for the school with the understanding that if I were accepted, I would re-enlist for another three years.

I still had some leave time left, so I decided to take a trip to the Bavarian Alps, or more specifically, Berchtesgaden, a resort city in the southeast corner of Germany, just across the border from Salzburg, Austria. I put in for a week's leave, then I asked Liz (Elizabeth) if she would like to go. She had not done a lot of traveling in her lifetime, so she said she would love to go. Her problem was that she might not be able to get time off from her job. She worked at the U.S. Army Supply Facility at Katterbach, which was just outside of Ansbach. I think she finally told her boss that she was going whether they liked it or not. She almost lost her job over it.

We boarded the train and headed to Berchtesgaden in August. The city and surrounding area were beautiful. The number one attraction was the "Eagle's Nest", a summer home which had been donated to Adolf Hitler, I believe early in 1945. It sat atop a high mountain peak overlooking the city. The nest can only be reached by taking a special bus, geared for the very steep ascent, or by a strenuous two-hour climb. The bus parks about 200 meters below the summit, and then you take an elevator which is cut through the rock for the final distance. Once on top, you have a 360-degree view of the surrounding area. The "Eagle's Nest" is almost as original as it was in 1945, as it was not damaged during the war. It was my understanding that Hitler only visited the nest once.

Toward the end of our weeks' vacation, I decided to go to Salzburg for a day. Liz said, "I can no go to Austria." It was something about not having the necessary documentation. I said, "Sure you can go. Come on!" So, we boarded a tour bus and took the 20-minute ride to Salzburg. We took in some of the sights, had a great lunch, and headed back to Berchtesgaden. Suddenly the bus stopped. We were at the German border, and a border agent boarded the bus and began checking papers. We were seated about midway the bus with me by the aisle. Now I was worried. This could be bad! I had better think of something, and quick! When the agent approached my position, I handed him my military identification card. He glanced at it, handed it back, and looked at Liz. I quickly said, "Oh, this is my wife." He nodded and continued on his way. But before he had gotten more than two steps away, Liz said, "Heh, heh, you say I'm your wife." I whispered, "Shhh! Be quiet! I'm trying to get you out of this country!" It was a great vacation, and I could tell that Liz was having a wonderful time. It was likely the most enjoyable week of her entire life.

When I returned to work on Monday morning, I had a surprise waiting. I had received an answer to my request to go back to school at Ft. Sam Houston. But it wasn't what I expected. They had turned me down! The explanation was that the school would give me a MOS of 931.20, and because I already had a 931.20, it was contradictory to Army policy. I thought that was so stupid! The only reason I had a 931.20 was because it was automatically awarded with my promotion to Specialist-5. Well, that settled it. I would not be re-enlisting. I would get out of service and find a civilian job. However, I did have an option. If for some reason that didn't work out, I had 90 days to go back in the Army and retain my rank of E-5.

Once back in Ansbach, Liz was never the same again. She was no longer just my friend. She wanted a lot more. This I had not anticipated. The girl had fallen madly in love with me and didn't want to give me up. I only had ten days left before I would be leaving for the States. She begged me, "You go back, you make finish with your wife. You come back for me." I said, "Liz, I can't make you that kind of promise." I told her that it had been almost two years since I had seen my wife, and I didn't know what it would be like when I got back, but I would write to her and let her know. I finally told her that if my marriage didn't work out, I would come back for her. She then made me a promise that until she heard from me, she wouldn't go to the "Black Bear" any more or go to the post gate and try to meet someone.

It was difficult as I said good-bye to Liz for the last time. There were four of us boarding the train for Nurnberg, and we would be on our way to Bremerhaven the following morning to board the U.S.N.S. Patch and sail to New York. But when we arrived in Nurnberg, we learned that our departure had been delayed for a day. Someone suggested that we go back to Ansbach for one last evening. We all agreed, so we caught a train and headed back. We walked the couple of miles from the train station to the Hindenberg Kaserne and headed over to the bowling alley where we rolled a few games. Someone said, "Let's go down to the "Bear", meaning the "Black Bear" bar, so we head down that way. As we were approaching the "Bear", a gentleman, whom I didn't know, approached me and said, "She's in there." I said, "Who's in there?" He said, "Your girlfriend." I couldn't believe what I was hearing. She had made me a promise, and I had believed her. I walked in ahead of the others, and there she was, sitting at a table and having a drink with a G.I that I had never seen before. She was facing my way, and you should have seen the look on her face when she saw me. I walked directly to her and said, "Come, we need to talk." Without speaking, she got up and followed me outside. I said, "Let's go to your apartment to talk." Again, we walked without talking. She had a two-room apartment on the 2nd floor of a building about 100 meters from the "Black Bear". Once in her room I said, " Liz, I can't believe this. Why did you do this to me. You promised not to go to the "Black Bear" anymore until you heard from me. I believed you. I trusted you." All she would say was, "Why you lie to me. You say you go. You no go." I could not convince her that my schedule had been changed and that we had decided to come back to Ansbach. I knew that she would always believe that I deliberately came back to try and catch her. I told her how disappointed I was in her and told her that I would not be seeing her again or writing to her.

I then wished her the best and left her crying. I went back to the "Bear" to join my friends. It had been maybe 20 minutes when another stranger approached me and said, "There's someone outside that wants to see you." I cautiously walked out but saw no one. As I scanned the area, I spotted a figure standing in a dark corner. As I got closer, I realized it was Liz. I said, "What are you doing here?" She didn't speak but raised her arm. Then I saw it. Blood was dripping from her fingertips. I said, "My God, Liz, what have you done?" She began to collapse. I caught her and picked her up in my arms, and glancing around I saw a friend, Tom Cooley, from the dispensary, who had followed me outside. I said, "come with me Tom, I need your help." I carried Liz to the apartment where I laid her on the bed. I examined her wound. She had cut her wrist, but the bleeding had almost stopped, and I was very much relieved to see that she had not cut the artery, only some veins. It didn't appear that any tendons were severed. I cleaned her hand and arm with warm, soapy water and cleaned the wound with peroxide. The cut was about two inches long and fairly superficial. With my experience in the emergency room, I knew how to take care of such a wound. It could have used a few stitches, but I had no way to do that, so I did the next best thing. I made a couple of butterflies from adhesive tape and applied them tightly to hold the wound together. Then I applied some antibacterial ointment and wrapped it with a sterile bandage. I told Tom he could leave, but I stayed with her all night, afraid of what she might do if I left. We spoke very few words that night, and I left around 6 AM to catch a train back to Nurnberg, realizing I would never see her again or know what might happen to her. I was sad and thinking that maybe I shouldn't have been so hard on her.

CHAPTER 11

Back to the Good Old U.S.A.

MY TRIP BACK to the Good Old U.S.A. was nothing compared to the trip over. The sea was much calmer in September than it had been in December. I only felt a little queasy a few times. I was put on duty as sergeant of the guard. I was assigned a group of men, and it was my duty to see that they were posted at various locations around the ship.

Eight days of sailing and we were docking in Brooklyn, New York. From there, we were taken by bus to Ft. Dix, New Jersey to be processed out of the Army. I was one of the few E-5s in the group, so I was always being put in charge of various details. A lot of the men didn't like me, because they thought I was being too "Gung Ho." They kept calling me "Lifer." I told them, "Look, I'm getting out just like the rest of you guys. But for now, I'm still in the Army, and I've been given a job to do, and I'm going to do it. That's why I'm an E-5 and you're not." One evening I was assigned 15 men to be put on KP (Kitchen Police) at 4 AM the following morning. So that I could identify them, I had them tie a towel to the end of their bunks. Well, when I got them together the next morning, I only had 11 men. Four of them had removed their towels during the night. I had no way of knowing who they were, so I had to arouse four men from their sleep and put them on duty. I marched them a few blocks to the mess hall and turned them over to the mess sergeant.

On September 16, 1960, I was finally discharged from the Army. I rode a post bus to the Trailways Station and bought a ticket to Weston, Georgia. On the ride home, I noticed two young ladies sitting across the aisle from me, and I realized they were speaking German. By now, I had come a long way with the German language, so I listened for a while and finally asked in German where they were from. They weren't from Germany at all, but from Switzerland, and were headed for Winston-Salem, North Carolina. I think from that point on they were a little more careful about what they said.

At around 3 PM the following day, we were closing in on Weston, and my hand was on the rope, ready to signal the driver that I wanted to get off at Thurmond's Store. As we slowed down, I saw Brenda run out of the store. She had no idea what day I would be arriving, and this was a week before my scheduled ETS (estimated time of separation). As soon as I got off the bus, she was in my arms, and we stood there holding each other for a long time. It was so good to be home! We walked into the store, and I was greeted and welcomed home by Trapie and C.P. We hung out in the store until closing time; I think 9 or 10 PM. Brenda and I would be spending the night here, and tomorrow we would go to my parents' home. They too, did not know exactly when I would be coming in.

Trapie, Brenda, and I walked from the store over to the house. We sat and talked for some time, then Trapie handed me the key to the store and asked me to go over and bring back Cokes for us. On the way over to the store, I realized that I didn't ask which door this key opened. There were four doors: two in the back, a front door, and a door under the car port. I went to the nearest back door and fumbled with trying to get the key in the lock. It didn't fit. I went to the other back door, same thing. Then I walked to the car port and tried that one. Bingo! It fit. The store was in total darkness, so I felt along the wall for a light switch. As the room lit up, I suddenly realized that I was looking down the barrel of a 12-gauge shotgun. "Jesus!" said C.P., "You scared the crap out of me! I thought someone was breaking into the store!" I had no idea that he slept in the store. I assumed he had been in bed at the house. He had heard me trying to get in at the back doors and had no idea it was me. I think it scared him more than it did me. It was a miracle that he didn't pull the trigger before the light came on.

After finishing our Coke, Brenda and I retired for the night. Then Elizabeth flashed across my mind. I thought, "This is not good." I think Brenda sensed that something was not right but didn't know what. Well, tomorrow would be another day, and Elizabeth would soon be erased from my mind forever, I thought.

We slept in kind of late the next morning, then walked over to the store. Trapie had breakfast ready for us, and after chatting for a while, we prepared to go to see my family.

My folks were happy to have me home again. It had been almost two years since I had seen them. Don was now 15, and Jimmy would be 12 soon. The biggest change at home was that Mama now had a television, and she loved it. She had gotten addicted to the soap operas. Every day at noon, she would stop whatever she was doing to watch "The Guiding Light" and others. I spent several days at home, and I had become interested in them also. Everything was pretty much the same at Dad's upholstery shop. I spent lots of time with him also. During the next couple of weeks, I spent all my time rotating back and forth between my family and Brenda's family and also visiting other relatives.

During my time in Germany, I had taken many pictures with my 35 mm camera and had a purchased a slide projector. I enjoyed showing the slides to all my folks. One day I was showing slides when up popped a picture of Elizabeth in that bright yellow dress, walking toward the camera. I didn't realize there were any pictures of her in the tray. Brenda commented, "Who is that, Miss Hollywood?" I did not have a very good answer.

It was time for me to start looking for a job. I went to all the hospitals in the area, but no one had an opening in the laboratory. I was beginning to get discouraged and began to think re-enlistment. Mama didn't really like that idea and told me that Brenda and I could stay there as long as we wanted. But I didn't want that. I was now 21 years old. Trapie had commented that I had lost that little boy look and now had the look of a young man. That made me feel good, and I wanted to be that man.

I had made my decision. I would re-enlist. I went to the recruiter and asked him to find me an assignment somewhere in the Southeastern United States. He called me a couple of days later and said the best he could do was Ft. Knox, Kentucky. It was an assignment with the U.S. Army Medical Research Laboratory. I told him I would take it, so on October 26, I re-enlisted. I had about 15 days until I would report for duty.

I needed a car. Brenda had sold the 1950 Ford to J.T. Everette while I was away. J.T. had married my 3rd grade teacher, Miss Fussell. C.P. and Trapie went with Brenda and me to Americus to look at cars. We found a new 1961 Chevrolet Bel Air that we liked. The price was $2400.00. The payments would be a little more than $100.00 per month for 24 months. C.P. and Trapie signed with us, and we drove it away.

This thing with Elizabeth was really preying heavily on my mind. I couldn't get away from this feeling of guilt. I knew I was going to tell Brenda, but I didn't know how. While I was gone, she had attended nursing school and was now a Licensed Practical Nurse. As far as I knew, she had been true and faithful to me while I was gone. I knew it would hurt her, but I was at a point where I could no longer stand the pain and guilt within me. So, one day when we were alone, I said, "Do you remember the picture of the girl in the yellow dress?" Her answer was in the form of a question, "Yes?" I said, "She was a friend of mine." It was as if she already knew and had been waiting for me to tell her. She said, "I suspected that." I told her how sorry I was that it happened, and I begged her for forgiveness. She said she could forgive me, but it would take a little time. What happened next was totally unexpected. She spread the news to everyone! Now it was poor little Brenda and terrible Johnny. I don't remember anyone acting any differently toward me, but I thought it would have been better If we could have just kept it between the two of us.

I believe it was the next day that C.P. said to me, "Johnny, "Let's go bird hunting this afternoon." A thought entered my mind, " Is he having second thoughts now about pulling that trigger?" But I said, "Yeah, sure." C.P. had a great love for hunting quail and had two of the finest bird dogs anywhere. His dogs were named "Hound" and "Dixie." Dixie looked like a first-class bird dog, but Hound, well, that's what he looked like, an old hound dog. We went out to the dog pen, C.P. opened the door and said, "Come on Hound." He said we would go on the tractor. He had a Ford Tractor with a seat attached on the rear, that he could raise up and down with the power lift. I got on the back seat and away we went, with Hound following along behind. We both had an automatic 12-gauge shotgun. As we were passing through a wooded area, suddenly a covey of quail flew up from in front of us. C.P.

116

stepped on the clutch, stood up, and took aim. As one of the birds flew between two trees, C.P. fired and the bird went down. C.P. said, "Dead Hound, dead bird!" Hound ran over, retrieved the bird and brought it to C.P. When we reached the field where we would be hunting, Hound ran over to a tall weed, peed on it, and continued on his way. He ran about 20 feet, stopped and raised his foot. C.P. said he's already found the birds. I thought, "Right." We walked slowly ahead as Hound held his position. Suddenly a large covey of quail flew up and spread out in every direction. C.P. brought down two of them before they got out of range. C.P. said that now we would hunt down the single birds. We followed Hound for a way. Suddenly he stopped and raised his foot. C.P. said, "OK, it's your turn." I slowly walked forward, and a single bird flew up. I took aim and fired, but the bird kept going. Hound ran ahead as if to retrieve the bird, but then realized that a bird didn't fall. Hound turned and looked at me as if to say, "What the heck are you doing?" C.P. said, "Hound doesn't like for you to miss. If you miss again, he'll most likely go lay down in the shade of a tree and go to sleep." I told him that he'd best do the rest of the shooting, because this was my first time to go quail hunting. Well, Hound found most of the other birds that had scattered, and C.P. didn't miss. At the end of the day, we had 9 or 10 birds. We went home, C.P. cleaned the birds, and Trapie fried them for supper, along with a big pot of grits. It just doesn't get any better than that!

CHAPTER **12**

On to the Blue Grass State

BRENDA AND I left a few days early for Kentucky. We wanted to have time to find a place to live before I had to sign in. Ft. Knox was almost due north of our parents' homes in Georgia. Our trip would take us through Columbus, Chattanooga, Nashville, and finally Elizabethtown, Kentucky, where we would spend the night and go house hunting the following day. The distance was approximately 530 miles and would take about 10 hours.

We reached Chattanooga around noon, and after stopping for a quick lunch, we continued our journey. Just north of town I saw a sign for Jasper. I said, "Hey, that's where Kevin Gram lives. Let's stop by and see him." Kevin had been my best friend in Germany. He had told me exactly where he lived, his parents' names, and the names of his siblings, all of them being sisters. We drove directly to the house which was on a dirt road. The house was not much more than a shack, and there were several teenage girls in the yard wearing plain dresses, and all were barefoot. It was easy to see that they were an extremely poor family. I told them who I was and asked if Kevin was home. About that time, Mrs. Gram came out, and I told her that Kevin and I had been best friends in Germany. She said that Kevin and his father were working in a cement plant in Chattanooga. She gave us directions, and we drove to the plant. We asked to see Kevin, and when he came out, he looked to be made of concrete. He was completely wrapped up in gray powder. Kevin had left Germany a few weeks before me and had brought back a German wife. We talked for about half an hour and he kept saying,

"So you went back in?" I told him we were on our way to Ft. Knox and told him what unit I was with. I asked him about his wife, Chris, and he said she was home at their apartment a short distance away and that I should stop by and see her. I had become acquainted with Chris while they were dating. Chris was a very smart girl. She spoke fluent English, and her grammar was excellent. We visited her for a few minutes and then headed north again.

We were in the vicinity of Bowling Green, Kentucky when I saw water spray on the windshield. Then another spray. I said, "What's going on?" I knew it wasn't raining because it was a clear day. Then I noticed the temperature hand had moved all the way to hot. I couldn't understand it. This was a brand-new car with only a few hundred miles on it. I pulled off the road at the nearest house. When I stopped, steam was rolling from under the hood. A gentleman came out as I was raising the hood. The problem was immediately obvious. There was a split in the upper radiator hose. We filled the radiator with water, and he patched the hose with duct tape. He, said, "I sure hate to see a car this new get so hot." I was hoping that no further damage had been done. We made it to Elizabethtown without any further problem. It was already 5 PM so I decided to check in at a motel, and we would take the car to the Chevrolet Dealership the following morning and have the hose replaced.

We were up bright and early the next morning. As we had breakfast, I was looking in the classified ads when I found, "apartment for rent, 4 mi. south of Ft. Knox, on Hwy 31-W." We had to get that hose replaced first, so we headed for the Chevy Dealer. Fortunately, they were able to get on it right away, and we were out in about an hour. We found the apartment with no problem. It looked to be fairly new. It was a three-apartment complex and the middle unit was vacant. We found a pay phone and called the number in the ad. The agent said he would meet us there, so we could look it over. It was fully furnished and nicer than expected. We signed the papers and told him we would move in the following day, which we did.

Ft. Knox is the U.S. Army's home of the armor, The Patton Museum, and probably most of all, known for the U.S. Treasury Gold Depository. Highway 31-W runs by Ft Knox and is the main route between

Elizabethtown and Louisville. As you enter the Post from the south, one of the first things you notice is the Gold Depository sitting on a hill some 500 feet off the road. That's about as close as you can get, because it is surrounded by a high security fence. The single entrance is heavily guarded.

Traveling a little further north, you reach the main gate on the right. I found my way to the AMRL (Army Medical Research Laboratory), which was near the new Ireland Army Hospital. AMRL was in the old hospital which was a series of wooden buildings built during World War II. The only brick structure was the headquarters building, which I assumed was part of the old hospital. After signing in, I was taken to my workplace. There were about as many civilians working at AMRL as military personnel. I was introduced to my boss, Henry Batsel, Ph.D. He was currently doing research on the brain, and I would be his assistant. This was totally different from anything I had ever done before, but I would come to enjoy my work. Our subject was cats. My job each morning would be to select a cat, anesthetize the animal, and prepare it for surgery. Dr. Batsel would carefully cut two 10 mm holes in the skull, being careful not to puncture the dura. Electrodes would be inserted in each opening. The brain stem would then be severed and an EEG (electroencephalogram) would be performed to measure brain waves. Various drugs would be administered to see what effect, if any, they might have. I discovered that brain waves would vary greatly by altering the body temperature of the subject. At the end of the day, I would euthanize the subject, place the body in the proper container, and place it in a freezer for later disposal. This same procedure would be repeated daily until the experiment was complete. The doctor would write a report to be included in various medical journals. My name would be included for technical support. I also assisted a surgeon, an army captain, with many experiments on dogs. The doctor taught me to do surgery. Once he was confident that I could perform the procedure, he left it to me to do the surgery. Most of his work was testing the effects of various drugs on the kidney. I actually became a pretty good surgeon and probably could have become a good doctor had I had that opportunity.

We also did a lot of experiments on human subjects, and they were always asking for volunteers. I volunteered for one of them. It was an experiment where I was seated in the center of a turntable in total darkness, and they would spin me for 15 minutes, during which time I would be given problems to solve in my head. Then they would stop me, and I would give them my answer, and they would give me another problem, and I would spin again. I was never told at what rpm I was spinning. I would also be wired to an EEG machine to measure my brain waves. I would be on the turntable for four hours per day, and the experiment lasted for about two weeks. We weren't told much about what these experiments were for, but I had heard that this one was related to the space program; after all, we had had the first two monkeys to go into space: Abel & Baker. That was a couple of years before I arrived there.

There was one interesting experiment that I was not going to volunteer for, and that was the electric chair. The subject was wired up, and a small amount of current was passed through his body. The amount of current would be increased each day to determine if he would build up a resistance. As far as I know, we never lost any subjects.

Probably the most useful experiment we did on humans was acclimatization. There were two parts to this experiment: the hot room and the cold room. The experiment lasted for three weeks. A group of men were placed in a 95-degree room for one week, then on week two, it was 105 degrees, and finally on week three, it was 120 degrees. In the cold room, it was 65 degrees on week one, 55 degrees on week two, and 45 on week three. The men only wore a pair of shorts, and they were given certain jobs to do. At the end of three weeks, they switched rooms and were given the same work. Their performances were then compared. The acclimatization was highly successful, the purpose being to acclimatize troops that might be sent to war zones in various parts of the world. They could be acclimatized for better performance before being deployed.

Dr. Batsel and I were in a single-story building along with two other Ph. D.s, Dr. Turner and Dr. Clark. Next door was a two-floor building, where the kennel was on the 1st floor and the medical laboratory on the 2nd floor. On occasions, I would have to collect blood samples from a dog or cat. Dogs weren't too bad, because I could usually draw blood from the front leg, but cats were different. Small samples could be obtained by making a small cut on the ear, but if larger samples were required, I would have to go directly into the heart.

Unlike humans, most dogs have the same blood type, and are therefore compatible with each other. They all type as B+. There's maybe a 1 in 100 chance that two dogs will not be compatible. We had one very important subject that needed a transfusion, and the doctor did not want to take a chance, so I was called on to do a type and cross-match, the only one I did while at AMRL.

Brenda and I had decided to move into military housing, so early on we had applied. It was two or three months before a unit was available. We were assigned an apartment in Rose Terrace, which was directly across highway 31-W from the main gate. The apartment was unfurnished, so we had to go out and purchase a bedroom and a living room suite. After making payments on these plus the car payment, we would have $15 per month to live on. We got a lot of help from the folks back home, and occasionally Brenda would get a baby-sitting job. We managed to get by and didn't complain.

One day someone knocked on our door. I was so surprised when I answered. There stood my old buddy, Kevin Gram. He had re-enlisted and requested to be assigned to Ft. Knox. Kevin was only an E-4 and didn't qualify for government housing, so he and Chris had found an apartment in Radcliff, a little town adjacent to post. Kevin was still playing his guitar, and we visited each other often. He was assigned to one of the armored divisions, and his job as clerk typist was not as easy as it had been in our small unit in Germany.

I bowled my first game ever while in Germany and joined a league. It was made up of two-man teams. My partner and I won first place, the only first place finish I would have in my lifetime. In the process, I had carried a 155 average. I joined a four-man team at Ft. Knox and carried a 168 average, second best in the league, but team-wise, we didn't do so well. I also entered the All Army Bowling Tournament in 1961. It was open to persons with a 165 average or better. That was a big mistake. I should have stayed home on that one.

I recall very well the day my wife said, "Johnny, would you come here please?" I walked to the bathroom and saw her staring at the commode. I said, "What's wrong?" Then I saw it. The commode was filled with blood, and there appeared to be tiny pieces of tissue or blood clots. I said, "Baby, I think you just had a miscarriage." She began to cry, saying, "I lost my baby." I embraced her and tried to comfort her. I said, "Honey, it's OK, we'll try again." I took her to the emergency room. The doctor kept her overnight and performed a D&C the following day.

The month was February 1961. The situation in Southeast Asia, or more specifically Vietnam, was becoming unstable. A number of "Military Advisors" had already been sent to the area. The Pentagon was concerned that the possibility existed that a large number of troops might have to be deployed. So, they decided to make a practice run. The 101st Airborne Division at Ft. Campbell, Kentucky was chosen for that exercise. The AMRL was called upon to do a study of the troops to determine their mental and physical condition prior to departure and during the long flight. They would first fly to a staging area in Okinawa and then to the Philippines for a training exercise. The Medical Study Team would be made up of five individuals. I was asked if I would like to be a part of that team. I considered it for a moment and was thinking, "This could be my only chance to see that part of the world." So, I accepted the invitation. A captain, who was a medical doctor, was in charge. We also had a 1st lieutenant and a master sergeant who had served in the Philippines during World War II and had married a Filipino. PFC Ben Hadd of Brooklyn, NY and I, rounded out the team. We would be gone for approximately two weeks.

We arrived at Ft. Campbell on a Saturday and would be flying out on Monday morning. I was assigned to a barracks, and my job was to observe and take note of the mood of the men; what they were doing, and what they were talking about. I had been warned that I might not be well accepted by the men because I was a "leg". A "leg" is a soldier who is not airborne qualified, and they are generally looked down upon. A few of them asked what I was doing there, but overall, I was pretty well accepted.

That Sunday, Ben Hadd and I decided to take a look around the post. We went to the Army Airfield where we would be leaving from and with my 35 mm camera, made some pictures of aircraft. That afternoon as we walked around the post, we came upon a strange area. It was a very large field with grass covered mounds of dirt inside, and more interesting, the area was surrounded by not one, but two very high fences with barbed wire on top. A sign between the fences said that the inner fence was electrified. I said to Ben, " What the heck is this?" At that moment, a military vehicle pulled up beside us and two MPs jumped out. They put us spread eagle against the hood of the vehicle, frisk us, and told us not to move. They questioned me about my camera. One of them got on a walkie-talkie and said, "Sir, two men walking along the fence, one of them with a camera with telephoto lenses." They told us to get in the vehicle, and they drove us to a building and took us inside. We were escorted to a major's office where we stood at attention and saluted. He asked what we were doing here. We were in civilian clothes, so we presented our military ID and AMRL ID cards. We told him this was our first time at Ft. Campbell and told him why we were here. He asked about my camera and wanted to know if I had taken any photos. I told him, "No sir, only a few pictures from the airfield this morning." He said, "I could confiscate your film, but I believe you." He said he would have the MPs escort us from the area and told us not to come back. On the way out, I asked the MPs what this area was, and their answer was, "I don't know." They dropped us off, and we walked away, completely puzzled.

At 4 AM on Monday, the 101st Airborne was up preparing and beginning to assemble for the trip to the airfield. There were 21 planes lined up and ready to go. We would be flying on C-121 Constellations; military transport planes which carry 75 passengers each. The plane was propeller driven, powered by four engines. The planes would be leaving at 15-minute intervals, and it would take approximately 50 hours of flying time to reach the Philippines. I boarded my plane which was somewhere in the middle. All the planes were named after world cities. My plane was the "City of Karachi". At the time, I had no idea where Karachi was. Once we reached our altitude, my work began. The two officers on our team had prepared questionnaires to be filled out on each leg of the trip. I passed them out to all the men and took them up about half an hour later.

Our first stop was San Francisco. It was already dark when we arrived, and it was cold and raining. We were allowed to depart the plane for a few minutes while we were refueling. On every stop we made, I would try to pick up some little souvenir, an ashtray if possible. I had started a collection in Germany. Our next stop would be Hawaii. We arrived in Honolulu about mid-morning. I thought, "Wow! What a beautiful place!" The weather was warm, and the palm trees were blowing in the breeze. Then it was on to Wake Island. The runway seemed to stretch out over the entire length of the island. Then it was Guam, and finally we touched down at Kadena Air Force Base in Okinawa. We would be there for three days before going on to the Philippines. The climate was nice, with temperatures in the 60s and 70s. We turned in all our questionnaires to the captain, and our work was done for the time being.

The three of us enlisted men took a bus and headed for town that afternoon. It was unlike anything I had ever seen before. There was a ditch beside the road, which had a little water trickling down it. Men and women were openly using it as a restroom, and no one seemed to pay any attention, that is except for us.

We arrived in downtown Kadena, and after walking around for a while we ended up in a bar. All our Sergeant wanted to do was find some girls, but for Ben and me, we had no interest whatsoever. Finally, three girls came and sat at the table with us. Later, they got up to go to the restroom. We waited and waited and kept an eye on the door, but they never came out. Finally, it was closing time, and we were the only ones left in the place. The owner came to us and told us we had to leave. Our Sergeant said, "We're waiting for the girls to come out of the restroom." He said, "What restroom?" The Sergeant pointed to the door and said, "That one." The owner said, "That not restroom. That back door." Talk about mad, old Sarge was really put out! We got on a bus and went back to the base.

The following night, which was our last at Okinawa, Sarge wanted to go out on the town again. I went with him, but Ben said he had had enough of going out. Sarge wanted to go to that same bar to see if he could find those girls. We went but never saw them. We left and went to a very small bar. Old Sarge met a girl, and they left together. I told him I would wait there for his return. After two hours, he still wasn't back, and I was getting a little concerned. An attractive young lady who was tending the bar came to me and said, "It's closing time." I told her I needed to wait for my friend. She said she had nothing more to do because this was her night off, and that she would wait with me for a while. She sat across from me at a booth and said, "Would you like to play a game of Casino?" I said, "I don't know, I've never played." She began dealing the cards and she taught me a very simple, but fun card game. I 've never forgotten that game, and my wife and I still play it occasionally. Old Sarge still wasn't back, and I told her I was really worried about him. She said, "Come. I show you where he be." We walked down a trail that led to a house sitting on a hilltop, when suddenly I saw him come staggering down the hill, drunk as a coot. I got him on a bus and back to the base.

Looking out the window of the C-121 as we touched down at Clark Air Force Base in the Philippines, I could see in the distance a perfectly shaped volcano towering high above an otherwise flat horizon. I don't know where the 101st went for the night, but the three of us enlisted men were given a sleeping bag and taken to a building and told to bed down there for the night, that they would find quarters for us the following day. You could hardly call it a building. There was only a partial roof, and the floor was dirt, rocks, and grass. Swarming around the floor were what looked to be thousands of bugs, some larger than anything I had ever seen. There was some kind of large tree outside, and what I saw under that tree, amazed me. There was a small man wearing nothing but a loin cloth, holding a bow. He drew an arrow from his quiver and shot it at something in the tree. His arrow lodged in the treetop. I said to the sergeant. "Who is that guy?" He said, "Oh, that's a Negrito. The Air Force has hired them to do guard duty on the base." I said, "Wonderful! I feel so secure!" But I was thinking, " I would sure love to have his picture standing by our plane, holding a bow and arrow." Then another one shows up, and they stood there pointing to the treetop and jabbering in some tongue that I couldn't understand. I was thinking, "No one back home will believe me when I tell them this story." But there's no way I could make this up. I asked the sergeant what a Negrito was. He said it was a tribesman that lives here in the Philippines. I have since learned that there are many of these ethnic groups that live in the Philippines and other parts of Southeast Asia. Well, we survived the night and were assigned to a very modern barracks the following morning. Our work was now essentially done so we would be on our own for a week while the troops were in the field. The sergeant was thoroughly familiar with the Philippines, and he was going to show us around.

On our first full day in the Philippines, we took a bus for the short ride to Manila. My first big surprise was the vehicles. Almost all were Jeeps, and were painted in every shade of the rainbow, and then some. I learned that at the end of the war, General Douglas McArthur had given all the Jeeps to the Filipino people and that they liked them so much that they began manufacturing them. These vehicles were called Jeepneys. We hired a Jeepney driver to show us around the city. Our Jeepney was something like a pick-up truck with benches in the back. There were four or five lanes of traffic, and most intersections had no traffic lights. The right of way belonged to whoever got there first, or to the one that didn't chicken out. Hundreds of horns were constantly blowing. It was as if the horn was the most important part of driving. To my surprise, despite the unorthodox method of driving, I don't recall ever seeing an accident.

That evening we went to a little restaurant for dinner. I ordered fried fish and to my surprise, when they brought it out, there was a whole fish: head, eyes, everything. The sergeant said the eyes were really good, but I couldn't quite stomach that. Otherwise, the meal was great.

After dinner, our Sergeant took us to a dance hall. On one side of the room was a group of girls. Sarge told Ben and me to go over and pick out a girl, and she would be ours for the night. Neither Ben nor I wanted a girl for the night, but he went over and found one for himself. Then he did something that was unreal. He had all the girls line up in single file and slowly walk by us, giving us a big smile as they passed. Sarge said, "Just grab the one you like." I guess we really made them feel unwanted because the last one passed by, and we didn't grab one. So, the Sergeant just went over and chose one for us. It was rather embarrassing, but they sat at the table with us, and we did an occasional slow dance. I was surprised at how well they spoke English. They said that English had been required in their school. It was quite enjoyable just talking with them. At the end of the evening, we thanked them for their entertainment, told them good-bye, and headed back to the base.

The following day Ben and I went our own way, and the old sarge did his thing. We spent some time walking along the waterfront of Luzon. It was a common sight to see mothers bathing their children as we walked along the beach. We also had the opportunity to talk with some Filipino soldiers. I even exchanged addresses with one, but I don't think we ever corresponded.

Our trip to the Philippines would not be complete without a visit to Baguio City, a city located high in the mountains of Northern Luzon. Its elevation is more than 5,000 feet, and because of that elevation it had a much milder climate than Manila. We boarded a bus that took us up a steep and winding road. We made a stop somewhere along the way and a young girl, maybe 12, came up to my window, which was down. She asked if I would like to buy candy. She held a tray of what looked like long green cigars. I gave her 25 cents for one and as I unwrapped it, I found that it was some type of homemade, shredded coconut candy, wrapped in a banana leaf and toasted. It was very good.

The one thing about Baguio that really stood out was the marketplace we visited. I was puzzled when I saw this large cage full of dogs. Some of the animals looked almost wild, and they were climbing up the sides of the cage. A lady walked up, picked out a dog, paid the equivalent of five dollars for it and led it away. I took my camera from the case, and as I prepared to take a picture, the merchant yelled at me, "Hey Joe! No can do! No pictures!" I put away the camera and asked the Sergeant what that was all about. He said, "This is a dog market. People come and buy a dog, take it home and butcher it, and enjoy some great meals." I couldn't believe what I was hearing, but it was a fact. They just didn't want me taking pictures and advertising it.

Today was our last day in the Philippines. We would be flying out tomorrow. Our Sergeant decided he should call the Captain to make sure our schedule hadn't changed.

The schedule had changed. When Sarge finally reached the Captain, his words were, "Where are you? Get your butts to the airfield now! The schedule was moved up a day. Half the planes have already left. The last plane will be leaving in about two hours. If we're lucky, we might be able to get you on one of the last flights." I was worried. I didn't want to be stranded in the Philippines, not knowing when I might be able to get out. Even if we took a bus at that moment, we still couldn't make it back in time. Our only hope was to fly back. The Air Force had a small airfield at Baguio, so we headed there as fast as we could. We all but begged for a pilot to fly us back to Clark AFB. Fortunately, a pilot was available. He fired up a C-47, a small twin-engine plane from World War II, and we got on board. The runway was cut into the side of a mountain and was very short. The C-47 was the only military plane that could land and take off here. The runway ended at the edge of the mountain, so you better be flying when you reach that point, or otherwise, you go off the side of the mountain. A half hour later we landed at Clark, grabbed our bag, and headed out to where the planes were loading. Fortunately, we were all able to get on a manifest.

Less than an hour into our flight, I felt the urge to go to the toilet. I had a case of diarrhea. I went back to my seat and it hit me again. What was the problem? We had been cautioned about drinking water while in Okinawa and in the Philippines, and I hadn't drunk any water except on the base. Then I remembered something. The candy! The candy I bought from that little girl when I was on the bus. That had to be it. It was contaminated with something. I was having to go to the toilet every 15 to 20 minutes. I must have spent half the flight home in the toilet. I wasn't eating anything, so by the time we reached Hawaii, the frequency had slowed down some. It was a good thing too, because in Honolulu we were taken by bus to the USO where we watched a group of hula dancers put on a great show.

One thing that was of interest during the flights was the crossing of the International Date Line. It was around midnight when we crossed it. Therefore, one way we had the same day twice in a row, and on the opposite flight we all but skipped a day.

I was in bad shape when I got home. I still had a terrible case of diarrhea, sometimes with bloody stools. I went to the emergency room the day I returned, and the doctor ordered a stool culture. It showed that I had a Shigella infection and was put on antibiotics for 30 days. I did not want that again!

Big news had come to AMRL while I was gone. The research facility at Ft. Knox would be moving to a new facility in Natick, Massachusetts. The move was still several months away, but they were already asking and deciding which personnel would be going. Dr. Batsel asked me to go with him and I agreed, but unfortunately, I never got the chance.

The Captain who was in charge of our team that went to the Philippines wrote up a report saying that the troops were ready, both

129

mentally and physically, once we reached our destination.

Our Captain was also the same doctor who had taught me how to do some surgical procedures, and I had the opportunity to work with him a few more times. One day I told him about Ben and me wandering into that restricted area at Ft Campbell. He said, "Wow! You guys wandered into the "Bird Cage". I asked, "What's the "Bird Cage?" He told me it was a storage facility for nuclear bombs. He said they were stored underground and that there was an underground railway to deliver them to the airfield to be loaded on planes should that become necessary. That gave me a much better understanding of what had happened.

Sometime in May 1962 my commander called me to his office. He said, "I've got good news for you and I've got bad news for you." I said, "Give me the bad news first, Sir." He said, "Orders have come down from Washington, transferring you to Germany." I said, "Sir, I just came back from Germany less than two years ago." He said, "Yes, I know, but that's the way the Army works. There's nothing I can do about it. We appreciate the outstanding job you've done for us here at the Army Medical Research Laboratory and to show our appreciation, here's a little going away present for you." He handed me a sheet of paper and it read, Sp-5 Johnny D. Wills is hereby promoted to the rank of Specialist-6 (E-6). I was overjoyed. I had only been in the Army 4 1/2 years, and I had already made E-6. Some soldiers are lucky to make E-6 by retirement. I saluted him and thanked him for his kind words and for my promotion. I couldn't wait to get my new stripe sewed on my uniform.

My orders said that I was assigned to the 2nd Evacuation Hospital in Bad Kreuznach, Germany. I also would have a 30-day delay in route before reporting to New York to board the U.S.N.S. Rose.

Brenda was now four months pregnant with our first child and by the time I would be leaving, she would be six months along, and that would be too far along for her to travel with me. We would have to wait until the baby was six weeks old before they could join me. That would mean sometime in December. So, we began to prepare for leaving Ft. Knox. There was a lot of work to do: arrange for our household good to be shipped, get the apartment cleaned, and ready to pass inspection so we could clear quarters. In June, I said good-bye to my friends and co-workers, and we headed to Georgia for our 30-day vacation.

CHAPTER 13

Back to Germany Again

WE SPENT MOST of the month of June visiting with our families, but there was one important item of business that had to be attended to. We had to find a name for our first child. Brenda's mother, Trapie, had long made it known that if our first child was a girl, her name would be Echo. I had never heard that name before, but Trapie once had a friend while growing up, somewhere in the Shellman, GA area, whose name was Echo Patterson, and she loved the name. She and Brenda said that If I would agree with that, I could choose whatever name I wanted for a boy child. I thought to myself, "Oh Yeah, I'll have a little fun with that." So, the next day I told them I had a great name picked out. I said, "If it's a boy, his name will be "Sylvester". They both said at the same time, "No, no! You can't do that!" I said, "But you promised." All they could think about was that cat chasing Tweety Bird. I had to leave the room to keep from laughing in front of them. I let them suffer until the next day and then told them that I was only joking. I said, "My son will be named Harvey Clinton Wills." As far as I knew, no one in our family had ever had either of those names. As a great fan of baseball in my teenage years, I had come to like Harvey Kuenn, star player with the Detroit Tigers. His career began in 1953. He could play shortstop or outfielder, and he had a lifetime batting average of over .300. I really liked the name "Harvey." Clinton came from a good friend of mine with that name, while serving my first tour of duty in Germany. Clinton ended up being the brother-in-law of my good buddy Kevin Gram, as they married sisters while in Germany.

With the baby's name all settled, it was time to begin planning the trip to New York. I would be shipping our car to Germany, so Brenda and my 17-year old brother Don, would be riding with me, and they would take a bus back home. We decided to take a scenic route. We would leave a couple of days early, drive through the North Georgia mountains, into Cherokee, NC, then pick up the Blue Ridge Parkway, a scenic route through the Appalachian Mountains, for most of our journey.

Our trip started out as planned. We stopped in Cherokee and had our picture made with the Indian Chief, then proceeded to the Parkway. Before we reached the Virginia State Line, we realized that this route was going to take much longer than we had anticipated, so we decided to leave the Parkway, and take the interstate highway for the rest of the way. From that point on, everything went as planned. We spent that first night somewhere in Maryland and made it to New York the following day. After dropping the car off at the Army Terminal in Brooklyn, I hugged by brother and kissed my wife good-bye as they boarded a bus for their trip back to Georgia.

This would be my third voyage across the Atlantic, on three different ships, and I expected that it would be very much like the last, but I was so wrong. Once aboard the ship, I heard my name being called, and upon checking in I was told that since I was an E-6, they had a cabin available for me. I was beginning to think, "Man, I love these E-6 benefits." With my duffle bag in hand, I headed up the stairs. The cabins were at the top of the ship. I couldn't believe it when I got to my room. It was like being on a cruise ship. I wore my class "A" uniform every day, I had maid service, the dining room tables had white tablecloths, there were waiters, and there were no duties to pull. At age 23, I was by far the youngest person in cabin class and was the only SP-6. In fact, I may have been the only Sp-6 on board. All the other E-6s were staff sergeants. I didn't really care about being a non-commissioned officer anyway. After all, my benefits were the same as theirs.

After arriving in Bremerhaven, I took the train to my destination. Bad Kreuznach was not as far away as Ansbach. It was more in the middle of the country and to the west of Frankfurt. There were several on board who were headed for the 2nd Evacuation Hospital. I had not liked the sound of 2nd Evacuation Hospital, and when I arrived my fears became a reality. It was not an operational hospital, but a field unit staying prepared for combat. We arrived on a Friday, and I met First Sergeant Singer. He was one tough looking character, the kind that you're afraid of just from looking at him, but I have to give him credit. He was always fair and respectful to me. I was assigned a room, and he said I would be processed in on Monday. With nothing to do but just hang around and talk to people, it would be a long weekend. Then late Saturday afternoon, someone asked if I would like to go down to the Victoria Bar for a while and listen to Johnnie Smith. I asked, "Who is Johnnie Smith?" I was told he was a dental technician in our unit. He had a country music band and would be playing tonight. Of course, I was always interested in country music, so I said, "Sure, sounds like fun."

The band was taking a break when we walked through the door of the Victoria Bar. The place was packed with G.I.s enjoying their favorite beverages. Suddenly, I heard a loud voice say, " You're the best woman I've ever gone out with, and I want to go out with you again!" Then I heard a female say in a firm voice, "Well, I'm not going out with you again!" I said to my companion, "Who is that?" He replied, "That's Johnnie Smith." I thought, "Oh my God! What am I getting into?" The band started playing, and I realized that Johnnie was a good singer and a pretty good guitar player. We listened until they took another break, and then I was introduced to Johnnie Smith. I told him that I did a little picking and singing, and he insisted that I take his guitar and play a few songs. I did, and apparently, he liked me pretty well, because he wanted me to take over for him the remainder of the evening.

The girl that Johnnie was after was Maria, one of the waitresses, and he continued to harass her the entire evening. However, she continued to resist him and let him know that she wasn't going out with him. At 11 PM, I told Johnnie I had to leave. He thanked me and said he would see me on Monday.

On Monday morning, I met the company commander, the hospital commander, head nurse, and personnel officer. They were all surprised to see me as a Specialist-6. They had expected a Specialist-5. I explained to them how I had been promoted after I received my orders. They said it was a good thing, because I could never have been promoted here.

My department was the P, L, & X (Pharmacy, Lab, and X-Ray), and they already had two E-6s'. I said, "Great, how about transferring me to an operational hospital." But that wasn't about to happen. The lab sergeant was a 46-year old alcoholic and was known as the "yodeler". Every night he would stand in the hallway and yodel, disturbing everyone's sleep. The other E-6 was an X-ray technician in his 40s, and he had terminal lung cancer. They saw me as young, full of energy, and apparently a good soldier, otherwise. I wouldn't be an E-6 at age 23. They decided to transfer the two old guys and keep me. Then they told me that I couldn't be a Specialist-6, that they would convert me to staff sergeant, so that's what I became in a couple of days. I had to sew new insignia on all my uniforms and was made head of the department.

About two weeks after I arrived at the "Dirty Deuce", I received notification that my car had arrived at Bremerhaven and was ready for pick up. I had the newest car in the company, and many of them had not seen a 1961 Chevy.

Directly across the street from the 2nd Evac Hospital, was U.S. Army Hospital Bad Kreuznach, the operational hospital for the area. It was operated by the 14th Field Hospital. We ate in the mess hall of the hospital. They had a special chef for the NCOs, and we could have whatever we wanted at mealtime, and he would cook to order for us. I really liked that.

One morning I was sitting beside First Sergeant Singer at breakfast, and I said, "First Sergeant, how about giving me a weekend pass for this weekend. I'd like to drive down to Ansbach." He said, "What the hell for? To see some of your old girlfriends?" I said, "No, I'd like to visit some of my old co-workers." He was giving me a hard time, but I got the pass.

I ran across Johnnie Smith that Monday, whom I had met at the Victoria Bar, and he was attempting to glue the neck back on his guitar. I said, "Johnnie, what the heck happened?" he said, "Aw, I acted the fool after you left that night, and slammed my guitar to the floor. I was mad because Maria wouldn't go out with me." It was a shame, because Johnnie's wife had just recently given him that guitar for his birthday.

Early Saturday morning, I began my drive to Ansbach. I don't remember exactly, but I believe it was about a two-hour drive. First, I would go to my old barracks and see if anyone I knew was still around, then I would go and see Frau Pruess, my co-worker at the laboratory. On the way, I couldn't help but think about Elizabeth. I was not going to see her, nor did I want to see her, but I had hoped that she hadn't done something foolish after I left her that September morning, almost two years ago.

Arriving in Ansbach, and at the Hindenberg Kaserne, nothing seemed to have changed since I had left. There were few in the barracks when I arrived, and I saw no one I recognized. As I was walking along, I saw the door to my old room open and out came a Sp-5 that I recognized as the dental assistant. He had only been there a short time when I left. He remembered me and told me he would be returning to the States very soon. We talked for a little while, and then I asked, "Do you remember Elizabeth, the girl I was dating?" He replied, "Oh yes, she recently married one of the guys from the dispensary. They left for the States about two weeks ago, along with her little girl. I believe they were going to Ohio." He told me the guy's name. I didn't know him, but I had heard his name before. He had been someone due to arrive at the dispensary the same week I had left. I said, "Nice to have seen you again", and I left. I felt so happy for Elizabeth, that her dream had finally become a reality.

I walked over to the dispensary and met the person on CQ. We talked for a while, and I took a walk around the place. Nothing had changed. From there, I went over to the snack bar and had lunch, then headed over to see Frau Pruess. She was so surprised to see me standing there when she opened the door. Her son, Hartmut, was now 14 years old. He was the kid I once bought tomato catsup for. He put catsup on virtually everything he ate. On several occasions, I had bought catsup for him at the commissary, because he liked American catsup better than German catsup. We spent the afternoon talking about old times and about new things that had taken place. She invited me to stay for dinner and to spend the night. I told her I wanted to go and see Nurse Elizabeth Ruedel, and she said she would go with me the following morning.

Just before noon on Sunday, we were knocking on Nurse Elizabeth's door. No answer. Frau Pruess said she was probably at church. As we were walking away, we spotted her coming up the sidewalk. It was so good to see her again. We visited for a couple of hours, then I dropped Frau Pruess off at home, then headed back toward Bad Kreuznach.

That same week we got the word that President John F. Kennedy was coming to Germany to visit the troops. There would be a big parade and review of the men at Hanau, Germany, near Frankfurt. A full armored division with some of their tanks, and other vehicles, plus a color guard from every unit in Germany, would be there for him to review. That was a total of 18,000 men.

A color guard was made up of four men: one carrying the American flag, one with the unit flag, and a rifleman on each end. To be in the group you had to be between five feet eleven inches and six feet one inch, and your weight must be between 170 and 190 pounds. I was just a fraction of an inch under six feet, and I weighed 185. It was such an honor for me to be chosen to carry the American flag, plus, as the highest-ranking soldier, I was in charge of the detail.

One week before the President was to arrive, we all moved into a tent city a mile from where the event would take place. We were in a large, grassy field, but it rained every day, and by the end of the week, with 18,000 men tromping around, it was nothing but a field of mud.

The day of the big event, we were up at 5 AM and marching toward the review stands by 6 AM. We took a towel with us to wipe the mud from our boots before we reached the bleachers. The President would be arriving at 10 AM. The tanks and trucks were put in place the day before, and once they were parked, the tires were blackened right to the ground. The President would have lunch with the troops at the mess hall, at one of the nearby kasernes. He would come to the grill and pick the steak of his choice. That was so no one could poison him without poisoning everyone. Also, everything on the post that didn't grow, had to be painted.

It was very hot that day. Some soldiers began to pass out in the sweltering heat. The secret service was everywhere. We were warned not to make any sudden moves once the President was in sight, because the secret service had the authority to take out anyone whom they thought might be threatening the President. All weapons were checked to make sure they were not loaded. By 9 AM, the outside fence of the kaserne was lined with Germans, hoping to get a glimpse of the President they were so fond of.

At 10 AM, we could hear the helicopter. It was a large, solid white marine chopper, and it sat down about a hundred yards from the stands. You could hear a loud roar from the outside crowd when the President stepped from the helicopter. He waved at the crowd several times. President Kennedy then walked the entire length of the parade field, stopping to shake hands with all the commanders. The field stretched for about 1000 feet, with the tanks and trucks parked in front of the bleachers. I felt so honored to be a part of this event and a day I'll always remember.

Being assigned to the 2nd Evac was usually pretty boring. We had a formation each morning, then went on police call, which means picking up and cleaning up the outside area, then hanging out at the warehouse where our equipment was stored. My department had a deuce and a half for loading our equipment, which was stored in the warehouse. Once a month they would call an alert, and we would have to get to the warehouse as quickly as possible, load the truck, and prepare to move out. An alert could come anytime day or night, and you never knew how long it would last. It could be an hour or less, and we wouldn't go anywhere, or we might move out and be in the field for a week or more. This was the part I disliked most of all, being in a field unit.

About a week after honoring President Kennedy, I was sent on TDY (temporary duty) to the hospital to work in the lab for two months. That was a welcome change from the daily routine. There were three German civilians working in the lab: one in hematology, one in chemistry, and one in bacteriology. I was able to rotate through all the departments. On October 9, while working in hematology, I received a telegram. It read, "Harvey Clinton Wills, born Oct. 9 at (I don't remember the time). Mother and baby doing well." Wow! I was now a father, and my family would be joining me in about six weeks.

Toward the end of November, I received word that my family would be arriving on flight number so and so, on a certain date.

At the Frankfurt airport, I was in a large waiting room, along with many other soldiers who were also waiting for their families. One by one they came through a door at the back of the room. Finally, I saw

Brenda come through that door. Someone said, "Boy! There's a little one." I ran to meet my wife. I hugged and kissed her and saw my son for the first time. He was so little, and Brenda had him wrapped snuggly in a little bundle. We drove back to BK and to the military housing area. I had procured an apartment and had it ready for them.

We had been at home every bit of ten minutes when we heard a knock on the door. "Who could that be?", I said. It was Bobby Melton, his wife Betty, and two-year-old, Julie. Bobby was one of my lab techs and also a very good friend. They had come to get acquainted with my family. Bobby was from Alabama and liked to play the dumb old country boy role, but he was anything but that. He was older than me and had been in the service longer but was only an E-5. We had a short visit and they left.

Right after Christmas, I was notified that I would be attending the 7th Army Non-Commissioned Officers Academy. I hadn't wanted to be an NCO, but I was one, and would be one as long as I was in the service. If I had to be one, I wanted to be a good one, and the academy was designed to help me do just that. It was a four-week course, located at Bad Tolz, a little city in extreme Southern Bavaria, in the foothills of the Alps. It was also home to the 10th Special Forces Group.

Arriving at the academy, the cadre was made up of the sharpest soldiers I had ever seen, boots spit shined to a mirror-like surface, starched fatigues every day, absolute perfect appearance. We were expected to be the same. Days were long. We were up till midnight every night and arose at 4 AM every day. Four areas were stressed at the academy: leadership, instructor training, map reading along with compass courses, and physical training. Just days before I arrived, Bad Tolz had seen its biggest snowfall in many years. More than six feet of snow had fallen, cars were completely covered, and it was difficult to get around except where the snow had been cleared. It had its greatest effect on the compass course. On that course, from a starting point, you had to travel a certain distance in a certain direction, locate a stake and write down the number found on it. Walking in four feet of snow made it extremely difficult, but I maxed the course. I missed one question on the map reading final exam, due to carelessness, but I still finished number one in the class of 138. I also did great in instructor training, finishing in the top five. I also did well in physical training and was in line to be an honor graduate.

If I could just do well in my leadership role, I had it made. But, in my first leadership position as squad leader, I made a grave mistake, and it cost me dearly. I didn't think I had done that badly, but when I received my score that evening I was devastated. My score was 29. I went right away to the cadre member who had given me that score and questioned him as to why I received such a low grade. He told me it was because I had reported all my men present that morning, when two of them were not yet in formation. I told him that they were only a few feet away from being there. He said that didn't matter, that the commandant had instructed him not to give anyone a grade of over 30 for such a mistake. He said, "I know you're doing well in all the other areas, but unless you pass in leadership, you won't graduate." I said, "I've never been a failure at anything in my five years of service, and I can't afford to fail now." He said, "You'll have one more chance in a leadership position. If you do well, you'll be OK." Well, a couple of days later I was made company commander of the entire school, the biggest job of all. I was worried. I was scared. But I put forth everything I had and came away with a grade of 85. I was so relieved. I ended up graduating 18th out of the 138 students. Back at BK I received a letter of commendation from the commanding officer of the 62nd Medical Group. That was the headquarters for all the medical units in that part of Germany.

I had become friends with Johnnie Smith, and although I didn't approve of some of his conduct, I was still playing music with him at the Victoria Bar. I was invited to his home several times. He had a beautiful wife who was also a good wife, as far as I could tell. Johnnie was extremely jealous of her and at the same time openly cheating on her. She knew it also. One day I asked her how she could stay with him. She told me that she was very much afraid of him. She said that once back in California he had shot at her while she was innocently riding with another man. The bullet had shattered her window and barely missed her.

Johnnie Smith had a pet snake. I'm not sure what kind, but a nonpoisonous one that crawled around freely in the house. One night he put the snake inside his shirt, buttoned it tightly around the collar and went to the Victoria Bar. As he was doing one of those belly-rubbing dances with a young lady, he opens the top button on his shirt, and the snake's head popped out into the lady's face. She let out a blood-curdling scream and ran from the bar. One day Johnnie couldn't find his snake. He thought it had gotten out of the house. A week went by and still no snake. Then a foul odor began to be detected around the sofa. Johnnie removed the dust cover from the bottom of the sofa, and there tangled in the springs was the snake, dead. Apparently, someone had sat on the sofa while the snake was in the springs, and it was fatal to his beloved pet.

Johnnie also had another talent. He was an excellent marksman with the M-14 rifle. He represented our company in the All Army shooting matches.

Playing my guitar at the service club one night, someone asked where I was from. When I told him Georgia, he said, "Do you know Stoney? I don't remember his last name, but he's from Georgia too." That didn't mean anything to me, because there were thousands of people from Georgia in the Army. Then I remembered something. I had only heard the name Stoney twice in my life. I said, "It wouldn't be Stoney Patterson, would it?" He said, "Yeah! That's him! He's over at the club now. His friend is over there playing music." We headed over to the club and sure enough, there was Stoney. He had been a basketball player at the Chattahoochee County High School in Cusseta, GA, a team in the same conference as Webster County High, and we had played them twice each year. Stoney was a Warrant Officer and a helicopter pilot. He introduced me to his friend who was playing guitar and singing, only as Kris. Kris was a captain and also a helicopter pilot. He invited me to play some songs with him, and I did on several occasions. I thought Kris was a better guitar player than a singer. Little did I know that I was playing with someone who was to become one of the great superstars in country music, especially as a songwriter.

In April 1963 I had been at the "Dirty Deuce" for nine months and had already done a lot: President Kennedy's parade, TDY, NCO academy, among other duties, and I was ready for a little vacation. I suggested to Brenda that we take a trip to Holland to see the tulips. They would be in full bloom now, and we could also visit Belgium and Luxemburg at the same time. We would also invite Bobby Melton and family to go. They said they would love to go. For the most part, we decided to camp out in order to save a little money. I also took along 10 extra gallons of gasoline. We only paid 15 cents per gallon at the quartermaster gas station, but there were no quartermaster stations in that area, and we couldn't afford the high cost of gas on the economy. There was not enough room in one car, so we each drove our own.

The large fields of tulips were beautiful, and we even bought some bulbs and had them shipped back to our families in Georgia. We drove along a major dike that seemed to stretch for miles. Large pumps were pumping thousands of gallons of water per minute, but even so, it would take years to drain the land. I bought myself a pair of wooden shoes, but I don't wear them. They are definitely not comfortable! The second night out we camped in a bombed-out building in Belgium, but after that we stayed in hotels. Betty Melton just couldn't handle roughing it. Harvey was now six months old, and he did nicely on the trip. Before we would leave Germany, we planned to visit many more European countries.

My brother Don graduated from Terrell County High School that May, and shortly afterwards, bought a motorcycle. He loved that bike, but it almost cost him his life. One day he was heading south on Hwy 55 when he decided to turn around and go home. He didn't see anyone behind him at the time, so he attempted to make a u-turn in the highway. Thinking all was clear, Don started his u-turn. A white Oldsmobile came over the hill and attempted to pass on the left. Not seeing the car, Don turned into the side of it. The motorcycle was slammed against the side of the car and spun around. Don ended up in the road a few feet from the motorcycle. The car went off the highway on the left side of the road. The driver of the car jumped out and immediately ran to check on him. Apparently having heard the accident, Herbie Majors, a nearby resident drove up and offered to take Don to the hospital. Instead, he asked Herbie to take him to the church where our mom and dad were. Daddy took him to the hospital. Don was very lucky to have survived the accident with only a broken ankle, contusions, and lacerations of the left leg. The motorcycle was repaired, but Don never rode it again. He ended up selling it to the Honda Dealer.

When I received word of Don's accident, I was happy to know that it wasn't a lot worse. I sat down that evening and wrote him a letter, urging him to get away from motorcycles and get into performance cars. And that he did. I couldn't believe how knowledgeable he was on high performance cars. The first weekend I was back home, he took me to the U.S. 19 Drag Strip in Albany, GA where I watched my first series of drag races.

I was approached one day by a gentleman who said that a fellow named Al Kelly wanted to talk with me after work, down at the 517th Medical Company. I had no idea what he wanted, but I went to see him. He said, "I understand you can play the guitar." I said, "Yeah, I've been known to do a little picking." He explained that he had just gotten here from Arizona, and that he had a country music band back there. He had just purchased a new Gibson Guitar, an electric Fender Base, and a drum set. He was looking to form a band, and start playing as soon as possible, so he could make payments on the equipment. He said the equipment would be arriving in two or three weeks. Actually, he wanted me to audition for him. So, I got my guitar and began playing various songs which he seemed to like. Then he said, "Can you play "Rainbow?" It just so happened that I had been working on that song, an instrumental by Chet Atkins. Before I got through the song, he said, "You're hired! I've asked a lot of people to play that song, and you're the first to do so."

We needed a place to play. I knew that Johnnie Smith would be rotating back to the States in about two weeks and that the Victoria Bar would be needing a new band. I took Al down to the Victoria and introduced him to Leo, the bar's owner. Leo said he would hold the job open for us. I believe he did it because he knew and respected me. Now we needed a drummer. I had made friends with Louis Riviera-Rolon, a nice young man from Puerto Rico who had mentioned that he could play drums. We talked with him, and he agreed to play with us. Now all we had to do was wait for the equipment to arrive.

While we were waiting for the equipment, Al had to find a job in order to make a payment. The only thing he could find was a dishwashing job at the NCO club, washing dishes every night from 6 PM till midnight. He said there was enough dirty dishes each night to fill a deuce and a half.

The equipment finally arrived, and we began playing six nights a week, 7 PM till 1 AM, except we had to stop at midnight on Saturday. We were off on Sunday. We were paid 30 Deutsch Marks each, per night, which was equivalent to $ 7.50 in U.S. currency. Al played the electric bass and was the lead singer. I played lead guitar and sang occasionally. Louis wasn't the greatest drummer in the world, but he could keep decent time. I think Leo liked us because we were strictly business and didn't conduct ourselves the way Johnnie Smith had done. Being a part of the band was fun, and I enjoyed it very much, but I was forgetting that I had a family at home. I was seeing very little of my wife and my son, and that would eventually turn into a grave mistake. That summer we picked up another lead guitar player, Tommy Benson, a rock and roll player and singer, but he also played country music. That would allow me to take a little time off.

So, in early September, Brenda and I decided to take another vacation. We decided to make a round trip of Italy. We invited another of my good friends, Peter Kim, a wonderful individual from the state of Hawaii, to go with us. We decided to camp out along the way and to take along most of the food we would need. We had two military pup tents, one for Brenda and me, and one for Kim. Then we obtained a map of all the campsites along our planned route, and all was set to begin our trip. The first night out we camped somewhere in Northern Italy. It was a very small campsite, in fact, we were the only ones there. The site was actually in a grape vineyard and once our tents were pitched, there were literally large clusters of grapes hanging over our tents. We couldn't resist the temptation to pick a few. I don't think the owner appreciated it very much, although he didn't say anything. We wouldn't have understood him anyway, because I don't believe he spoke a word of English. He kept walking back and forth by our site for the entire evening to keep an eye on us. The following morning, we gave him a generous tip for the grapes.

We parked the car in the huge parking lot near the entrance to the Grand Canal in Venice. From there we hired a Gondolier to take us the entire length of the canal, making a few stops along the way. We passed under the famous Rialto Bridge and made a stop at St. Mark's Square. It had the only tree we saw in the city, and there were thousands of pigeons everywhere. There were quite a few shops in the Square, and it was the only land we saw. Everything else appeared to be built in the water, and every street in the city was a canal. It seemed odd to see a city without a single automobile. Before returning to our car, we stopped for lunch at one of the many sidewalk cafes. Our visit to Venice was definitely something I'll never forget.

Leaving Venice, it was just a short distance to Verona. There we had our only problem on our trip. As I was driving down a center lane, suddenly the traffic on either side of me began to close in and I was running out of space to drive. I had no choice except apply my brakes, rather sharply. Wham! The little Fiat that was tailgating me crashed into my rear. Upon examination, I was surprised to find that our car wasn't damaged, while the front of the Fiat was severely damaged, including a busted radiator. Using my translation booklet, I asked the driver to call the police. He said, "No, no. No police!" It was obvious for some reason he didn't want to report the accident. I drove away a little concerned, wondering if he had taken my license number and might try to make trouble for me later. With that thought in mind, I stopped at a U.S. Army post in Vicenza and reported the accident to the military police. That was the end of it. Our next stop was Milan, where we spent a few hours visiting some of the points of interest. Heading south, we stopped at a large campsite. It was already dark by the time we pitched our tents.

Sometime during the night, we were awakened by a downpour of rain that must have lasted two hours. No water came into our tent, because we had dug a drainage ditch around the tent, as we had been taught in basic training. At daybreak, we began to smell a very foul odor. Looking out, we saw a lake that wasn't there the night before. There were turds floating in the lake. It was apparent that a cesspool had overflowed, and it was headed our way, probably 15 feet from us. All around us were large, beautifully colored tents, quite a contrast to our little OD pup tents. We quickly tore down our tents and got out of there. We reached Rome around mid-morning. I don't recall if we planned it that way, or if it was purely an accident, but we had gotten to Rome on Sunday morning. The Vatican was our first stop. There were literally thousands of people gathered in St. Peter's Square. We didn't know what was going on, but we asked and were told that the Pope would be coming to a window to bless everyone in the Square. We decided it might be a good idea if we stuck around and got blessed also. I may be wrong, but I believe the Pope was John Paul, VI. He came to the window, raised his arms and spoke for a few minutes. It was quite a moving experience. Afterwards, we toured the Basilica and saw some of the paintings and sculptures of the great Italian artists. Later that afternoon, we threw some coins in the Fountain of Trevi and visited the ancient Roman Colosseum.

We would have visited Naples, but it was much further down the boot, and we didn't want to chance having a problem with gasoline. There was a quartermaster gas station between Rome and Milan, and by filling up there we could easily make it back to Germany. Our trip to Italy wouldn't be complete without seeing the Leaning Tower of Pisa. Our next night of camping out was uneventful, and we got an early start, heading toward Pisa. We were able to climb to the top of the Leaning Tower and made a lot of photos as we had done the entire trip. Leaving Pisa, we took the Autostrade out of Italy. The Autostrade is the Italian equivalent of our interstate highways. The biggest difference is that the Autostrade is a toll road, and there was bumper to bumper traffic, mostly trucks. The going was extremely slow. We were glad to finally get back to Germany.

Returning to the 2nd Evac, I was assigned an additional duty. I was made the re-enlistment sergeant. There weren't very many people who wanted to re-enlist, but It was my job to talk to them and let them know what options might be available. I had a nice office in the administrative section, and I divided my time between there and taking care of business in the warehouse. I was the first person to re-enlist after I got the job. So, in October, I signed up for another three-year hitch. I joked with people and told them I had to re-enlist myself in order to meet my quota. Of course, I didn't have a quota to meet.

Al Kelly's band was constantly changing. After picking up Tommy Benson, he dismissed Louis and hired a much better drummer. Then he hired a saxophone player from England. The band was definitely getting much better, and he began to get gigs at clubs all around the Bad Kreuznach area. I continued to play with the band almost full time.

In early 1964, I got burned out from playing, and all but quit the band, but I took on other activities. I began taking some college courses through the University of Maryland, at the Army Education Center. I also began teaching Sunday school and eventually became head of that department.

There was another Evacuation Hosp at Idar-Oberstein that closed down, and many of its personnel were assigned to us, including a Staff Sergeant Robinson, an X-Ray technician. He was a coin collector as I was, but he had other interests as well, one of which was firing a pistol. He talked me into joining the unit pistol team, and we spent lots of time on the range firing the Army .45. At one point we spent a week training at Ramstein Air Force Base. With his help, I actually became good enough to make the team. Then we began to travel to matches all around Germany.

Meanwhile, Brenda was really feeling neglected and becoming depressed. She had gained quite a bit of weight while in Germany, so she had the doctor prescribe some diet pills. I'm not sure what they were, but they were highly addictive, and she became hooked on them. She lost weight because she all but quit eating. Then she took a job running the snack bar at the bowling alley. We had hired a little 14-year-old, red headed German girl named Ulrika to baby sit Harvey. That's when our marriage really began falling apart. Brenda felt neglected. She was lonely, and she needed companionship. If I couldn't give it to her, there were plenty of others who could and would, especially now that she had lost weight and was looking good.

On the way home from work on November 22, 1963, a news flash come on my radio, which was always set on the Armed Forces Network. It said that President John F. Kennedy had been shot in Dallas, Texas and had been taken to Parkland Hospital. A few minutes later, it was announced that he was dead. It was a very sad time for the military, because we all loved our Commander in Chief.

By now, our marriage had reached a point of no return. I believe the drug she was taking was largely responsible. I tried talking with her, but she was not rational and would not listen to reason. I even took her and Harvey on a few weekend trips to places like Heidelberg, but it didn't seem to help. There were rumors that my wife was seeing other men, but she flatly denied that. Then, late in the year she didn't even try to hide it anymore. I was still playing in the band occasionally. One night while I was playing, she came into the Victoria Bar in the company of two officers: a captain and a warrant Officer from the 14th Field Hospital. It was an embarrassing situation for me, but I didn't make a scene at the bar. I confronted her at home later that night. That's when she told me it was over, that she didn't want to be married to me anymore. That was in November 1964. Then she wanted to leave Germany and go home to Trapie. I still had six months left on my tour of duty. When I got home, we would apply for a divorce.

I had been able to save a little more than $2,000 while in Germany, so I generously split it with her, so she could buy tickets home for her and Harvey. I drove her to the airport in Frankfurt in December for their trip back to the States. Then she said, " I've got something I've got to tell you. I think I'm pregnant." I said, "Are you sure?" She said, "No, but I'll let you know." I said, "Please do." I was sad, because I felt that I had failed them. I had no idea what was next.

It was not a very Merry Christmas, and after the holidays I was sent on TDY to work at the hospital lab again, this time for three months. All the personnel at the lab were still the same, except for a new civilian employee in the chemistry lab. She was introduced as Vera. I thought she was an American, but she told me she was from Switzerland. She had no foreign accent whatsoever. I asked her how she happened to end up in Bad Kreuznach. She told me that a doctor friend of hers had gotten the job for her. He was a pathologist at one of the General Hospitals in Germany, about fifty miles away. I gathered that he wanted her as close to him as possible. She had met him while living in the States. I enjoyed talking with her, and I made it a point to stop by her department every day to see her. Then one day just before we got off work, I said, "Vera, would you like to have dinner with me tonight?" I had no idea she would, but she surprised me by saying, "I'd love to."

After work, Vera and I drove the short distance to the small village of Bad Munster. Like Bad Kreuznach, Bad Munster was located on the Nahe River which flowed south to the Rhine, some forty miles away. The Nahe Valley is famous for producing some of the finest wine made in Germany. We went to a nice little restaurant that I had been to once before. We ordered dinner and a glass of that fine Nahe Valley wine.

Leaving the restaurant, we sat in the car for a few minutes and talked. One thing I liked about Vera, was that she could talk on a wide variety of subjects, almost anything except sports. I don't believe she had ever been much of an athletic person. As we talked, she suddenly said something totally unexpected. She said, "It is so hard for me to sit here on this side of the car." It stunned me at first and I hesitantly said, "You don't have to." That was all she needed to hear. She was instantly by my side. I put my arm around her, and she laid her head on my shoulder. I drove to a secluded area on the hill, high above the valley and parked at a site overlooking the city of Bad Kreuznach below. We stayed there for hours talking and getting to know each other. I was really interested in knowing about her doctor friend, whom I had assumed she was going steady with. She told me she had met him while in Cambridge, MA. Apparently, he was very much in love with her and had asked her to marry him. She didn't have the same feeling for him. She liked him as a friend, but he was a doctor, and she said she couldn't be happy with being the wife of a doctor. She felt that a doctor's work would demand too much of his time, and she would be neglected. She couldn't handle that. She needed lots of love and attention. She went on to say that within the next few weeks she would be moving back to Zurich and to her old job in medical research. I held her close and kissed her that night, as time seemed to pass by so quickly.

Sometime around the end of January, I received a letter from Brenda, confirming that she was, in fact, pregnant, and that her due date was around the 1st of July. That would be about the time I would be returning to the States. She mentioned nothing in the letter about wanting to get back together with me. I assumed she didn't. I wrote back and told her to keep me informed. I never heard from her again before I left Germany.

Vera Sturzenegger was a 28-year-old virgin. She grew up in a well-to-do family in Zurich, Switzerland. Her father was a high-ranking official in a Swiss bank. She had graduated from the University of Zurich, received her master's degree from Stockholm University in Stockholm, Sweden and finally finished her education at Harvard University in Cambridge, MA. She was just short of a Ph.D. She was fluent in five languages: German, Italian, French, English, and Swedish. She was a brilliant woman. She was also very pretty with brown eyes, short brown hair, and a lovely smile, which was something between mischievous and inquisitive. She was five feet six inches and weighed about 125 pounds. She had a friendly personality and a beautiful voice which she spoke with perfect grammar and without an accent.

There were still two places I wanted to visit before I left Germany, and that was Paris and London. I had made plans along with a friend in my department to go to Paris for three days. Around the first of March 1965, we boarded a train for Paris. It would have been a lot more fun if Vera could have gone with me, but plans had already been made. Paris was a great city. We climbed to the top of the Eiffel Tower, walked across the Arch of Triumph, visited the Louvre, saw the Mona Lisa, and even went to some of the famous night clubs at Pigalle.

Back in BK I spent as much time as I could with Vera. I would play music in some of the local NCO and EM clubs, and she would come with me.

It was almost time for Vera to return to Zurich. I wanted to help her with packing her belongings and preparing to move. Her landlady did not want military people in her home, but Vera got special permission for me to help her. We promised to write each other often. She told me that when I wrote to her, I would have to write in German, because she wanted to help me learn the language better. I had completed two college courses in German, so at least I had a good start. My letters weren't perfect, but at least she got my messages. I promised to come and visit her as soon as I could.

After Brenda and Harvey left Germany, I was no longer authorized to continue living in the apartment. I would have to move back into the barracks and would have 30-days to clear quarters. One afternoon as I was leaving the apartment and was walking down the stairs, I met a familiar looking face coming up the stairs. It was none other than Ronald Weld, the first person I had made friends with in Ansbach, six years earlier. He was taking some time off from his teaching job in Minnesota and was going to be in Europe for about three months. I invited him in, and the first thing I noticed was how big he had gotten. Apparently, he liked to eat and didn't waste any time letting me know. Since I was clearing quarters, I had no food at all, so he suggested we walk over to the commissary and get some ice cream. I didn't really want any, but I went with him to buy some. He bought a half gallon. I don't recall what flavor, but we went back to the apartment, sat down at the bar, and he proceeded to eat the entire half gallon. It was easy to see how he had gotten so big. He told me that sometimes when he was hungry, he would eat a whole loaf of bread, or at breakfast he would eat a large box of cereal and use a half gallon of milk. I was thinking, "I'm glad I don't have to feed him." He stayed that night, and the following day he left. He told me he would see me again before he left Europe.

He came back again about the time Vera was leaving to go home to Zurich, and I introduced him to her. Somehow, without my knowledge, he got her phone number or address, I'm not sure which, and a couple of days later he went down there to see her. Then he came back to Bad Kreuznach smiling and telling me how he went to visit Vera and what a good time he had. I couldn't believe it! I was mad! I told him, "Look, she's my girlfriend, and you leave her alone." He said, "Gosh, I didn't know. I thought she was just a girl you worked with. I'm sorry." That was the last time I saw Ron.

I called Vera and asked her about Ron coming to see her and asked what went on. She told me that he had asked her to go for a walk that night, and they sat on a park bench and he held her hand. I said, "Why did you do that?" She said, "I thought he was your best friend, and I was just being polite. Is he not your best friend?" I said, "He's a friend, but not that good!"

My good friend Bobby Melton had volunteered for the Special Forces and was being transferred to Ft. Bragg, NC. I hated to see him go. He was a very good soldier and a great laboratory technician. He had the reputation of being the best technician around in bacteriology. I was regarded the same in parasitology.

Louis Riviera, my buddy from Puerto Rico, had also left, leaving behind the girl that loved him so much. Her name was Ilke, and she was absolutely beautiful. She was also the big sister of Ulrika, Harvey's babysitter.

Our company was having some kind of a banquet, I don't recall the occasion. I needed, or at least I wanted a date to take, so I invited Ilke to go with me. She accepted, and I ended up with the prettiest girl at the banquet. I've often wondered if she and Louis ever got together again.

I received a letter from Vera saying that she was settled in with her parents, and she invited me to come to see her the coming weekend. I couldn't wait, so I asked for Friday afternoon off, got it, and left for Zurich shortly after lunch. It was about a six -hour drive, and I arrived just before sundown. Her parents lived in an up-scale neighborhood. Their home was very nice, but small by American standards, as were all the houses in Switzerland. After meeting her parents, who were very receptive of me, Vera said she wanted to take me to a very special restaurant.

The restaurant was very old, and the wooden tables and chairs appeared to look like something I would have seen a hundred years ago. We found an empty table, sat down, and I looked for the menu. Vera said there was no menu, and that they only served one item. That item was fondue. This was the original fondue restaurant. I asked, "What is fondue? I've never heard of it." She explained that they would bring a pot of hot, bubbling, melted cheese, and with a special fork, we would dip pieces of bread in the cheese and eat it. I said, "That sounds interesting." The waitress brought out a huge pot of melted cheese and placed something like a candle under it to keep it hot, along with a large bowl of hard pieces of bread that looked something like large croutons. We also had wine. It was a totally new experience for me, and I thoroughly enjoyed it.

Back home, she took me to her room which was packed with her belongings, I assumed because she had no other place to store them. She said, "This is where you will be staying tonight. I will see you in the morning." I said, "I wish you would stay with me." She said, "You know I can't do that." I knew it, but I wanted her to stay anyway. She gave me a little kiss and said, "Good-night." As I was preparing to go to bed, I heard a light tap on the door. It was Vera. She said, "I came back to visit for a little while." I said, "I'm glad you did." She showed me her picture albums from Sweden and from the United States and also showed me some items she had collected from her travels. Vera was a very loving person, and she needed to be alone with me for a little while. There were three things she wouldn't do, and she had made that clear from our first night together. She would not have sex, she would not sleep with me, and she would not tell me she loved me unless she was absolutely certain. Love was a very special word to her, with a very special meaning and not something to be used loosely. She had never told a man that she loved him. I told her that I respected her wishes, and that's the way it would be. She stayed with me for maybe a half hour, said good-night again and left.

Sometime during the night, I woke up with the worst stomach ache I had ever had in my entire life. I was in pure misery for a couple of hours. The cheese had been good, but I had eaten too much, and it didn't agree with me.

The next morning, I felt OK, and after a light breakfast we went outside. If I'm not mistaken, this was Easter weekend, and there was plenty of snow still on the ground. Vera had on a beautiful Carolina Blue ski jacket with a white scarf. She looked so pretty. We took her sled and began pulling it up the road. Zurich is not in the mountains, but in the foothills. The road we were on led up a hill for about half a mile, maybe a little more, until we reached the top. There was a little restaurant there, and we went in and got something hot to drink. Outside, we sat on a little bench out behind the store. The sun was shining directly against us, and it was so warm we had to take off our coats.

The reason for pulling the sled up the hill was so we could ride it on the way down. This was going to be the fun part. As we began sledding down the hill, Vera said, "Don't go too fast." There were dozens of people now walking up the hill. The sled began to pick up speed. I was having fun, but I began to see where it could also be dangerous. I tried to slow it down by dragging my shoe, but it didn't work. I only succeeded in tearing the sole off my shoe. I began shouting, "Achtung! Achtung!", in order to warn the people in front of us. Vera was sitting at the front of the sled, and I was behind her. She was really frightened. We were going very fast and were approaching the bottom of the hill. The problem was that the road curved rather sharply to the left near the bottom of the hill. We could guide the sled to some extent but not enough to make it around that curve. We were going off the road. On our right was a heavy snowbank and a barbed wire fence. This was not looking good. We crashed into the snowbank, coming to an abrupt stop, with Vera going over the front of the sled and me landing on top of her. She had previously broken her leg skiing, and I was so afraid that she was hurt again. Fortunately, we had avoided hitting the barbed wire, and neither of us were hurt. We pulled the sled back to the house and never got on it again.

The remainder of the weekend was pretty much uneventful, and I left around noon on Sunday and headed back to BK. I promised to try to come to see her again in about two weeks.

I kept my promise, but I didn't get to leave as early as I had the last time. I was now living in the barracks and was asked to be in charge of the Friday night G.I. party. By the time the party was over, and I could shower and change clothes, it was almost 10 PM. I quickly packed my bag and was out of there. It was late April, but it was very cold, and a light rain was falling.

Around midnight, and after driving about a hundred miles, I got sleepy, very sleepy. I pulled off the road, cut off the engine, and lay down on the seat to take a nap. About the time I was getting to sleep, it got so cold I couldn't sleep. I started the car, turned the heater to high until the car got very warm, cut off the engine and tried again. Same thing. It got cold in a hurry. I didn't want to go to sleep with the engine running, so I said, "The heck with this!" I started the car and headed down the Autobahn, the Autobahn being the equivalent to our Interstate Highways. I was still very sleepy when I came up on a car going rather slowly in my lane. I jerked the wheel to move to the left lane, and as I was straightening up, the car didn't respond. Turning the steering wheel did nothing. My thought was, "My steering has gone out." The car continued on its path, and I realized that I was headed for the guardrail. I was thinking that if I hit the guardrail, it would straighten the car's path. Instead, as I crashed into the guardrail, it turned the car sideways, and I continued skidding down the road, finally coming to a rest. As I looked out my left window, I saw a car in the left lane headed straight toward me. I didn't like the idea of a car plowing into my door. That could hurt, or maybe even be worse, so I jumped out of the car and got out of the way. However, the driver was able to stop. He got out, and in his broken English, asked me what the problem was. I said, "My steering has gone out." He told me to get in the car and turn the wheel. When I did, he said it seemed to be working fine. I still didn't believe it, but I got in my car and continued driving, but very slowly. I pulled up to Vera's apartment about 6 AM. I went into her new apartment totally exhausted from lack of sleep. I told her what had happened, and she said the forecast had been for freezing rain. That had not crossed my mind, but now I realized I was skidding along on a sheet of ice. I lay down and slept for about four hours, waking up at 10 AM. Shortly afterwards, we heard a knock. She opened the door and there stood two Americans. Both were army captains and doctors. Vera's friend, Dr. Jay, had told them to stop by and see her since they were in Zurich. I introduced myself and they were respectful. Then when one of Vera's friends stopped by, and I began speaking German, the doctors were really impressed. After they all left, Vera said, "Let's go for a drive." We got in the car and drove away. I said, "Where are we going?" "Bern" she said. "I want to take you to a very famous restaurant there." I don't remember the name of the restaurant, but it was large and very crowded. We had to wait two hours to be seated and then another hour before the waitress took our order. Then, it took another hour for our food to arrive. What started out as a late lunch, ended up being our dinner meal. Afterwards, we returned to her apartment, and the two of us spent a lovely evening together.

I didn't have a lot of time left, so in order to make the most of it, Vera said she would come to see me at BK in two weeks. I received a letter from her a couple of days before her arrival, to let me know that a friend of hers, Gretle, was coming with her. She suggested that I might find someone to entertain Gretle so that we could have some time alone. I was all for that, so I asked one of my X-Ray technicians, John Kennedy, if he would like to join us, and he readily accepted.

John and I met the girls at the train station late Saturday afternoon. After checking in at their hotel, we took them to one of the finest restaurants in BK, where we had a wonderful dinner, complete with a bottle of 1959 Nahe Valley wine. 1959 was a dry year in Germany and the drier the year, the better the grapes and subsequently, the wine. I'm sure Vera had told Gretle that she and I would like to have some time alone, so she didn't mind when we suggested we split up and meet at a certain place at a certain time.

I asked Vera, "Where can we go to spend some time alone together." She didn't hesitate, "Back at the hotel room." "What if they come back there also?", I asked. "They won't", she said. As we lounged on the bed that evening, she said something I never expected to hear from her. She said, "Johnny, I love you." I knew then that she was totally committed to me, otherwise, she wouldn't have said it. Those three hours with her were so special, and time went by so quickly. We met John and Gretle and walked them back to the hotel. Vera and Gretle left for Zurich early the following morning.

With only four weeks to go, I finally received my orders. I had been assigned as the NCOIC of the laboratory at the U.S. Army Hospital, Ft. Ord, California. I was not pleased with this assignment, but that's just the way it is in the Army.

I still wanted to go to London before I left Germany, and time was running out. If I could take a week off, I would have enough time to visit Vera once more and also go to London for a few days. The First Sergeant approved my request, and I was off to Zurich. I stayed with Vera for two days, and we mostly spent our time talking about what the future might hold for us. We talked about getting married, assuming Brenda went through with her plans for a divorce. But there were other considerations. Some of her closest friends had told her not to marry me because we were not in the same class. That was certainly true when it came to education. She was very highly educated, whereas I was a high school graduate. Vera didn't really see it that way, because we were able to communicate on the same level. It probably wouldn't matter as long as I was in the Army, but if I got out, I could never get the kind of job she could, because I didn't have the credentials. Another thing that bothered her was where we would live. She didn't think she could handle living in the South because of the heat. She would prefer to live in New England where the climate was more like it was in Zurich.

Vera had seen much more of the United States than I. While living in Cambridge, MA, she and three of her girlfriends had taken a month-long vacation and toured the country, first traveling across the northern part to Seattle, then south to Los Angeles, and then across the southern part of the country to Florida and then back to Massachusetts. They had made the trip in a 1962 Ford Falcon, which she loved.

My car would need to be taken to Bremerhaven as soon as I got back from my trip, so it could be in New York when I got there. However, I had made plans to sell the car to Sergeant Thomas, who had been on the ship with me coming over, and we would be on the same ship going back. I would be buying a new car when I got back to Georgia, and I already knew what I would get. I would buy a white Falcon with red interior, just in case Vera and I managed to get together again.

I kissed Vera, and we said good-bye for what just might be the very last time. As I left Zurich and headed north to Frankfurt, I thought how wonderful it would have been if she could have gone to London with me. We had never gone on an overnight trip together, but even if we had, she likely would have insisted on having her own room.

I parked the car at the Frankfurt Airport, went in and bought a round-trip ticket to London on Lufthansa Airlines. The plane would make a stop in Paris before arriving in London around 6 PM. I had not made any reservations for a place to stay, so after arriving at Heathrow Airport, I found a pay phone and had no trouble finding a hotel. I took a cab to the hotel, had dinner at the restaurant, then retired for the night. I wanted to get an early start the next morning.

I arose early and took in a lot of sights that day, including The Tower of London, London Bridge, Big Ben, 10 Downing Street, Trafalgar Square, and much more. There were many tour busses on which you could visit many places outside of London, and I would take a tour the following day. I would read about all the tours and decide on which one to take, after I got back to my room that night.

It was a pretty easy decision. I decided to take the tour to Stratford-upon-Avon, which was located on the Avon River, a hundred miles northeast of London. The most exciting part of the trip was visiting the home of William Shakespeare. Our tour took up the best part of the day, but we were back in time for me to make my evening flight back to Frankfurt.

Back in BK the following day, I completed the transaction with the car, and Sergeant Thomas headed to Bremerhaven, so it could be shipped back to New York. I didn't do much those last few days except pack my belongings for shipment back to my home address in Georgia. The biggest thing I had was my guitar and amplifier. I packed everything else in a large trunk.

The old house where I was born in 1939.
This picture was taken around 1975.

Mama and Daddy on their Golden Wedding Anniversary in 1977.

My 2nd grade picture.

Me and some of my brothers and cousins on my mother's side of the family, 1951. L-R: Wayne Dillard, brother Jerry (back row), brother Don, brother Jimmy, Tony Black, Linda Black, and me with the bat.

Me, #5 with classmate Gerald Smith.

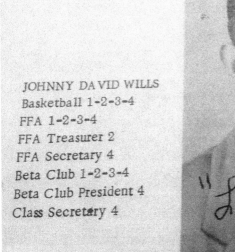

JOHNNY DAVID WILLS
Basketball 1-2-3-4
FFA 1-2-3-4
FFA Treasurer 2
FFA Secretary 4
Beta Club 1-2-3-4
Beta Club President 4
Class Secretary 4

"Love Always"
Johnnie

My senior photo, 1957.

Me and my first wife Brenda, 1961.

2nd Evacuation Hospital color guard for President John F. Kennedy's parade at Hanau, Germany, 1962. I'm carrying the American Flag.

Our first band in Germany, 1962. Me, Louis Riviera, and Al Kelly.

*Me and my two children from my first marriage,
Harvey and Wendy Echo.*

Juanita, 1969, the woman of my dreams. This photo sat beside my bed every night before we were married.

*A song for **Juanita**.*

Above: My 1969 Mustang. I was the North Carolina State Champion in bracket drag racing in 1970. Below: Me in front of the Lafayette Ford dealership in Fayetteville, NC. I was president of the Ford Drag Club in 1969 & 1970.

Me and Kelly doing a little mowing, 1974.

Me and Juanita in front of our new business, 1978.

The Wills Brothers, 1987. L-R: Jimmy, Don, Johnny, and Melvin.

This is my family at my 70th birthday party in 2009. L-R: Wendy, me, Harvey, Kelly, and Juanita.

Me and my 9-month old grandson, Blake David Sears, 2008.

Wills family members at my 70th birthday party, 2009. Back Row L-R: Pam Wills Keller, Carolyn Wills, Jason Wills, Harvey Wills, Faye Wills, Wendy Wills Kronberg, Juanita Wills, and Kelly Wills Sears. Ftont Row L-R: Don Wills, Melvin Wills, Johnny Wills, and Jimmy Wills.

All my grandchildren. Upper Left: Wendy's daughter, Nichole. Lower Left: Harvey and Shirley's girls, Jennifer and Shelby. At Right: Kelly's son, Blake.

CHAPTER 14

Good-Bye Germany, Hello USA

AS SOON AS I found out when I would be boarding the train for Bremerhaven, I called Vera to let her know. She said, "I'll be there to see you off." I said, "You know I would love to see you, but you don't have to do this." She replied, "I know, but I want to be there." And she was there, waiting at the station when I arrived. The train would travel to Frankfurt, which was about an hour away, then we would change trains for Bremerhaven. Vera bought a ticket to Frankfurt, so she could go with me, but the problem was, she couldn't ride in the same car as me. There were at least 50 or more G.I.s, and we had our own military car to ride in. As soon as we left the station, I got up and started walking. I knew she was up ahead of me somewhere. I had to find her. Searching the faces of everyone as I went from car to car, I finally found her in the fifth car. She gave me that pretty smile as I sat down beside her. We held hands all the way to Frankfurt. As we began slowing down for the Frankfurt station, I made my way back to the military car. I was surprised to learn that we had a two hour lay-over before we boarded the train for Bremerhaven. Vera and I took a short walk to a little park where we sat on a bench and enjoyed each other's company for the last time. I told her how much I loved her and how wonderful it had been to be in her company these past six months. She said that she felt the same and went on to tell me that I was the only man she ever told, "I love you." We both had tears in our eyes as we kissed good-bye for the last time, then I stepped aboard the train.

In Bremerhaven, I boarded the U.S.N.S. Upshore for my fourth trip across the Atlantic, on four different ships. Speaking with Sergeant Thomas while on board the Upshore, he invited me to ride with him after picking up the car. It made a lot of sense, because he was going to Alabama, and I was going to Georgia. That way I could help with driving and gas expense. It would be a lot better than taking a bus and a heck of a lot quicker. We would be going through Atlanta, and he could drop me off at the bus station, and I would take a bus the rest of the way home. I had 30-days before I would have to report to Ft. Ord, California. That would give me plenty of time to see the folks and also time to shop for that new car I planned to buy. As we were traveling through North Carolina on Interstate 85, I happened to remember that my good buddy Bobby Melton was over at Ft. Bragg. I told Thomas, "I think I'll get out in Charlotte and catch a bus over to Fayetteville for a visit with Bobby." Arriving at the bus station in Charlotte, I called to make sure the Meltons would be home. They were, and Bobby told me to call when I got to Fayetteville. I thanked Thomas and said good-bye to him and the old Chevy which had served me well for nearly five years.

Twenty minutes after I called, Bobby picked me up, and we headed to his home. Bobby and Betty had purchased a nice little three-bedroom brick home in a neighborhood off Country Club Drive. That was most impressive to me. It was sure good to see my friends again. Bobby said that tomorrow he would take me out to his workplace.

Entering Fort Bragg the following morning, we headed to the old hospital area and pulled up to one of those old wooden buildings. I had seen plenty of those before at almost every post I had been on. Bobby was assigned to the Special Forces Training Group, and he was in the laboratory department. He taught basic laboratory procedures to the medics going through their year-long training course.

Bobby introduced me to his supervisor, Sergeant First Class J.V. Hickman, head of the laboratory department. The only thing I knew about the Special Forces was that they were an elite group of soldiers that wore green berets. Bobby and J.V. were more than willing to tell me all about the training that the medics went through. Their one-year course was equivalent to that of a physician's assistant. Special forces soldiers have a very dangerous job. There are often casualties, sometimes many casualties, and the medics have to be trained to care for them as a doctor normally would, but there are no doctors, so the medics are on their own.

Special Forces groups are made up of small groups of men called "A" Teams. The team is composed of 10 or 12 men. I don't recall the exact number, but each man is trained in a specific area such as light weapons, heavy weapons, communication, medical, and others. Each man is cross-trained, so he can do another job if necessary, and each is taught a foreign language. That's why they are the world's finest fighting men.

It is the job of the Special Forces Training Group to train all these men. The different areas of training are called committees, and Bobby and J.V. were a small part of the Medical Committee. The part of the medical course that impressed me most was the surgical part. Each student is assigned a patient, the patient being canine. The dog is put to sleep and taken to the "tank", a concrete structure containing a .50 caliber machine gun. The dog is carefully placed in position and a single round is fired through the fleshy part of the animal's hind leg. Great care is taken not to hit the bone. The medic then rushes his patient into the operating room for a debridement of the wound, that is to say, clear the wound of any foreign material such as hair, skin, pieces of tissue, etc. The wound is then bandaged, and antibiotics administered. Pain medication is given as needed. It is the job of the medic to nurse his patient back to health. Most of the students kept their patient beside their bed, although some of them put their patient in their bed, and they slept on the floor. The rule is that if the patient expires, the student does not pass the course and is dismissed. Near the end of the course, after the patient has completely recovered, he is taken back to surgery and the leg is amputated. After a successful amputation, the animal is euthanized.

I said, "Wow! Sounds like a great program you have here." Then Bobby said something I never expected. He said, "Why don't you stay here and join us? You're a great instructor, and we could use you here." J.V. agreed. At the NCO academy, I had been one of the top five students in instructor training, and I was tops in map reading. Subsequently, I had been given the job of map-reading instructor at the 2nd Evacuation Hospital. I said, "Yeah, that sounds great, but I'm on my way to Fort Ord, and there's no way they're going to change my orders." "I'm not so sure", said J.V. "The Special Forces have top priority. They can get anything or anybody, just for the asking." "OK", I said. "Let's give it a try." I didn't want to go to California anyway, so I would be very pleased if I could stay at Ft. Bragg. J.V. told Bobby to take me over to headquarters and speak with a certain major in the personnel department. Staff Sergeant Barry Sadler was also working at headquarters. He's the soldier who wrote and sang, "The Ballard of the Green Beret." Later he would autograph my 45-rpm record.

We got permission to speak with the major. We walked into his office, saluted, and I introduced myself. Bobby told him that he had known me for several years in Germany and that I was a very good instructor and that I would be an asset to the Medical Committee. I told him that I had orders for Ft. Ord and would be reporting there in about 30 days. The major said, "In other words, we need to get those orders rescinded and have you assigned here?" "Yes, sir", I said. He asked if I was jump qualified. When I told him no, he asked if I was willing to go to Jump School and to go through the Special Forces basic training course. I said, "Yes, Sir!" He said, "OK, it's done. Go on home and enjoy your delay in route. In about two weeks you 'll be receiving a manila envelope in the mail, assigning you to Ft. Bragg." This was too good to be true. I still had some reservations that this could actually happen. I said, "Thank you sir!" He said, "Welcome to our team, Sergeant. Enjoy your time off." I saluted and left his office.

The following day Bobby took me to the Fayetteville Airport, and I bought a one-way ticket to Albany, Georgia on Piedmont Airlines. The cost was $50.00. After a short lay-over in Atlanta, I would be arriving in Albany at around 9 PM. I called my parents and told them what time I was arriving, and they said that my brother Don would meet me at the airport.

When I walked into the terminal at Albany, I got a huge surprise. Standing there with my brothers, Don and Jimmy, was my wife Brenda. "What is she doing here? How did she know I was coming in today?", were my thoughts. I had only heard from her once in the past six months. I thought she didn't want to be with me anymore. I greeted everyone, but I was stunned. She tried to act as if everything was normal and well. She said she had called Don to learn when I was coming in. Sitting in the back seat as we drove home, we spoke very few words. Don was doing most of the talking.

After three years, it was great to see my parents again. We talked for quite some time, then retired for the night. Brenda had come prepared to spend the night, so we slept together as if everything was fine and dandy. She was very large and told me that she was due to deliver our daughter in about ten days. It was obvious to me that someone had influenced her decision about leaving me, and I had a pretty good idea who it was. She flatly denied that anyone had influenced her, that she had changed her mind on her own. She asked me if we could just forget about being in Germany and try to start all over again. That was not going to be easy for me. I had a decision to make. If I had to choose between Brenda and Vera, it would have been an easy decision, but it wasn't that simple. I had a three-year-old son who loved his Daddy, and his Daddy loved him. I would soon have a daughter to love also. Who should I put first in my life, Vera or my children? I couldn't stand the thought of my children growing up without a father, so they had to come first. I knew that Vera's heart would be broken, and I didn't know if the wounds would ever heal, because she had totally committed herself to me. On the other hand, there was the possibility that a marriage to Vera might not work out. Telling Vera of my decision would be the most difficult thing I would ever face. I would put it off as long as I could.

It was time to shop for that new car. I knew exactly what I was looking for but couldn't find it. I went to the Dawson Motor Company, the local Ford dealer and had them order a white Falcon with red interior. They told me it would arrive in two weeks. That was Vera's car, but I never revealed that secret until now. I needed something to drive, so they let me have a 1958 Ford Fairlane, while I was waiting for my new Falcon.

I wanted to do something special for my mother. She had always wanted to go to the Grand Old Opry, so the following Saturday, we packed a bag and headed for Nashville. We got a hotel room about two blocks from the Ryman Auditorium, then walked over to see about getting tickets. The early show was already sold out, so we had to get tickets for the late show which started at 10 PM. We got a bite to eat and hung out in our room until show time. It was a great show, and Mama got to see many of the Opry Stars that she had been listening to every Saturday night for years. We slept late the following morning, had breakfast, then headed home. Between Nashville and Chattanooga, we kept seeing signs for "Crystal Caverns" and "See Rock City". I thought Mama would like to go in a cave, so we stopped at "Crystal Caverns", but I was wrong. She did not like it at all and said she would never go into another one. We made a stop at Lookout Mountain and she enjoyed that much better. We visited Rock City, Ruby Falls, and Lover's Leap.

Just before we reached Columbus, we had a flat tire. As I was beginning to change it, a car with four soldiers from Fort Benning stopped and insisted that they change it for me. I let them know that I was also in the military. They said they were happy to help a fellow soldier.

On July 4, 1965, Brenda gave birth to our daughter, Wendy Echo Wills at the Stewart County Hospital in Richland, Georgia. Trapie's dream had come to pass, a granddaughter named Echo.

I don't know if my letter that I wrote to Don two years earlier had any bearing on him at all, but he had certainly turned his interest to fast cars, and he had gained much knowledge about them. He could tell me the year of any car on the road, what engine it had, and how much horsepower it had. He also knew many specifications such as compression ratio, cam duration, and a lot more. He amazed me. On the first Saturday I was home, he took me to a drag race in Albany. I was amazed at the power of some of those cars, and I was liking what I saw.

At the end of week number two, I received that manila envelope that the major had promised. I was assigned to the Special Forces Training Group, and I still had almost three weeks before I had to sign in. Two weeks went by, no car, three weeks, no car, four weeks, still no car. I couldn't wait any longer. I only had a week before my reporting date.

I went to the Ford dealer and cancelled my order. Don took me to the Ford Dealer in Albany. I found a white Falcon Sprint convertible. It had gold interior, and it was powered by a 289 C.I., V-8 engine. The price was $3100. That was a lot of money for a car, but I wanted it, so I paid them the $1000 I had saved, financed the balance for 24 months with a payment of $102 per month, and drove away. It drove so good and felt so powerful with those 200 horses under the hood. I loved it.

I couldn't wait any longer to tell Vera what I was doing, so one afternoon I took my pen and paper and went outside and sat under one of those large oak trees and began to write. My dad came out and asked what I was doing. I told him I was just writing to a friend. He gave me that little grin and walked away. He knew better. I finished my letter, took it to the post office, and mailed it. It would be reaching Vera about the time I was signing in at Ft. Bragg. I knew it would be heart-breaking for her, and I wasn't sure she could handle it; I could only hope she could. I was deeply concerned.

Brenda didn't go with me initially to Ft. Bragg. I knew that I would be going to Ft. Benning very soon for jump school, so we decided to wait until that was over, and then we would find a place to live and get settled in.

I left for Ft. Bragg right after lunch, two days prior to my reporting date. I wanted to have plenty of time, and I wanted to stop by and see Bobby first. I wasn't sure how long it would take me to get there, but my plans were to stop somewhere for the night and finish my trip the following day. I stopped somewhere around Aiken, SC for the night. I figured that was about the halfway point. Interstate 20 was not yet completed, so I took U.S. 1 as far as Camden, SC. I stopped at some little town and got a haircut. I didn't want to sign in looking like a shaggy dog. Around the middle of the afternoon, I saw the sign, "Fayetteville City Limit". I was on U.S. 401, and I knew Bobby was just off the 401 By-Pass on the other side of town. Somehow, I missed the By-Pass, and I continued on Business 401. Suddenly, I was driving through a residential neighborhood. How did this happen? I backtracked until I saw the U.S. 401 sign, then turned around. Same thing again. Finally, on the third try I saw the sign where 401 turned to the right. It must have taken me an hour to find my way across town. I thought, "Boy, the roads in this town are really screwed up." I was later to learn that there was no logical pattern to the streets in Fayetteville. They just paved a bunch of pig trails.

I arrived at Bobby and Betty's home late that afternoon. They invited me for dinner and to spend the night with them. I would be signing in tomorrow morning.

I couldn't get my mind off Vera. I knew she would be receiving my letter about now, and I was deeply concerned. During the course of our conversation that evening I said, "Bobby, do you remember the new girl that started working in the chemistry lab just before you left Germany?" He said, "Vera?" I said, "Yes." I told him how Brenda had left me soon after he had departed and how I had become involved with Vera. He said, "Man! I had no idea." I told him I was very concerned about her and wanted to call her. Zurich time was five hours later than it was here, so it was too late to call tonight. I asked if he would let me call from his phone the coming weekend. He said, "Sure, not a problem."

At 2 PM on Saturday, I was dialing Vera's number. She answered, and I knew right away that she had received my letter. She was so hurt that she could barely talk. The last thing she said before hanging up was, "I don't know what I'm going to do." That scared me because it could have meant many things, but I feared the worst. I had already had one girlfriend cut her wrist, and I surely didn't want something like that happening again. I didn't know what to do. There was nothing I could do.

The following weekend, I called again. No answer. Then I remembered Vera's friend, Gretle. I dialed her number. Someone answered, and I asked in German if this was Gretle. She told me she was Gretle's mother and that Gretle had gone on vacation in the Azores. I asked if Vera was with her. When she said, "Yes", I thanked her and hung up. I felt much better now.

It didn't take long to get my orders for jump school. I would be leaving for Ft. Benning in about three weeks. I had to start getting in shape, because at jump school you don't walk, you run everywhere you go. So, every afternoon when I got off work, I would run around the block, which was about a mile. At first, I could only make it about half way, but it got a little better every day and after three weeks, I was running the full mile.

A few days before I was to leave for jump school, J.V. walked in to the lab and said to Bobby and me, "Boys, I just got word that we're going on vacation. The Pentagon wants to form a medical study team of medics and lab techs to do a little job. We'll be parachuting into the jungle of Vietnam to study things like malaria, plague, and parasitic infections." I didn't say it, but I thought, "Wow! Sounds like the dream vacation I've always wanted." J.V. went on to explain that we would be training for this mission for about a year before being deployed. That would give me plenty of time to finish jump school and go through the tough Special Forces course.

I left for Georgia on Friday afternoon. It was around the middle of August. I would spend the weekend with Brenda and the kids, then she would drive me to Ft. Benning on Monday. It was only about an hour's drive away. Despite our differences, Brenda and I were getting along pretty well. I was trying to put Vera behind me, and I had not mentioned her to Brenda and was not going to. I had made that mistake once before and was not going to make it again.

Jump School was a three-week course. The first week was ground week, the second week was tower week, and the final week was jump week. At age 26, I was one of the oldest students in the class, and most of the guys called me "Pop". However, I was not the oldest guy in the class. We had a gentleman in the class who was 46, called the "Old Man". He was in a National Guard unit and his life-long dream was to become airborne, so he had volunteered to come and fulfill that dream.

I did very well during the first week. We did things like jump from a four-foot platform to practice our PLF (Parachute landing fall), jumping from a 34-foot tower and sliding down a cable at the speed to simulate a parachute landing, and then we had to stand on a 10-foot platform, wearing a parachute harness. The instructor stood behind us holding a rope to support us. When we would jump from the platform, we would swing back and forth like a pendulum. The instructor would slowly lower us toward the ground, and at some point, when we were about four feet from the ground, he would release the rope and we would fall to do our PLF. On that particular exercise, the instructor strongly stressed that we must take up the slack in the rope before we jumped, so that it wouldn't jerk him. He was very upset if someone forgot to do so. Well, when it was the "Old Man's" turn to jump, he forgot to take up the slack. The instructor said a few choice words and as the "Old Man" swung out to the furthest point, the instructor dropped him from 10 feet up. The "Old Man's" heels hit the ground first. He fell backwards with his head hitting the ground very hard. He didn't move. His steel pot (helmet) had broken his neck at the base of his skull. The "Old Man" was dead. This was probably the saddest thing I saw in my 10-year military career. This guy was trying to fulfill his dream and it cost him his life. I'm not saying the instructor killed him deliberately, but he should have controlled his temper better. I never saw him again after that, so I have no idea of what might have happened to him.

On Wednesday morning of week two, I woke up thinking, I've reached the halfway point of the course. This was also the day that I would jump from the 250-foot tower. The tower had four arms at the top that reached out in each direction. On the ground the jumper was placed in a parachute which was already opened and then hoisted to the top. Then he would be released and dropped to the ground. I was apprehensive as I was placed in the harness and hoisted to the top. To be honest, I was scared. The wind was blowing toward the tower, and there was the possibility I might crash into it. On the ground, my instructor yelled, "Pull down the two risers on your right." I did so. This would cause me to drift into the wind, away from the tower; however, I would be falling much faster. In class we had been taught that in such a case we should hold that position all the way to the ground. I was prepared to do just that. The instructor released me, and I felt that I was falling very fast. Then he shouted, "Prepare for a normal landing." I had my knees together and bent, my toes were pointed downward, and I thought I was ready. Then he yelled again, "Prepare for a normal landing!" I didn't know what else to do. Seconds later, I made contact with the ground. As I did, I heard a loud snap as if breaking a broom handle, and I knew what it was. My instructor said in a sarcastic voice, "I heard bones breaking." I said, "Yes, I broke my leg." There was no pain, and as I tried to get up, he told me just to lie still. He motioned for the ambulance to come over. I was placed on a stretcher and taken to Martin Army Hospital. By now the pain had set in. After X-raying my leg, they put on a walking cast and gave me a pair or crutches. I asked for a ride back to my company and was told to take the bus. Problem was, the bus didn't go by my company. They dropped me off at the closest point which was still about a mile away. I would have to walk the rest of the way. By now the pain was excruciating, and the temperature was 100 degrees. They had given me nothing for pain. I was in pretty good physical condition, but the heat and pain were taking its toll. I was totally exhausted by the time I came within sight of my company. Then, two of the men in my company who knew me, came and picked me up and carried me the remaining 200 yards. I was most grateful for that. Then I was told that since I couldn't continue the course, I would be put on CQ (charge of quarters) for the remainder of my time. I was hurting, and I was in no mood for that kind of talk. I said, "Like hell I will!" I got on a pay phone and called Brenda. I said. "Honey, come and get me, now!" She laughed and jokingly said, "What did you do, break a leg?" I said, "Yes, as a matter of fact, I did." She was there within the hour to get me. I picked up my records, signed out and was out of there. We went back to my parents' home to spend the night. She would have to drive me back to Ft. Bragg, so we packed what we could in the little Falcon and headed out the following day. Arriving in Fayetteville, we checked into a motel, and the next day, we went house hunting. We found a nice little four room house on Pine Meadow Drive. It was a dead-end street and there were maybe a dozen houses along the street, all built the same. We moved in, and that would be our home for the next two years.

Back at the lab, I was told that since I didn't make it through Jump School, they would have to take me off that team going to Vietnam. Broke my heart. They told me to wait about a year and let my leg heal, and maybe I would get another chance to go. Oh, joy! At Benning, they had told me to check in at the hospital when I got back to Ft. Bragg. When I checked in at Womack Army Hospital, the doctor said, "Who in the hell put this cast on?" I told him it was done at Ft. Benning. He told me that I shouldn't have a walking cast because it could make the fracture worse. So, it was removed and a new one put on that didn't have a walking heel. He said for me to comeback in six weeks. After that, they put on what they called a jello cast. They told me to wear it for two weeks, then it was removed for good.

Once I was driving again, I started going to the drag strip. The more I watched, the more I wanted to participate. Finally, one Sunday afternoon, I entered my Falcon in the race. I only had one car in my class to run against, a 1956 Ford Station Wagon. Being my first race, I was a little nervous, but the race was very close, and I ended up losing by half a car length. It wouldn't happen again. The next day I visited Lee's Speed Shop and told him I needed to do something to the car to make it run a little faster. He knew what to do. He set up the distributor for maximum power and installed cut-outs on the exhaust system. That increased my elapsed time by 0.2 seconds. That doesn't sound like much, but it's more than 20 feet at the finish line. Later, I would do more to make it run even faster. From that point on, I was the one to beat. Then I taught Brenda to drive, and she was equally as good as me. During the next two years we would win almost 100 first place trophies.

During the fall of 1965, I thought of Vera's birthday. It had been three months since my last contact with her, but she was still very much on my mind, and I wanted to send her a present. I bought her a sterling silver charm bracelet with a single, heart-shaped charm. On one side, I had it engraved "Happy Birthday 1965", the other side said, "I Love You". Two weeks later, it was returned to me with a note saying she couldn't accept it. I removed the charm and several months later, buried it at the base of a pine tree at the edge of our pond.

The first Special Forces soldiers to go to Vietnam in the early 1960s were sent as advisors and that's pretty much what they did. But by 1965, things were really heating up over there, and they were very much engaged in combat. The life expectancy of a Green Beret in combat was not very long. We were losing men every week. I recall one week when a camp was overrun, the entire team lost their lives. Many of the men were trying to live their lives to the fullest, and some were pretty wild. The men on that medical study team that I was supposed to be on, were now training for their mission, and they would come back with some pretty wild stories. Here's a couple of my favorites.

While training at Ft. Dix, NJ, four of the guys were driving along when the car ahead came to a screeching stop. A lady jumped from the car, turned around and said, "I'm going to sleep with every man on post!" The car left her standing there and the Special Forces men pulled up beside her and one of them said, "You might as well start with us." She got in the car with them and they drove over to the NCO club where they sat at a table and had a beer. She told them that she and her husband were not getting along well and that she was very unhappy. She went to the lady's room, and while she was gone, the men drew straws to see who would take her home. Jack won, and the other three left. While she and Jack were sitting there talking, her husband walked in and started trouble with Jack. Jack got up and politely beat the hell out of him. The M.P.s showed up, and after a short discussion, told Jack to take her home. Jack said, "Now, wait a minute, she belongs to him, not me." An M.P. said, "We were told that you brought her in, so you get her out of here!" Jack had no choice but to take her home. Sitting at the kitchen table and having coffee, she told Jack that things were so bad, she once tried to commit suicide by cutting her wrist. It didn't work because the bleeding stopped. Jack told her that next time she should fill the bathtub, sit down, cut her wrist and hold her arm over the water. He told her that when her arm got tired, it would drop in the water, and the water would keep the blood from clotting, and she would bleed to death. Jack said they spent a wonderful evening together and that he left around midnight.

The following day the men were having dinner at the mess hall when they happened to pick up a newspaper. The headline read, "G.I.s' WIFE COMMITS SUICIDE, FOUND DEAD IN BATHTUB". Jack said, "Oh, my God! That's the lady I was with last night. We've got to get out of here!" They left Ft. Dix, returned to Bragg and never heard another word about that incident.

On a training trip to the Desert Southwest, I believe Arizona, Sam met a girl in a bar. She was a teacher from Baltimore who was there for a year. He talked her into taking a ride out to a nearby state park. He was unable to get to first base with this lady. Suddenly, he spotted a sheep dog standing on a mesa, silhouetted against the sky. He said, "Look!" She said, "What is it?" He told her it was a wolf. She wanted to leave, but he said, "No, if we start the car or turn on the lights, we could be surrounded by an entire pack of wolves." He said she was so frightened that she climbed all over him. The dog left, and they got out of the car and spread a blanket on the ground. They ended up falling asleep on the blanket. Sam said he was awakened by someone kicking his foot. He opened his eyes, and a big park ranger was standing over him. The ranger said, "It's 9 AM. Tourists will be coming out to the park soon. You guys need to get up and put on some clothes." The girl woke up and realized she was naked and started wrapping the blanket around herself. She said, "This is so embarrassing! He'll go back to town and tell everyone. I can't stand to go back and face anyone."

In early 1966, I walked over to nearby Womack Army Hospital to visit the lab, and to my surprise, there was Sergeant Bill Knight. He had been the NCOIC at the lab at Bad Kreuznach and was now assigned here. During the course of our conversation, he mentioned that Cape Fear Valley Hospital in Fayetteville was looking for some lab technicians to work part time. He said he was going to inquire about it and asked if I was interested. I said, "Sure, why not?" We drove down to Cape Fear, went in and talked with Ruth Meissner, the Lab Chief. We told her about our training and experience, and she ended up hiring the two of us. We would be working on Saturday mornings and part of Sunday. We would be starting the first week in February. I was excited. This would be my first civilian job.

With Bobby and J.V. training for their vacation to Vietnam, I was teaching all the medical laboratory classes to the students. I was also responsible for doing any lab work that might be needed, and there was plenty. It was almost all parasitology. We had to do three stool specimens on every Special Forces soldier going to Vietnam and three on every soldier coming back. I had two young boys who were just out of lab school helping me. I recall one week we had 700 men going to Nam, and we had 2100 specimens to test. They brought us case after case of stool specimens. One of the guys said to me, "Sergeant, this is a lot of crap" I said, "You're absolutely right." There was nothing else to say. It took the three of us 10 full days to complete that job.

I was enjoying working at Cape Fear Hospital on the weekends. There were less than ten employees working in the lab, and only five of them were qualified to be on call at night. One day Mrs. Meissner asked me, "John, would you be interested in taking call some week nights?" I said, "Tell me about it." She told me it paid $10 per night and that included the first two calls. For any additional calls I would be paid $5 per call. She said I would be able to stay at home and they would call me if needed. I said, " Hey, sounds good to me. When do I start?" She said, "Tonight. You can take my place." She went on to tell me that she liked my work and that I was the first G.I. she had ever trusted to take night call. I felt honored. It wasn't long before some of the others asked me to take their nights. I was making about $100 per week, which was more than my army pay.

Brenda and I were getting along very well, and we began talking about getting our own home. At that time a nice 3-bedroom brick home could be built for well under $20,000. I didn't want to live in the city. Being a country boy, I wanted a place in the country. So, I started looking for a little piece of land, something big enough that I could plant a garden. Every day I checked the classified ads under "Land for sale". After about two weeks of searching, I found it. The ad said, "19 acres, mostly wooded in young timber, fish pond, house and barn. $6500." I couldn't dial the number fast enough. I asked the agent to hold it until I could take a look at it. He agreed. I drove 20 miles north of Fayetteville to the northern sandhills region of North Carolina. This piece of land was located on a dirt road a mile and a half off of N. C. Highway 24. I found a wood frame house with an elderly colored couple living there, only they weren't called colored anymore. They were now Negros. They had an outdoor toilet and a well which was only about 20 feet deep. The old barn was in decent shape, and there were horses grazing in the back yard. There was a lot of trash and debris and old wire fences all over the place. There was a lot of work that would need to be done, but I saw great possibilities. I could tear down the house and barn and build a new brick home on the slight rise above the pond. The timber would be ready to harvest in about 25 or 30 years. I asked the agent if he could finance the place for me. He reluctantly said he would. He said that several people had called after me and was ready to pay cash for it, sight unseen. I had been lucky. He got it financed for me for seven years with a payment of just over $100 per month. Jessie, the Negro who lived here, was very nice. I told him he could stay at no charge until I was ready to build my house. I rented a pick-up and began to clean the place up, hauling away trash and tearing down old wire fences. The previous owner moved his horses away, and I began to tear down the old barn, saving the lumber that was still in good shape. I might have plans for it later. The old house was a different story. It was too big a job for me to tear down and dispose of. I got lucky. Mr. Gilbert Brown, a neighbor stopped by and asked if I would sell it to him, and he would have it moved. He said the house was worth about $1000 to him and it would cost about $700 to move it, leaving about $300 for me. I said, "Deal done!" He had the house moved about a mile down the road to a piece of property he owned. Thirty days later the house caught fire and burned to the ground.

Brenda and I had already picked out the floor plan we wanted; seven rooms, hallway and two baths. The kitchen and dining room were actually one large room which was later separated by a bar and overhead cabinets. Then there was a living room, three bedrooms, a study which could have been used as a fourth bedroom, and a single carport. All floors would be hardwood except the kitchen and dining area. We picked the tile for the bathrooms and the wood paneling for the kitchen and dining area. We would have no central heat and air. We would have electric baseboard heat. The total price would be $16,600.00 and that would include landscaping with shrubbery, paved driveway, and a 75 foot deep well.

We went to the contractor in Fayetteville and told them we were ready for them to start building. They said, "We can't start with that old house in the front yard." I said, "It's gone." They didn't believe me and had to send someone out to take a look before they would agree to get started. They finally began work in the summer of 1966.

In the spring of that year, I had been called in by the Company Commander and received a promotion to sergeant first class, E-7. I had now been in the service for 8 1/2 years. There were about a half dozen of the men on the Medical Committee to be promoted to E-7 that day, and we all went to the NCO club that night for a big celebration.

I was about to have a big decision to make. My enlistment would be up in about six months. Did I want to re-enlist again or become a civilian? I wasn't sure. I loved my job at the hospital, and my pay was equivalent to my military pay; I just wouldn't have that early retirement benefit. If I stayed in the army, I would surely end up in Vietnam sooner or later, and that was a dangerous place to be, not that I was afraid to go, but I might not be around to retire in eleven more years.

It had been a year since Brenda and I had gotten back together. It had been a good year. We had two nice kids who were happy, we had bought the land, and they had finally started building our new home. We would be moving in next spring. Harvey would be starting to school next fall. I had received a promotion and had a nice part-time job at the hospital. Although I had not forgotten my wonderful relationship with Vera, it was no longer preying on my mind. I was finally putting it behind me.

Brenda had a good friend in our next-door neighbor. She had always made friends easily, in fact, I don't think she'd ever met a stranger. One Saturday morning we finished our work early at the lab and I decided to go home. I was still on call, but I didn't have to stay at the hospital. As I pulled into my driveway, the gentleman next door was standing outside. I stood there chatting with him for a few minutes when he said, "My wife is running out on me." I said, "Man, I'm sure sorry to hear that." Then he said something that hit me like a sledge hammer. He said, "It's not just my wife, It's your wife too." A thousand things flashed through my mind. I said, "Are you sure?" He said, "Yes, without a doubt. She and my wife are seeing men almost every day while we're at work. They are out somewhere right now." How could this be? She had begged me to take her back and had vowed that nothing like this would ever happen again. I can't begin to describe the feeling that came over me. I barely remember driving back to the hospital and had trouble concentrating on my work. Where were the kids? Very likely with a baby sitter somewhere. I would confront her tonight.

After dinner that evening, I said, "How did it go with your friend today?" She said, "Great, she invited me to go shopping with her this morning." I said, " Not that friend. I mean the boyfriend you went to see." She flatly denied having a boyfriend. I kept the pressure on her and she continued to deny it, until around midnight. She finally broke down and admitted it. I said, "How could you do this?" The best answer she could give was, "It just happened." I said, "This has to stop now, or we're finished." She was crying and saying how sorry she was. I asked when she would be talking to him again. She told me that he called her every morning about ten minutes after I left for work. I said, "I want to talk with him." She thought I wanted to threaten him or cuss him out. I told her I just wanted him to know how things stood.

The next morning, I didn't leave for work. He was right on time. Brenda answered the phone and told him that I knew and that it was over. Then she said, "My husband wants to talk to you." He was hesitant at first but agreed when she told him I wasn't going to be mean. I took the phone and told him that it had to end, and that I wanted his assurance that he would not call or see her again. He agreed to do just that, and then he had to tell me what a wonderful woman she was. I said, "That I know", and hung up. To the best of my knowledge, they never made contact again. I told Brenda that she should go to Georgia and stay with her mother for a couple of weeks. She and the kids left the following day. While she was gone, I cleaned the house room, by room, from top to bottom. When she returned, she commented on how nice the house looked. I thanked her and asked her to try and help keep it that way. Unfortunately, that didn't work out too well. She was simply not a good house-keeper.

I still hadn't made up my mind about whether to re-enlist or not. Time was quickly running out, so I went to headquarters and applied for the longest extension I could get, which was eleven months. That would give me until September 25, 1967 to make my decision.

Everything was progressing smoothly with our new house. We would drive up every few days to check on the progress. We would also drive up on the weekend for a picnic by the pond and to do a little fishing. We caught mostly small bream and small bass, but one day Brenda caught a Bass that weighed 1 1/2 pounds. Her record wouldn't last long, because a few weeks later I caught one that was 2 1/2 pounds. Old Jessie, the Negro who had lived there, told me he had seen one so big and old that it had moss growing on its back. Unfortunately, I never saw that one.

For the remainder of 1966 and into the spring of 1967, Brenda and I were very active in drag racing, and she was becoming increasingly popular, because she was the only female driver. We were bringing home trophies every weekend. I hardly ever got to drive anymore. Whenever I would attempt to drive, the officials would say, "Let Brenda drive. It'll help turn this into a family event". I couldn't help but notice that she was also becoming popular with some of the male drivers.

Our new home was finally completed, and we moved in around the end of May. Being so far out in the country and with hardly any neighbors, I hated to leave Brenda with no car, so I went shopping. I bought a 1967 Pontiac Tempest Sprint. It was white with blue interior. It had an overhead cam six-cylinder engine rated at 207 HP, and it came with a three-speed transmission with a Hurst shifter on the floor. It was a fun car to drive. So I took it and left the Falcon for Brenda.

One afternoon I went to the hospital to see Dr. Harold Steffee. He was the pathologist in charge of the lab and the one who did the hiring and firing. I told him I was considering getting out of the Army and asked about the chance of getting a full-time job. He assured me that a job would be open for me should I make that decision. I thanked him and left. My mind was now made up. I would be leaving the army at the end of September.

I was continuing to teach classes every day to the Special Forces Medics, and I enjoyed it. Soon the guys on the Medical Study Team would be returning and if I had decided to re-enlist, I would be going back to Jump School very soon. It had been an honor for me to wear that Green Beret for the past two years. At that time, we were the only U.S. Forces wearing the beret. I would always treasure the time I spent with those brave men.

I didn't have any concrete evidence, but I was beginning to be suspicious of some of Brenda's activity. I took the afternoon off from work one day and went home. Brenda was there with the kids as I expected she would be, but around middle of the afternoon a car pulled into the driveway. I didn't recognize the car, and Brenda jumped up and ran to the door and out onto the small front porch. A man got out of the car, that I recognized from the drag strip. He was a master sergeant in the army. His eyes were glued on Brenda, and I knew he was reading her lips. Then he saw me and said, "They told me you had gone home." The problem was, no one knew I had gone home, and besides, he didn't even know where I worked. I said, "Who told you?" I asked what number he called, and he started getting really uptight, so I let it go. Then he took a newspaper from his pocket and showed us a picture of a car that had been hit by a train. The driver had been killed. He said, "isn't that the boy that's been racing at the drag strip." We looked at the picture and said, "Yeah, that's him." He was a 19-year old soldier, and his parents had just recently bought him a new car. Now he was dead. I was sorry to hear about it, but I just couldn't believe this guy drove 15 miles one way just to show us that picture. It didn't make sense to me.

I was going to class two evenings per week, taking a course in basic auto repair. I enjoyed doing minor work on the cars. Class was cancelled one evening, and I came home early. There was a teenage girl sitting on the sofa and an older man with his arm around her. That looked strange to me because she was the daughter of our closest neighbor, and I had never seen this guy before. I later learned that there was a second man, and he had run out the back door and into the woods as I drove up. Very weird.

Then, there was the time my parents came for a visit. I had been working the night before, and Brenda had been home with the kids. When my parents arrived, my mother noticed a bloody T-bone in a plate. Mom said, "Who ate that?" Brenda said, "Oh, I like my steak rare." Funny thing, I'd never seen her eat one that way.

CHAPTER 15

Back to Civilian Life

ON SEPTEMBER 25, 1967, I received an honorable discharge from the U.S. Army. That was only two days short of my 10th Anniversary of enlisting in the service back in 1957. That was half-way to a retirement that would have paid me half of my monthly base pay for life. I received a lot of criticism for getting out, but I thought it was the right decision at the time, and I still think so today. I have never regretted it.

Before starting my new job, I had promised Brenda and the kids, that I would take a week off to visit our families in Georgia. Upon returning, I went to Dr. Steffee, and told him I was ready to go to work full time. To my surprise he said, "I'm not sure if I have anything available for you at this time." I felt like my heart fell to my feet. I said, "Dr. Steffee, I just gave up my 10-year military career because I was confident you would stand by your word and hire me. He said, "Let me think for a minute." After a short pause he said, "I can put you at Highsmith, or I can put you in charge of the blood bank." Highsmith was a smaller hospital across town, and I had no desire to go there. I said, "I'll take the blood bank job." The technician who was in the blood bank was very unhappy and wanted to be transferred to another department. He said, "OK, you're hired, and you can start to work right away." I thanked him and went to the chief lab tech, Mrs. Meissner, who took me to the blood bank and told me that she wanted me to work with the other technician for a week in order to familiarize myself with everything.

I loved my new job. I was responsible for making sure we had an adequate supply of blood on hand at all times and that included all the blood types. More importantly, when someone needed a transfusion, it was my job to make sure that the blood was cross-matched properly and was compatible with that patient. There was no room for error in the blood bank. An error could be very serious or possibly fatal. I had a big responsibility.

The thing that made this job different from all the other labs I had worked in was the fact that all my co-workers were female. We had a few military guys working on weekends, but I rarely saw them. I enjoyed working with all those women, and most of them were friendly. There was one who really caught my eye. A pretty, 19-year-old brunette named Jo Ann Sykes. What I liked most of all was her personality. She was something of a Tom-Boy type and a joy to be around and talk to. She loved fast cars, motorcycles, guns, and sports. She could pass a football better than most guys. We became good friends, that's it, just friends. There was never any romantic relationship. We would remain good friends until she left for a new job about two years later.

In October, it had been two years since I had sent Vera that birthday present. My last contact with her was when she had returned it. I wondered how she was doing. I decided to send her a birthday card and a short note. I hoped she would respond. I used the hospital for my return address. Two weeks later I received a letter from Zurich. There was something unusual about this letter. Then I realized it was rimmed in black. A sick feeling came over my body. My hands were shaking. I managed to open the letter. The letter read, "I'm Vera's sister and I'm writing to let you know that Vera is dead." My heart was broken. How could this be? Such a lovely and wonderfully talented lady, gone. The letter went on to say that she had taken an overdose of sleeping pills. The sister said that her family was very bitter toward Dr. Jay for writing that prescription for her. The letter didn't say when she died. It could have been anytime during the past two years; I didn't know. I could only assume that she had gotten back together with Dr. Jay, the man she had met at Harvard. I never met him but had always assumed I would have to confront him someday. That never happened. I only know that I'll never forget Vera and the wonderful six months we had together. I may well have been the only man she ever loved.

The Cape Fear Valley Hospital School of Medical Technology was another function of the lab and pathology department. We would have about a half dozen or so students who were working on their degree in Medical Technology. Our program lasted a year as they rotated through all departments of the lab. I would always have a student to work with in the blood bank. In addition, I taught all the classes in parasitology. Those classes were the same as I had taught to the Special Forces Medics.

1968 was pretty much a non-eventful year. Brenda and I were getting along OK, but in my mind, there was always some doubt. I always had the feeling that our marriage was not going to survive. Harvey started in the first grade at Ben Haven School that fall. Echo was now three, and she was a Daddy's girl. She was the cutest little thing. The kids loved the outdoors, and they loved walking with me through the trails we had made in the woods. Harvey and I dug up a little long leaf pine, and he planted it in the front yard, by the driveway. We called it the "Good Boy Pine". Forty-nine years later it has grown into a beautiful, mature tree. We had a nice Christmas that year with Echo getting a tricycle and Harvey a little red wagon.

One memorable occasion in 1968 was the Georgia State High School Basketball Championships being held in Macon. This was of interest because my first cousin, Kay Chambers, who was graduating this year, had taken her team to the tournament. She had been a super-star throughout her high school career, scoring as many as 48 points in a single game. We were going to Georgia for the weekend, so we would stop by to see her play. What a thrill is was to see her perform! I was proud to call her my cousin!

The winter of 1968-1969 was very harsh. In January we had a terrible ice storm, followed by snow and frigid temperatures that stayed below freezing for five days. Because of the ice, power lines were down, and we had no electricity or water for almost a week. During that week we had to leave home and stay with some friends in Fayetteville.

Many of the girls working in the lab were military dependents. They would usually be there for a year or two, then be gone. We were constantly getting new employees. In addition to a student, I had an assistant helping me in the blood bank, plus a phlebotomist working in the donor room. We had two donor chairs. Dr. Steffee had recently organized a Blood Assurance Plan, and we were constantly trying to recruit as many members as possible. A member of the plan was required to donate one pint of blood per year. In return, if he or any family member would ever need blood, it would be provided at no charge. We did not yet have enough members to meet all our needs, so we would occasionally have to purchase blood from a commercial blood bank to make up for any shortages. The commercial blood bank we used was Knoxville Blood Center in Knoxville, TN. Whenever we had to order blood, it would be shipped to us overnight by bus.

During my time as the blood bank supervisor, I had many different assistants; the first being a young lady named Hazel. She was very nice to work with but had some strange ways and beliefs. She was a Seventh Day Adventist, and for example, she didn't believe that Neil Armstrong went to the moon in 1969. To her, it was a hoax, because God wouldn't allow that. She did her best trying to convert me to her religion, but I failed her. However, I did go to her church a few times.

I recall in particular one new girl that showed up in '69. She was introduced to me as Marlene Bartram. She was a brunette and very pretty, with a personality that matched. After being there for about a week, she began to ignore me. If I said, "Good morning", she would turn her head and not speak. I thought, "What the heck is her problem?" This went on for two or three weeks, and suddenly one day she walked into the blood bank with a big smile on her face, friendly as could be. She said things were not going well for her in hematology where she was working, so she thought she'd pay me a visit. I said, "I'm glad you did." She didn't know much about blood banking. I wasn't busy, so we sat and talked for a while about blood types. I had a way of making my little talks interesting, and she was impressed and excited. I was curious. So, I asked, "Marlene, why have you been avoiding me for the past several weeks?" She told me that some of the other girls had told her to stay away from me, that I was no good and would be bad news for her. She said, "I was so upset with the people in my department, I thought I'd come here for a little excitement." I laughed and said, "I'm sorry to disappoint you." She said, "You're just the opposite of what they told me. I am so happy that I came here and met you." She went home that evening and told her husband what a wonderful person she had met that day.

Perry Bartram was a highly trained Green Beret medic. He had attended some of my laboratory classes in 1967. He and Marlene had a two-year-old son. Before the week was over, they had come to our home and met my family. Perry saw our pond and said he loved to fish. I invited him to come back and go fishing. He did and caught more fish than he had caught at any other place he had been to around the area. That was the start of a lasting friendship.

My marriage was rapidly deteriorating, and I could sense that the end was near. What had gone wrong? Had I been a complete failure at being a husband? I didn't know. Sure, I had done her wrong during my first tour of duty in Germany, and I had greatly neglected her on the second tour because of being so involved with my music. It had now been four years since we got back together, and I had not been unfaithful to her, although some may have thought I had, after I started a friendship with Jo Ann.

Drag racing was becoming increasingly popular, and the auto makers were now sponsoring some of the professional drivers. Two such drivers, Ronnie Sox and Buddy Martin came to the local Ford Dealership to help organize a local drag club. I was at the meeting along with many others, and we all filled out application cards for membership. The dealership named a president who said he would be contacting us for a meeting. But it never happened. I kept going to the dealership, and finally they got tired of me bugging them. They gave me all the applications and told me to take it over. And that I did. I contacted all the potential members and called for a meeting to be held in the conference room of the dealership. We elected officers and now had a club with me as president. We were the Lafayette Ford Drag Club. I worked very hard and succeeded in making it a successful organization.

From the time I had begun working full time at Cape Fear Hospital, I had noticed something strange on many of the blood donor cards. My initials were appearing on many of them, only I wasn't the one doing the initialing. I began asking whose initials it was, but no one seemed to know. The initialing seemed to have stopped around February 1966 which was about the time I started working there part-time. It was a mystery to me.

By late summer 1969, Brenda was no longer sleeping with me, and she was ready to go her way. We didn't fuss and fight for sake of the children. She found a place to stay, I don't know where, but whenever I was home, she would bring the kids to me. I washed their clothes and fed them well when they were with me. Harvey started the 2nd grade at Johnsonville School, about three miles from our home. Johnsonville School had previously been a Negro school, but 1969 was the year the schools were integrated in North Carolina.

In Late August as I stood in the blood bank facing the door, I saw a young woman walk down the hallway that I had not seen before. I remember thinking, "Wow, that's a good-looking woman." I didn't think any more about it, until 20-minutes later when Mrs. Meissner walked in with her. She said, "John, this is Juanita White. She's your new assistant. I was stunned. I couldn't take my eyes off her. She was the most beautiful woman I had ever seen; beautiful dishwater blonde hair flowing almost to her waist, a perfect figure, beautiful blue eyes, and a Dolly Parton smile, dimples and all. I finally managed to say, "Hello." One word came to my mind. Sophisticated. I had never seen a girl with so much class.

As we began to get acquainted, I began to change my mind. She had grown up in the mountains of Southwest Virginia. Her family was poor, as was mine, and she had moved around a lot, going to schools in Virginia, North Carolina, Delaware, and Indiana. When she started talking about going to a one-room school, I said, " No Way! That's the kind of school my parents went to back in the '20s. "She laughed and said, "I'm not quite that old." The more we talked, the better I liked her. My current assistant was a petite little blonde named Betty. She invited Juanita to go to lunch with her in the cafeteria. Upon returning, she said, "Do you know how old Juanita is? She's 29! I thought we were the same age." Betty was 18.

When Juanita came to work the following day, she said, "I want to ask you something. Are you my boss or is Mrs. Meissner my boss?" I said, "Mrs. Meissner is over both of us, but technically I'm your immediate boss, but why don't we just say that we're co-workers." She liked my answer. We continued to talk and get to know each other better. We talked about our families. She said she had two brothers and three sisters, and that one of her sisters was mentally retarded. I said, "I've got no sisters, but four brothers, and one of them is retarded. We thought that was kind of unusual. I didn't see a ring on her finger, so I asked, "Are you married?" She said, "Yes, but my husband and I are separated." I said, " I'm in the same boat. My wife is in the process of leaving me." I didn't dare ask about any boyfriends. As pretty as she was, I figured she probably had all kind of guys after her.

As the president of the Ford Drag Club, I didn't think I should be driving around in a Pontiac. I decided to stop by the Ford place one afternoon to browse around. I had always liked the Mustangs, and there was one that really caught my eye. It was a solid black fastback model with the all-new 351 C.I. engines, 4-barrel carburetor, and rated at 290 horsepower. It had an automatic transmission. I thought, "Boy! This would be a fun car to put on the drag strip. The price was $3300.00. I returned the next day to talk with a salesperson. The deal was done. I traded the Pontiac and drove home in my new pony car. As soon as I could get it broken in, I would take it to the strip and see what it would do.

Juanita's primary job was to take care of the donor room, so her hours were slightly different from mine. Instead of eight till five, she worked from ten till seven. That way, people getting off work at five, could come by and donate blood after getting off work. Juanita liked those hours, because she could sleep in a little longer. One morning she came to work, and I almost didn't recognize her. She was wearing a gorgeous, blonde, Dolly Parton wig. She looked so much like Dolly. I could only say, "Wow! You look beautiful!" Her response was, "Thank You!" Later, as we were talking, she told me she had worked here before: once as the EKG technician, and more recently in the donor room. She said she had left in early 1966. That was the same time I had begun working here part time, but our paths had never crossed. Then a thought came to my mind. I said, "Would you initial this?" She made her "JW", then I made my "JW". She said, "They look the same!" Mystery solved. She had been the person putting my initials on all those cards when I didn't even work here. We both had to laugh about that.

Halloween was coming up soon, and I decided to have a party at home and invite my friends and co-workers. I was pleased that Juanita came, along with Marlene, Perry, and about a dozen others, all wearing their costume. I was a little surprised to see my wife there, although she was in and out with the kids. It was a good party, and everyone had fun.

When Juanita came to work the following morning, she said, "Johnny, there's something I think I should tell you." Without answering, I just looked at her, waiting. She said, " Last night your wife wanted me to leave the party with her to go to Ft. Bragg to meet some guys." I said, "I'm glad you didn't go." I had seen Brenda on the phone a couple of times and wondered who she was talking to. Now I knew.

A lot happened in 1969. My brother Don had graduated from Georgia Southwestern University in Americus, GA the previous year and had taken on a job with Firestone Tire and Rubber Co. as a chemical engineer at the Albany, GA plant. In 1969, Don married his college sweetheart, Carolyn Davis. Don asked me to be his best man at their wedding. When I showed up that day, Don handed me a pair of black socks. I guess he didn't want his red-neck brother wearing white socks. Don and Carolyn made their home in Albany. Don was not active in drag racing, but he loved the sport and fast cars. He and I would be going to a big National Ford Drag Club event at Capital Raceway near Baltimore in the spring of 1970, where I would be participating with my '69 Mustang.

By now, the word was out that Brenda and I were getting a separation. I began to notice that Gloria was starting to pay more attention to me than usual. She was a pretty brunette with a great personality. I didn't know what she was up to.

I had a habit of inviting some of my co-workers to lunch occasionally. We had a full hour for lunch, and there were dozens of eating places just minutes from the hospital. I mostly went with Jo Ann and Marlene, but one day I invited Gloria. She readily accepted and wanted to get something at a fast food place, then go sit in a park to eat. We did and had a good time. She told me that she was in an unhappy marriage and was thinking of leaving her husband. Then she suggested that maybe the two of us could become friends. I said, "We're already friends." She looked me in the eye and said, "You know what I mean." Well, maybe I did, and maybe I didn't.

Jo Ann moved back home to Mebane and took a job at a clinic there. I would miss her. We had been friends for a long time.

Not long after that, I was on call one night when I heard the phone. I thought, "More lab work to do." To my surprise, it was Gloria. She said, "How's it going tonight?" I said, "Not much going on tonight." She said, "Why don't you come over and visit with me for a while? My husband is in the field, and I'm all alone." I told her I'd think about it, and we hung up. A little while later, I told the switch board operator where I'd be, and I headed to Gloria's. We talked about all kind of things, and during our conversation, she told me her husband had recently returned from Vietnam. He told her that he got a great deal of pleasure from killing Viet-Cong soldiers but even more pleasure from cutting off their genitals and sticking it in their mouth. "I thought, "Holy shit! Let me out of here. If he comes home and catches me here, I'm in trouble, regardless of whether I'm doing anything or not." I told Gloria bye and left as fast as I could. I wanted nothing to do with her husband, Barry.

Not long after that, we were having some kind of lab function, and the husbands and wives were invited. I was seated directly across the table from Gloria and Barry, enjoying my salad. Suddenly, Marlene, who was seated beside Gloria said, "Gloria and I have been fighting to see who gets to go to lunch each day with Johnny." She continued talking, and I could tell that Barry was staring at me. Gloria was a big liability with Barry around. He was one mean dude. I didn't take my eyes off my salad. When Marlene stopped talking, Barry said, "Now, let's get back to that little thing about somebody fighting." I thought, "Oh God, how can she answer that?" But Marlene laughed and calmly said, "Oh, Gloria and I are the two prettiest girls in the lab, and we had a little joke about us fighting to see who would go to lunch with Johnny." Thankfully, he let it go at that.

Juanita and I had a great working relationship, and we laughed and talked together, learning more about each other and about our families. I asked what religion she grew up in. She told me Primitive Baptist, and I said, "You're not going to believe this, but my parents are also Primitive Baptist." She said, "You've got to be kidding. You're the first person I've met since I left home that has ever heard of a Primitive Baptist." Then we learned that one of the favorite games that our parents played was a card game called "set-back". I was the first one she'd met who knew about that game. We were finding all kind of common ground, and it was strengthening our relationship.

When lunch time came around that day, I was having second thoughts about inviting Gloria to lunch again, so I said, "Juanita, I'm going down to Chris's Steak House for lunch. Would you like to go with me?" She looked up with that big pretty smile and said, "I thought you'd never ask." I really didn't think she'd go with me, but she did, and we had a delightful time.

Juanita's parents were divorced, and her mother had re-married and lived near Hillsville, VA. She said that when she got off work on Friday, she would drive up there for the weekend. She said it was about a 3 1/2-hour drive. I said, "I'm on call all weekend. Have a safe trip. I'll see you Monday." It was the longest weekend I had ever had. I couldn't get my mind off Juanita. She was such a doll and so much fun to be with. I couldn't wait for Monday to get here.

And I didn't wait. I figured she would be getting home around 7 or 8 PM. I dialed her number at exactly 7 PM. No answer. I tried again every 15 minutes until 8:15, when she finally answered. I think she was a little surprised it was me. I asked about her trip and after chatting for a few minutes, I said, "If you're not too tired, why don't you stop over and visit with me for a few minutes. It's so boring over here." She said, "OK, see you in a few." Twenty minutes later she walked in. We sat in the chemistry lab and talked. After about two hours, she said she had to go, so I walked her out to her car, opened her door and she got in. Then I slid in beside her. She didn't seem to mind. I put my arm around her and kissed her warm and tender lips for the very first time. It was the sweetest feeling I had ever known. I walked back into the lab in a total daze. I remember thinking, "I'm in love."

We went through the following week as if nothing had happened. Then on Friday afternoon, she said, "What are you doing tomorrow?" I told her I had to work till noon, and then I was off. She said, "If you don't have other plans, stop by my place when you get off." I said, "OK. Thanks for the invite."

I couldn't wait to get off work. I found her place and rang the door-bell. She answered the door and gave me that big smile and stood there with the sexiest look I had ever seen. She was wearing a pair of brown hip-huggers with white flowers, with a two-inch-wide leather belt. Her short, white blouse showed her tanned, bare midriff. I thought, "Oh my God! I'm looking at the kind of woman every man dreams of, but few have." She said, "Well, come on in." I walked into her living room, and she said, "Can I make you a drink? I've got bourbon and Coke or Mountain Dew and gin." I said, "I've never had Mountain Dew and gin. I'll have one of those." Taking my first sip, I said, "Wow! You make a great drink, Juanita." We sat and talked. She told me at first, she thought of me as a bookworm or maybe a nerd, because I wore glasses and was so business-like. She said she began to change her mind after the party and because I had a Mustang and was a drag racer. During the course of our conversation, I mentioned that I had played in a band in Germany. She said, "You play the guitar?" I said, "Yeah, a little." She went into the bedroom and brought out an old guitar that her husband had tried to play. She said, "Play me a song." I tuned up the old guitar and started playing and singing Johnny Cash's "Folsom Prison Blues". Juanita was so surprised and very impressed. I think that was the moment I won her heart. When I left later that evening, I realized, "Hey, I didn't even know what love was until tonight." I also knew I wanted to spend the rest of my life with this woman, and I would do whatever I could to make that happen.

Gloria wouldn't give up. She kept calling and coming to see me at night. She told me of all the little plans she had for us, like making a stone walkway from the back door to the pond and planting flowers along the way. Problem was, she was a big liability with Barry around. I wanted no part of him. When she finally realized it was over, she said, "You liked me fine until someone prettier came along, then you dumped me." Maybe she was right.

For Christmas, I gave Juanita a hot-pink jump suit. She looked so pretty in it. I finally realized that clothes didn't make Juanita look good. She made clothes look good, regardless of what it was. I always said that she would have made a great model, but she said that at five feet one, no one would want her as a model.

In January, I met Juanita's youngest sister, Lois. She and her two-year-old daughter Cheryl stopped by the blood bank for a short visit. Like Juanita, she was a fun-loving girl, and we would have a good relationship throughout the years.

When Easter rolled around in April 1970, Juanita and I had a three-day weekend. We decided to take a trip to Florida. It would be our first trip together. We were ready to go when we got off work on Friday. A light rain was falling. The further south we went, the heavier the rain fell, and by the time we reached South Georgia, it was raining so hard we could barely see. We pulled off at a roadside park. As we sat there in the car, I had the urge to pee, really bad. I said, "There's no way I'm getting out in this weather." Then Juanita came up with one of the most brilliant solutions I had ever heard. She said, "Why don't you just hang it out the window." I said, "Baby, I don't think I can do that." We both started laughing, and we still laugh every time we think about that night.

We fell asleep in the car and slept for about four hours. The rain had stopped, and we made our way into Jacksonville, stopping at a Waffle House for breakfast. Then we headed for Marineland where we enjoyed a great show featuring the whales and dolphins. Heading back to St. Augustine, we checked in at the Holiday Motel. That had been the same motel I had stayed in on my class trip back in 1957. We were pretty well beat by now, so after dinner we retired early. We wanted to get an early start on Sunday, so we could take in all the many sites in St. Augustine.

We visited the Old Fort, Old Jail, Ripley's Believe it or Not Museum, an alligator farm, and much more. We made sure we drank from the Fountain of Youth, although I have come to realize that it didn't work.

On Monday morning, Juanita put on that pink jump-suit I had gotten her for Christmas. She was a real doll. As we headed north in the Mustang, the radio was blaring country music. When we started across the St. John's River Bridge in Jacksonville, Jerry Reed began singing, "Talk About the Good Times". It seemed so appropriate because we had certainly had a good time. We made one last stop at Jekyll Island, Georgia. I had Juanita pose for me, standing atop an old rusted cannon. It was a gorgeous photo. This was the first of many wonderful trips we would take together.

A few weeks later, my brother Don and I headed for the big Ford Drag Club event in Maryland. There were hundreds of participants from around the country. I felt confident that I could do well, because the '69 Mustang was running well, and it was consistent. The key to success in bracket racing is to run consistent and be able to cut a good light at the starting tree. I did both and was runner-up in my bracket. That qualified me to run in the eliminator, which meant that all the brackets would compete for an overall champion. On my first run, I had to run against a '68 Mustang with a 390 C.I. engine, which was much more powerful than my car. He had to spot me by a two-second handicap, which meant I got to start two seconds ahead of him. He was able to overtake me at the finish line, but we were both disqualified for breaking out of our dial-in time. If I had just slowed down, I would have won. My 2nd place finish had won me many prizes from the sponsors. I received a nice set of tools, at least six racing jackets, and other gifts. I left pleased and looked forward to next year.

The local drag strip in Fayetteville announced it would be hosting the State Championships that summer. It would be a two-day event with qualifying on Saturday and the finals on Sunday. As always, I was racing in the bracket division. There were four brackets: A, B, C, & D. I was in "C", and I easily won my bracket on Saturday, and I was ready to take on my competition on Sunday afternoon. I only had to run two cars. My first run was against the "B" winner. He had an El Camino with a 396 C.I. engine. He left the starting line too early, red-lighted, and was disqualified. One more run. I lined up against the "A" winner, a Ford Torino with a 429 Super Cobra Jet Engine. I knew he was very fast. He had to spot me about two seconds. That gave me a good head start, but he was coming on strong, and he roared by me, but too late. I had beaten him to the finish line by less than half a car length. That would be one of the highlights of my seven-year drag racing career. I was the North Carolina State Champion in bracket racing. I received a large championship trophy plus $100 in cash. Juanita was there to help celebrate my victory. I took my winnings and bought a new set of tires for the car.

By now, the entire laboratory department, and probably the whole hospital, knew that Juanita and I were lovers, and even though we were separated from our spouses, we were still married, and that didn't sit well with hospital administration. I was later to learn that Brenda had come to the lab and spread the word that Juanita had broken up our marriage, and many of them were convinced of that. The truth is, Juanita had nothing to do with our breaking up. Dr. Weaver, who was over the blood bank, approached me one day and told me that one of us would have to go. Juanita and I talked it over and decided that she would look for another job. It wasn't difficult. Our old boss, Dr. Steffee, had left and was now at Moore Memorial Hospital in Pinehurst. One call to Dr. Steffee, and Juanita was hired. She went to work in the hematology department right away. She needed a car, so she purchased a 1966 Mustang GT. It was blue with white interior. It had the 289 C.I. engine with a 4-barrel carburetor, rated at 225 horsepower.

Brenda and I were about ready to sign our separation agreement. I asked her if this was really what she wanted. I said, "I know we don't love each other anymore, but for the sake of the children, I'm still willing to keep the family together." She said, "No, things have gone much too far. You have Juanita now, and I hope it works out for you two." She was very generous with our agreement. All she wanted was the Falcon and her piano. She signed over her part of the house and the land, plus all the household goods. She would be moving back to Georgia soon and when that happened, Juanita would move in with me. Although she didn't have any children and probably never would, Juanita got along well with Harvey and Echo, and they loved "Miss" White.

I drove to Georgia one Friday when I had about three days off for a visit with my parents. They didn't know about Juanita, and I didn't know how she might be received, so she didn't go with me. She had given me a 5X7 picture of her sitting on a stool in a yellow dress, wearing one of her wigs and her beige boots. She looked so beautiful. That picture sat by my bed every night, and I had taken it with me to Georgia. My parents saw the picture and asked who it was. I told them she was a very special friend of mine and asked if they would like to meet her. They were receptive. I called Juanita that evening to say "good-night" and that I missed her. She said, "I miss you too." When I said it would have been OK with my parents if she had come with me, she said, "I'll be there tomorrow." I picked her up Saturday afternoon at the Albany Airport. She got along well with my parents, especially my dad.

This was my second year as President of the Lafayette Ford Drag Club, and Juanita had been elected treasurer. I had worked very hard to make it a good club. Every month I personally edited and published a newsletter that went out to all members, owner and general manager of the dealership, and a copy to our National Coordinator in Dearborn, Michigan. A national newsletter was also published, and there was almost always an article about our club. I was also actively recruiting new members at the drag strip every week, and I organized a special race each month for members only, called "King of the Strip". My hard work finally paid off when I received a call one day from Jon Brantmeier, National Coordinator, announcing that our club had been awarded National Club of the Month. I didn't accept a third term in office and unfortunately, the club folded in late 1971.

In the fall of 1970, Juanita moved in with me. It was almost the same distance to her job in Pinehurst as mine in Fayetteville, roughly 22 miles. The big difference was that most of her distance was through back roads, much through scarcely populated areas. One November evening as she was coming home from work, she spotted what looked like a group of eight or ten dogs crossing the road up ahead. As she got closer, she realized they were not dogs, but a herd of deer. She slowed down, and as they cleared the road, she speeded up again. Then as she reached the crossing, a straggler darted in her path, and there was no way to avoid hitting him. The grill of the Mustang was smashed, and the radiator was busted and shoved into the fan, and a young spiked buck was dead beside the road. As she was surveying the damage, a pick-up truck stopped and asked, "What's the problem?" She told him she hit a deer. Acting very suspicious, he said, "Well, where's the deer?" She said, "The little fellow is over there beside the road." The idiot wanted to know how she knew it was a fellow. She said, "Because he has antlers!" Then he told her he was the game warden and would have to take the deer. She had her doubts about that. Another car with two men stopped and the "warden" told her to get in the car with them and told them to take her to use a phone. She reluctantly got in the car with them, and they drove her to the nearest house, which was about a mile away. The driver told her to wait in the car while he went to the door. A lady came to the door, and the man asked, "Are you alone?" Juanita was already afraid, and when she heard that, she jumped from the car thinking this might be her only chance to get out of here before something really bad happened. She ran to the door and begged the lady to let her use her phone. She told me that she thought the lady saw the desperation in her face and thankfully, let her in. The men drove away. Juanita called me, and I rounded up a piece of rope and headed over there in a 1965 Mustang I had just bought. I tied the rope to her car and began towing her toward home, some 12 miles away. The rope broke several times before we reached home, and what started as a ten-foot rope was now only three or four feet between the two cars. The rope broke one final time as we pulled into the driveway. I was so thankful that my lovely lady was safely at home. We both gave thanks to the good Lord that night for keeping her safe. Instead of repairing that car, we got her another 1966 Fastback Mustang. This one was candy-apple red.

The day was Friday, December 18, 1970. It was one week before Christmas, and the laboratory was having its Christmas party that night at one of the local restaurants in Fayetteville. Juanita was off from work that day, and she had planned to get her hair done before we went to the party that evening. She was sleeping-in that morning as I kissed her forehead and walked out the door. My black '69 Mustang was under the carport, and her '66 pony car was parked directly behind. Rather than move her car, I decided to drive hers to work. We both carried keys to both cars, and she could drive mine when she got ready to leave. Little did I know that I would never drive my car again.

A light rain was falling when I left for work, and it was much heavier by the time Juanita headed out around mid-morning. My car was set up for maximum performance on the drag strip. It had 4.11 gears, positive traction, and cheater slicks on the rear. As she turned right on NC Highway 24, she began to accelerate up Cameron Hill. She noticed a stream of water flowing across the road in front of her. She did not realize that those cheater slicks had little to no traction on wet roads. When her rear wheels hit that water, the car began to fish-tail. Unable to control it, she went off the right side of the road, climbed the bank, and flipped upside down. Not wearing a seat belt, Juanita was thrown to the rear seat and as the car came to a rest, she was sitting in a pile of glass on the rear window. Crawling back to the front seat, she tried to open the door. It wouldn't open because it was jammed against the bank. She began to panic, then remembered there was another door. She tried it, and it opened. As she crawled out, she saw smoke rolling from the car and thought it was on fire and might explode. She quickly got away from the car. As it turned out, what she saw was steam from rain falling on the hot mufflers.

The accident occurred directly in front of the fire tower. The man who attended the tower saw the accident and came out to assist. He took Juanita to the hospital in Sanford. She was in shock, and her body had many scratches, bruises, and abrasions. After a thorough examination, it was determined that she had no serious injuries and was released. The man who took her to the hospital stayed with her and brought her home. She later told me that he tried to flirt with her at the emergency room and then tried to put the make on her when he brought her home. I said, "What a sorry SOB!"

As soon as she got home, she called me, and I rushed home to her. The first thing she said was, "I am so sorry about wrecking your car. I know how much you loved it." I said, "Honey, don't you worry about the car. I'm just glad you're OK. We can get another car, but I can't get another you." I hugged her, and she felt much better.

The State Trooper came to question her and to fill out an accident report. Then he charged her with improper equipment, because of the tires. I learned that the car had been towed to a garage in Lillington. I went to see it. It was destroyed. The top of the car was caved in on the driver's side, down to the headrest. It might have been a good thing she wasn't wearing a seat belt. Juanita lay in bed most of the day and then insisted we go to the Christmas Party. We went, and I think it was much to the surprise of some of my co-workers.

I needed another car quickly. We went to the Ford place and found a 1970 Mustang Fastback that had been driven as a demonstrator. The car was blue, and it had a 428 C.I. engine, rated at 335 horsepower. They offered it to us at a good price, and we took it. When we tried to get insurance, we ran into a problem. No one wanted to insure it. We finally found a company that insured it at a high premium, but at least we were able to get license plates.

Juanita had told me that she wanted to learn how to drive the car on the drag strip, and I promised to teach her the first of the year. I kept my promise. She learned quickly, and she was very good. In the spring we would go to the big National Ford Drag Club race in Maryland.

In February 1971, we were about to face another mishap. One

evening, Juanita took the '70 Mustang out for a joy ride. She loved all that power under the hood. While driving on a country road, she took, or tried to take a curve a little too fast, or maybe a lot too fast. The car left the road, missed a huge oak tree by inches, sailed through the air for 50 feet or so, and landed with such force that it broke the tie rod on the right front wheel. The wheel turned sideways, and the car skidded through a man's yard and stopped in the middle of his sweet potato patch. Juanita was afraid to get out of the car for fear of snakes in the potato vines. She began to blow the horn, and the man reluctantly came out and rescued her. We had the car towed to a garage for repair. Filing a claim with the insurance company, they told us that the policy had been cancelled. How could that be? We were not notified of any cancellation, nor was the NC Dept. of Motor Vehicles. We hired an attorney to look into the matter, and the insurance company produced some phony documents showing where we had been notified. It was obviously a fly-by-night company that would sell you a policy and then cancel it without notification. Unless you had an accident, you would never learn that the policy had been cancelled. We got the car repaired, but it was never the same again. I believe the frame was slightly bent. The wheels would never line up as they should have, and the tires did not wear properly.

Nevertheless, we took the car to Maryland in April and entered Juanita in the ladies' division race. There were quite a few entries, and the favorite was a lady who held the title of "Miss Universe of Drag Racing." The race got underway and Juanita was doing well, beating her first two opponents. Then she came up against "Miss Universe." The race was very close, but to everyone's surprise, Juanita nudged her out by a fender. One more run to make. On that final run, Juanita was up against a Chevy Vega. She had to spot the Vega by a full five seconds. By the time Juanita's green light came on, the Vega was almost halfway down the track. The Mustang broke traction badly off the starting line, and all you saw was a big cloud of blue smoke. With no chance to catch the Vega, it was over. Then the announcement came. The Vega had run too fast and was disqualified. Juanita was the 1971 East Coast Champion in the ladies' division. I was so proud of her.

At Moore Memorial Hospital, Juanita was working in the hematology department and was doing well. She was an excellent worker but was limited in what she could do because all her training had been OJT (on the job training). She had married at a very young age and never had the opportunity to attend any technical or vocational schools. She was always wanting to learn more, so when I was on call at night, she would come to my workplace, and I would give her classes, especially in hematology. She loved doing white cell differential counts, and she was an excellent student and learned quickly. That was actually her first experience at using the microscope. It paid off for her, because it wasn't long until Dr. Steffee had her reading slides on a cancer patient, because the registered techs didn't have the confidence. She was also able to work in the urinalysis department including reading the microscopics.

I had now been working at Cape Fear Valley Hospital for four years. In addition to working full time in the blood bank and teaching the students, I was accumulating a lot of overtime hours from working nights and weekends. There was one stretch where I worked 14 months without a day off. I recall one week where I worked 140 hours. That was a nice paycheck. Then one day, hospital administration decided to cut out all overtime. To help make up my lost wages, I took a job with the John Elliott Blood Bank, a commercial blood bank in downtown Fayetteville, as a phlebotomist. I collected blood from donors all day long each Saturday, earning $3.75 per hour, whereas I was earning $3.60 at Cape Fear. It was no doubt the hardest job I had ever had. There was always a line of people waiting to donate.

It still wasn't enough. We had two car payments, the house payment, land payment, and utilities. I went to Dr. Steffee, and he hired me to work nights at Moore Memorial. Juanita and I were getting by, but that was about it. Was our life always going to be a struggle? I didn't know. There were times when we didn't know what our next meal would be. There were few times when I would come home and shoot a rabbit for dinner; or we might go to the pond and catch a few fish. We loved each other very much, but I wanted so much more for my lovely lady. My divorce from Brenda was finally complete, but Juanita's husband didn't seem to be in any hurry to help her with their divorce.

In April 1972, Juanita came to me and said, "Honey, "I think I'm pregnant." I was stunned. "How can this be?", I asked. "I thought you couldn't get pregnant." Then she gave me another one of those brilliant answers. "I guess I just had the wrong man", she said. I couldn't argue with that.

It was confirmed. We were going to have a baby, and she already had the names picked out. A boy would be Johnny David Wills, Jr., "Little Johnny", and a girl would be Kelly Denise, a dream she had had for a very long time.

We made the decision to give up drag racing, and we sold the 1970 Mustang. That would be one less payment we would have. We still had three cars. In addition to Juanita's 1966, I had a 1965 and a 1967. All our Mustangs were fastbacks. I wanted to eventually have one from every year, because I just knew they would someday be a good investment, and they would have been, but unfortunately, we weren't able to keep them that long.

Juanita and I had both grown up in church-going families, but neither of us had gone in a long time. One day we said, " Let's start going to church." Since our parents had been Primitive Baptist, we began looking, and found several, all of which were some 40 miles away. We settled on two that we liked, one in Angier and one in Coats and started going regularly. They had a wonderful pastor, Elder Lawrence. We visited at his home a few times and talked about the possibility of joining the church. That didn't work out well, but we continued to go to church almost every Sunday.

At the blood bank, we regularly got visits from representatives of pharmaceutical companies, the ones who provided us with products for typing blood and for detecting and identifying irregular antibodies. We were still purchasing a small amount of blood from Knoxville Blood Center. One day their sales rep, Ty Foster, walked in, and during the course of our conversation, he said, "We are looking for a good quality Anti-Lewis-B antibody. Do you by any chance have one or know one?" I told him I had never even seen a strong Anti-Lewis-B. He said, "Well, if you ever run across one, let me know. You can just about name your own price for it." I said, "OK", and thought no more about it.

A week passed. Then one day I had a request to prepare two pints of blood for a 16-year old girl who had just delivered a baby. She was a type B+, so I selected two pints of B+ blood and performed a crossmatch. One of the pints was grossly incompatible. That told me that this girl had some type of irregular antibody. Now I had to identify it and try to find some blood that would be compatible. I was always guessing what the identify of an antibody would be, and many times I would be right, but this time I was dead wrong. It turned out to be an anti-Lewis-B, the strongest one I had ever seen. This was amazing! I remembered what Ty Foster had said, but then I thought; this girl is only 16, she can't be a donor until she's 18.

I got on the phone with Mr. Foster and told him what I had. He said, "Send me a sample. If it's as good as you say, we can get her parents to sign for her to donate." Later that day, I went to see the patient. She was a black girl, pretty, and just as friendly as could be. Her name was Gwendolyn Bratcher. I tried to explain what she had and told her that it could be valuable to her, although I don't think she understood. I got her address and phone number, and she said I could call if I needed to.

A few days went by, and I received a call from Ty Foster. He said, "We've got to get that girl to Knoxville." I said, "I assume you liked my antibody?" He said, "It far exceeded my expectations." She would have to wait six weeks after her delivery, then Ty would send two round-trip tickets, so she and I could fly to Knoxville for her first plasmapheresis. In the meantime, I would get a written consent from one of her parents, so she could donate.

I drove the twenty miles to the Bratcher residence, where I met with Gwen and her parents. Johnny Bratcher was a very nice and friendly young man, not much older than me. After I explained to the family what we wanted to do, they were agreeable, and Mr. Bratcher signed the consent form. I told Gwen that whatever we got paid, we would split the money. She was agreeable.

We boarded a Piedmont Airlines plane and headed to Knoxville. This was Gwen's first time to fly, and she was a little apprehensive, but she did fine. Arriving at the blood center, a medical history was taken, and she had a brief physical exam by the center's physician. Plasmapheresis is a procedure whereby a pint of blood is taken; a saline drip is started, and the blood is centrifuged to separate the plasma from the red blood cells. Then the plasma is transferred to another container, and the red cells are returned to the donor. A pint of blood will yield about 300 to 350 milliliters of plasma. That's where the antibodies are found. The procedure takes about half an hour. The FDA allows plasmapheresis to be performed twice a week. This is possible because all the red cells are returned to the donor. They only lose the plasma which is primary water with a little protein. The protein is rapidly replaced by the body.

Ty had the cashier cut me a check for $300.00, and we headed to the airport for our trip home. I paid her $150.00 in cash. She softly said, "Thank you" and gave me a big smile. I could tell she was very happy, and so was I.

The following week, Ty Foster called. "We need to draw this donor once a week", he said. Since we wouldn't need another physical exam for a year, he suggested that I perform the plasmapheresis and ship the plasma to him. I told him I would, but he would need to send me the necessary supplies. This was sounding too good to be true.

I immediately quit my Saturday job at John Elliott Blood Bank, so I could work with Miss Bratcher on Saturday afternoon when no one would be in the donor room. Earning $150.00 for a couple hours work was a whole lot better than the $30.00 I was earning at John Elliott for a full day's work. I called Gwen and told her my plan, and she was thrilled.

The anti-Lewis-B antibody in her plasma was used to manufacture anti-Lewis-B blood typing serum and was essential to every blood bank in the world. It was used to select compatible blood for those patients having the Lewis-B antibody, and there were many of them. At this time, Gwen was the only known donor in the world whose antibody was strong enough for commercial use. How lucky could I be?

Juanita's divorce became final in May, and we began making plans for our wedding. We decided on Saturday, June 3rd for our special day, and we asked the pastor of Hillmon Grove Baptist Church to officiate the wedding. We would be married at our home with my parents, my children Harvey and Echo, a few friends, and co-workers invited. To me it was a very simple, but beautiful wedding. Juanita walked down the hallway in her long, pink dress to meet me in front of the TV in the living room where the pastor conducted the ceremony.

Juanita had been transferred to the blood bank because of her experience, and her boss lady, Mrs. Jackson, set up a very nice reception in our kitchen and dining area. My parents and children spent the night with us. Since we had limited sleeping space, we gave our bed to my parents, and we spent our first night of marriage on the living room floor. There was no honeymoon, because I had to go to work the following morning. Our honeymoon would come later. I was so happy. My dream had finally come true.

Gwen and I continued to split that $300.00 for several weeks. It was exactly what Juanita and I needed because we were struggling to make ends meet, and our baby was due in November. Gwen had more money than she had ever dreamed of having.

Then one day my boss called me in and told me that I would have to stop collecting plasma in the hospital blood bank, because it was not in the best interest of the hospital. This was bad news for me. What could I do? I didn't want to have to fly to Knoxville every week. Then it dawned on me. "There was a large commercial plasma center downtown. Maybe for a small fee, they would let me draw my donor there." It was certainly worth a try.

I walked into the Beta Plasma Center and told them what I wanted to do. When they learned I was the Blood Bank Supervisor at Cape Fear Hospital, they were more than willing to oblige me at no charge. Then I realized that they thought this was a hospital function, and they wanted to establish a good relationship. I wasn't about to tell them that this was my own enterprise. I would continue to use their facility for more than five years.

In the latter part of summer 1972, I found what looked like a good quality ant-Lewis-A and wondered if it might be valuable. I called Ty, and he said it could be, but we probably couldn't use it as often as the Lewis-B. I sent him a sample, and we got an order for one donation per month. He also told me to send samples of any other antibodies I might have that was of good quality. I did, and it wasn't long before I was also collecting plasma from two more donors, an anti-c (little c) and anti-E (big E). Now, instead of $600.00 per month, I was earning about $1500.00 per month. That's when I gave up my night job at Moore Memorial Hospital. We opened a savings account and began to put some money aside. When I got my form 1099 from Knoxville

Blood Center, I had earned more from working on Saturdays than I had earned from two full time jobs. I couldn't believe what luck I was having! Juanita and I were thankful for our good fortune, and we continued to go to church almost every Sunday.

In the fall of '72, we got a big surprise. Juanita's sister Jewell showed up with her three children. Juanita had not seen them for quite some time. I remember showing her Kelly's room which we had prepared for her arrival in November. I recall Jewell saying, "I have a feeling she's going to be a very lucky little girl." Her prediction was right.

It was Saturday, November 4, 1972. Early that morning Juanita said, "Honey, I'm having labor pains." The time had come. We headed off to the hospital. After going through hours of pain, the contractions were getting closer and closer, and she was taken into the delivery room. Her obstetrician, Dr. Gardner, was called in off the golf course to deliver our baby. When he walked into the room, Juanita said, " Dr. Gardner, those surely are some sexy pants you're wearing." I was grinning and thinking, "Leave it to Juanita; she always knows what to say." I held her hand tightly as she suffered through death-like pain. Then the pain turned to joy as it was over, and I said, "Honey, Kelly Denise is here." Raising her head to take her first look at our baby, Juanita said, "She's got a pointed head." Dr. Gardner said, "I can fix that", and he began to mold her head as if it was modeling clay. We were both thinking, "Oh God, he's going to kill our baby!" But she was very much alive and crying to prove it.

On the OB ward, Juanita was receiving preferential treatment! Wow! We couldn't figure it out. Sure, I worked in the lab, but that wouldn't matter to them. Then it finally came to us. They thought she was the wife of the Chief Pathologist and Lab Director, Dr. Charles Wells. People were always getting my name wrong, calling me "Wells" or "Willis". I always thought my name, "Wills", was a pretty simple name, but I guess it wasn't. This was one time I didn't mind someone getting it wrong.

We spent Christmas at home and then decided to go to Georgia for New Year's and show off our new addition to the family. We packed our bags and headed out in our best car, Juanita's 1966 red Mustang. Kelly was snug and warm in her bassinette in the back seat. We had a nice visit with my parents and other relatives. I don't recall for sure, but I believe we left my parents' home right after lunch on Tuesday, January

2nd. We figured on being home in the vicinity of 9 PM. The weather was very cold. We reached Augusta around 5 PM, and it was already beginning to get dark. As we crossed the state line and into South Carolina, big, fluffy snowflakes began to hit the windshield. We had not expected that. It was obvious that we had not heard the forecast. The heater and defroster in the old car were not very good, and it was unable to keep the car warm or the windshield clear. Kelly was wrapped warmly in her bassinette, and Juanita draped a blanket loosely over the top of it to keep the cold air off her little face. The snow was very heavy, causing very poor visibility, and it was difficult to see the road. Going was extremely slow, and occasionally we would have to stop and scrape ice from the windshield. By the time we reached Cheraw, near the North Carolina border, there were at least five inches of snow on the ground, and it was already 10 PM. We continued our journey toward home. The snow didn't let up, and there was little traffic on the road. We became very concerned that we might become stranded and not be able to make it home that night. When we reached Cameron, we began to follow a snow plow on NC Hwy 24. Thank goodness! This would get us to within two miles of home. But when we reached the county line, just 4 miles down the road, the snow plow turned around and went back the other way. There were now seven or eight inches of snow on the ground, and on Rambo Hill, we hit two drifts that must have been two feet deep. I really didn't think we'd make it through, but I managed to build up a little speed, and we made it, with snow coming up over the hood of the car. Thank God! We finally made it home. It was 3 AM. What would have normally been a nine-hour drive, had taken 15 hours.

Late in the afternoon of May 6, 1973, the phone rang. I answered, and it was my Dad. That was unusual, because he rarely called. He told me that my brother's only son, Melvin, Jr., had been involved in an accident. He, his wife, and their seven-month-old daughter had all been killed. While driving near Albany in their Volkswagen Beetle, a car had veered into their lane and hit them head-on. It was the worst tragedy to ever occur in our family. I'll never forget the funeral. It was the saddest I have ever attended. First, they rolled in the two adult caskets, then the little casket with the baby. When that happened, my sister-in-law, Faye, completely lost it, crying out, "That's my baby! That's my baby." Melvin,

Jr. was just 22 years old. He had already served in the U.S. Army and had such great plans for the future. I had seen him four months earlier while we were visiting my parents. I remember how impressed I was while talking with him. He was a very smart man. Melvin and Faye never got over it. My brother, Melvin, passed away in July 2014, just days before his 86th birthday.

I was still doing plasmapheresis on my antibody donors, although it had slowed down a little. I often dreamed of someday having my own plasma center and specializing in nothing but rare antibody donors. I had heard that there were only 15 such centers in the world, and they were all in the United States. I knew there were lots of people walking around out there with gold in their veins, but most of them would never know it. That business was also tightly regulated by the FDA, and it was difficult to obtain a license. Oh well, I could still dream.

I was now working the one job at Cape Fear Hospital, but with the extra money coming in from my plasma donors, Juanita was able to stay home with the baby. She was a good mother and housekeeper, and she enjoyed working outside doing things like cutting the grass with our riding mower, planting flowers, and raking the yard. We also planted a large garden and a patch of corn. It was a lot of work tending the garden, but we always had plenty of fresh vegetables, and we had extra for canning and freezing.

As a member of the North Carolina Association of Blood Bankers, I always attended the state conventions and also the national convention whenever possible. In 1975 our state convention was being held in Charlotte. As we were preparing to leave home and head to the convention that Friday morning, I suddenly began to run a fever, and I was having chills. I was obviously getting sick and probably should have stayed home, but we went anyway. That was a mistake. I felt really bad the entire weekend, and my chills and fever continued. On Monday morning when I got up, I suddenly had a severe pain in my abdomen, worse than any pain I had ever had. I said to Juanita, "Honey, you've got to take me to the doctor." Arriving at my personal physician's office, the nurse made a snappy diagnosis that was completely uncalled for. She said, "Oh, you've got a stomach ulcer. Everybody's going to get one sooner or later." I didn't think so and neither did my physician. My pain was almost unbearable, and I received a shot of morphine. It stopped the pain, but I became extremely nauseated. I was admitted to Highsmith Hospital where I spent nine days. I was deathly sick, and my wife told me later that she thought I was going to die. I was 36 years old, but that illness seemed to have aged me at least 20 years. I lost 20 pounds, and I looked like an old man. Juanita and Kelly came to see me every day, but I looked so old and so bad that Kelly didn't recognize me and would run. My doctor couldn't make a positive diagnosis. He suspected Rocky Mountain Spotted Fever but couldn't prove it. Returning home, I had trouble sleeping. I would wake up every night at 3 AM and couldn't go back to sleep. It gradually got better, and after several weeks everything seemed to have returned to normal.

Several years later, I went to the doctor with a case of shingles. He also did a test for Rocky Mountain Spotted Fever, and I had an extremely high antibody titer, confirming that I had previously had the disease.

After I had recovered from my illness, I was outside one day when I noticed some people surveying the land next to us. I walked over and inquired as to what they were doing. The owner said that he was cutting off 20 acres next to me and putting it up for sale. Our home was isolated with no other houses in sight, and we wanted to keep it that way. I certainly didn't like the idea of someone building next door to me, especially not knowing who it might be. I asked, "How much?" He said, "$11,000." That was almost double what I had paid for my original 19 acres just nine years earlier. I wanted that land, but Juanita and I only had about $6000 that we had managed to save from our antibody donors. I knew the bank wouldn't lend money on undeveloped land, so my only hope was to get someone to share the cost with me. I got lucky. One of my co-workers was interested in investing in some land, so he agreed to put up half the money. As it turned out, when they finished the survey, there were only 17 acres. The owner still insisted on $11,000. We bought it and cut it in half with me getting the 8.5 acres next to us. A few years later we bought the other 8.5 acres from my friend. About a third of the land was cleared, so now we could plant an even larger garden.

Beginning in 1972, my children, Harvey and Echo were coming for a month-long visit each summer. Juanita was doing an excellent job with our daughter Kelly, but she had never had experience with children, and it was a different story with Harvey and Echo. I think they resented her trying to discipline them. She was doing the best she could by them, and I thought she was doing just fine, although I guess they didn't think so. Maybe it was because she was not their real mother, or maybe they were used to having their way at home.

Although Juanita looked like a perfect picture of health, she was not. As a child she had been diagnosed with a rare respiratory disease called bronchiectasis and had had lung surgery twice, at age 10 and again at age 25. She was on death's doorsteps in both cases. She was also a smoker, having started as a teenager. She was now smoking nearly two packs per day. When Kelly was two years old, Juanita began to feel bad and was losing weight. One day she realized, "If I don't quit smoking, I won't live to see my daughter grow up." With that thought in mind, she laid down the cigarettes, never to pick them up again. I was so proud of her. I couldn't bear the thought of ever being without my lovely wife.

In 1975, we got some new neighbors. C.W. and Edna Johnson moved into a mobile home directly across the road from us. They had two very small children, Ammia and Jamie. We developed a lifelong friendship with them. They were more like family than friends. Kelly was slightly older than Ammia and Jamie, but they were like sisters, and they spent many hours together as they grew up. Edna had a civil service job, working in housing at Ft. Bragg, and C.W. did all sorts of things from farming, working with heavy equipment, or just being a handyman. Edna's job eventually took them to Germany and finally to Ft. Knox, KY, where they bought a home in Radcliff and settled down there. We would continue our friendship and visits over the coming years.

Not only was Juanita a beautiful woman, she was also very friendly, and still is for that matter. I don't think she's ever met a stranger. She loves talking to people, especially when she's in a check-out line, and she loves talking to the cashiers, especially the grouchy ones and those who never smile. She will make them smile almost every time. The problem is, there are certain men who think that if a woman smiles at him or talks to him, she is flirting and wants to crawl in the sack with him. One such case comes to mind when Kelly was a baby. We had a

TV repairman come out to work on our TV. I'm sure Juanita was friendly and talked to him as she always did, but this guy drove back to see her the following day and tried to put the make on her. He gave her some story like his wife is in the hospital having a baby and he hasn't been with a woman for a long time. Thank God, she didn't unlock the screen door. She called and told me about it. To say I was mad would be an understatement. I had to find this guy. He had only given his first name and the receipt had three initials, S.S.S.

I called the store and asked for Scottie. He was on a service call and wasn't expected back that day. That night I looked in the phone book and found a Scot S. S----------. I dialed the number and asked if he was the TV repairman. He was, and I told him I knew he had been to my home that day. He said, "I don't know what you're talking about." I said, "You know damn well what I'm talking about. You better listen really good and you better not hang up. My wife is a decent lady. She's not like you. You should be ashamed of yourself. You have a good wife that just came home from the hospital with your new baby, and by the way, It's a cute baby." He didn't know what to say. I could hear his wife in the background, "Who is that Scottie? Who is that?" He said, "A customer." I said, "I'm going to forget about it this time, but don't you ever set foot on my property again, and I mean that." He said, "Thank you sir! I really appreciate that."

In the spring of 1976, my brother Jimmy called and asked if I would like to go with him and Daddy on a fishing trip to Florida. Several years earlier, Dad had bought a 16-foot boat with an outboard motor, and he enjoyed fishing along the Florida Gulf Coast every chance he got. We picked a weekend that would be convenient for all, and Juanita, Kelly, and I headed to Georgia on a Friday. Dad and Jimmy had everything ready to go, so we retired early, arose at 3 AM and headed out. We checked in at a fishing camp on the St. Marks River on the Florida Panhandle. From the camp, we traveled a mile or so down the river, where it widened to a half mile or more at the mouth and emptied into the Gulf of Mexico. Large oyster beds could be seen in the mouth of the river. Reaching open water, we headed east for a couple of miles. Fishing was great. By noon we had almost filled the cooler with speckled trout. We had a great lunch of pork and beans, sardines, and saltines. We continued fishing and had planned to go in around 3 PM and head home. At around 2 PM, the sky in the west began to turn dark. Dad said, "Boys, there's a storm coming. We need to head back." Jimmy and I were having such a good time catching fish, that we wanted to stay a little longer. That was a big mistake. The storm was moving toward us in a hurry, and we had to head in that direction to get back to the mouth of the river. Running at full speed, we were almost to the river when the wind picked up, and we had four to six-foot waves splashing over the side of the boat. Daddy never wore a life preserver, and I was becoming a bit nervous. I said, "Daddy, don't you think we should put on our life jackets?" He said, "No. I don't think that's necessary. We can ride this out OK." By now the rain was coming down in sheets, and we had virtually no visibility. We were being violently tossed around by the wind and waves. Suddenly I heard the sound of a motor behind us. I couldn't see it, but I knew it was close and only slightly to our left. I shouted, "Daddy, hard right!" At that moment, a boat running full speed shot by within 20 feet of us. A minute or two later the rain let up, and as I wiped the fog from mine and Dad's glasses, we could see again. We were dangerously close to an oyster bed. What could have been a great tragedy, turned out to have a happy ending.

Juanita, Kelly, and I traveled to Georgia for the celebration of my parents' Golden Wedding Anniversary on August 21, 1977. I had a special plaque made for them, from all their children and their families. Today that plaque hangs on the wall of our home. It was a wonderful celebration, and they received many nice gifts from family and friends. That visit might very well be the best memory that Kelly has of "Granddaddy Wills." That night as she was drawing, the point of her pencil broke. Granddaddy called her over, took out his pocket knife and sharpened her pencil. Kelly will always remember him for that.

Three months later, on a Sunday morning, in November, Daddy arose, had breakfast, got dressed in his suit and tie, then kissed Mama good-bye and headed off to the morning service at Liberty Primitive Baptist Church, near Americus. Mama couldn't go, because there was no one else to stay with Jerry, my mentally retarded brother. That would be the last time Mama would see my father alive.

That afternoon, I received a phone call from my brother, Don. He said, "Johnny, Daddy was in an automobile accident today. I hate to have to tell you this, but he didn't make it." My reply was, "Oh no, Don!" I was devastated. I have no idea what else was said, except I told him we would come as soon as we could. I was in no condition to drive that night, so we decided to leave early the following morning.

No one knows exactly what happened, but from the information I could obtain and the evidence I observed, this is what I think happened. My father had left the church to return home. As he approached the intersection with GA Hwy 45, the road that runs from Plains to Dawson, he failed to stop at the stop sign. A couple from Florida with their two grandchildren in the back seat, who had been visiting President Jimmy Carter's hometown, was traveling toward Dawson. They reached the intersection at the same time as my Dad. He crashed into the center of the driver's side of their car. The impact caused their car to veer off the right side of the road and come to a rest about 100 yards away. Daddy's Maverick was spun around 180 degrees and went off the road backwards. My father was a smart man, but there were two things he wouldn't do: wear a life preserver or wear a seat belt. Dad hit the steering wheel with such force that his chest was crushed against his heart and lungs. A church member stopped by minutes later and asked, "Bernard, how're you doing?" Dad said, "I'm hurting."

The driver of the other car was killed. His wife was injured; I believe the most serious was a fractured leg. Their two grandchildren were unhurt. An ambulance came and took my Dad and the lady to the local hospital in Dawson. The emergency room attendant took one look at my Dad and said, "We can't help him here." I don't know who made the decision, but they decided to take them to the Columbus Medical Center in Columbus, which was 64 miles away. It would take more than an hour to reach the Medical Center. The lady told us later that she talked with my dad all the way to the hospital, and as they pulled up to the emergency room, my father took his last breath. He was dead at the age of 69. Columbus Medical Center has a great reputation, but my father needed help in a hurry. They could have taken him to one of the large hospitals in Albany, which was only 23 miles away. Had they done that, they possibly could have saved his life. My mother was devastated. Even though they had a very hard life, my mother loved him very much, having married at age 17. He was the only man she ever had, and she never wanted another after that. She lived for nine more years.

By late 1977, my antibody business had really slowed down, and my dreams of ever having my own plasma center were dwindling away. Then, one day I received a letter addressed to the blood bank supervisor. The return address caught my eye. It was from the "Antibody Search of Florida". The letter said they were a highly specialized plasma center, and they needed and were looking for rare blood group antibodies. They were offering a finder's fee to anyone who could provide a donor to them. They gave a list of donors they needed, but the two at the top of the list were what caught my eye. It said that for an anti-C (Big C), they would pay $3000 and for an anti-e (Little e), $2000. I didn't have either, nor had I seen either, at least in commercial quality. The letter was signed, Dr. Bill Page, Immuno-hematologist. I was curious, so I gave him a call and told him I had been working with some rare antibodies for the past few years, and I told him what I had. He asked me to send him samples, and he would determine if he could use any of them. I never heard from him, so I assumed he wasn't interested.

Around the end of January 1978, something almost miraculous happened. I detected and identified an anti-C antibody, strong and pure. Then I remembered Bill Page. He would pay me $3000 for this donor. I got Bill on the phone and told him what I had. He said, "I'll believe it when I see it. Send me a sample." A sample went out in the mail that afternoon. In the meantime, I began thinking. If he will pay me $3000 for this donor, it must be a gold mine to him. Two days later, he received my sample and told his technician to test it while he was at lunch. When he returned and saw the results, he picked up the phone and began dialing. He said, "John, we've got to get together and talk. I want you and your wife to come to Jacksonville for the weekend, or if you prefer, I can come to North Carolina, and we can go on a skiing trip. Since I didn't ski, I told him we would come to Florida. He said, "Great, which airport will you be flying out of?" I said, "Raleigh-Durham." He said, "I'll overnight two fist class tickets to you and have accommodations for you for Friday and Saturday nights." I said. "Bill, we don't need to fly first class." He told me, "I don't fly anything but first class and neither do my clients." On Friday morning, we drove to Hillsville, VA. Our 5-year old daughter Kelly would be staying with Juanita's mother while we were gone. We drove back to RDU airport and boarded an Eastern Airlines flight to Jacksonville with one stop in Atlanta.

Tony, the Vice President of the company, met us at the airport in a Cadillac Deville and drove us to Atlantic Beach. The executive suite in one of the finest hotels on the beach was waiting for us. Tony said he would pick us up at 6 PM, and we would go out to eat. Juanita and I were not accustomed to this type of treatment, to say the least. Tony and his girlfriend were there at six, and we went to a fancy seafood buffet restaurant. They had every imaginable seafood dish, and we thoroughly enjoyed the evening with a fun couple. Tony said he would pick me up at 8 AM on Saturday and take me to meet with Dr. Bill Page. It was hard to believe this was happening.

While Juanita was sleeping in on Saturday morning, I was on the way to meet with Dr. Bill Page. I questioned Tony about the doctor, and I learned that in fact, he was not a doctor but used that in his letters that he sent out to hospital blood banks. Bill Page was a medical technologist who specialized in blood banking, as I did.

The center was very impressive. As I walked into the reception area, there was a fountain with goldfish and nice plants, definitely not your typical medical office. Bill Page was a handsome, blonde haired gentleman in his mid-40s. He was strictly business, and he got right to the point. He said, "I'll write you a check right now for $3000 for that anti-C donor." I said, " No, I don't think so Bill. I believe she's worth a lot more than that." He looked at me, probably remembering that I told him I had been involved with rare antibody donors for several years. He said, "OK, here's what we can do. I'll do the plasmapheresis and market the plasma. Then we'll take out the expenses and split the profit." I couldn't ask for any more than that, so I said, "It's a deal." I would fly with the donor to Jacksonville for her medical exam and first plasma donation. After that I would perform the plasmapheresis at the Beta Plasma Center in Fayetteville and ship the plasma to him. Bill sold the first two donations, and after expenses we each had about $3500. Bill said that there was such a high demand for this antibody that we could continue collecting plasma twice each week. I was so lucky to have found this donor and to have found Bill Page. Bill said that we would have to be very careful with this donor, because it was highly possible that one of our competitors might try to steal her away from us. He said that from his experience, the best way to keep her was to buy her a new car with the understanding that it was hers as long as she donated for us. That following week I took her car shopping. She finally settled on a 1978 Mercury Cougar, XR-7. The price was just under $10,000. She was thrilled with her new car, but no one could have been happier than Juanita and me. In our first month, we made more money than the two of us combined had made in a full year, when we were both working. Juanita and I were still driving her 1966 Mustang, and we had purchased a 1972 Pinto Wagon in 1974, so we decided it was time for us to have a new car. We went out and bought a 1978 Thunderbird. That was during the time when the Thunderbird was a full-sized car. What had we done to deserve our good fortune? Almost every Sunday we were at church, thanking the Lord for our blessings.

One day, I received a call from the Beta Plasma Center. They were having a meeting with the regional manager and he wanted me to attend. I had no idea why they wanted me there, but I went. During the meeting, the regional manager said, "John we want to offer you the job of manager of our center in Fayetteville. You will still be able to bring in your antibody donors for plasmapheresis." A thought went quickly through my mind, "If I become an employee there, my donors won't be mine much longer, or he will certainly want his share of the profit. I also knew this job was nowhere near as secure as the one at the hospital." So, I said, "Thanks, but no thanks. I'm happy with my job at the hospital." He went berserk at that point saying, "Then you are no longer welcome to draw your donors here!" Somehow, he had found out that my donors had no connection with the hospital. I walked away knowing that I now had a major problem. I had to have a place to draw my donors.

The next morning, I called Bill Page. I said, "Bill, I got a little problem. Beta Plasma Center will no longer let me use their facility for drawing our donors." He said, "That's not a little problem, that's a major problem. Let me think about it and I'll get back to you." There was only one solution. We would have to draw the donors in Jacksonville. Our anti-C donor, the big money maker, was being drawn twice a week, the maximum allowed by the FDA, however, it couldn't be on two consecutive days. There had to be at least one day between donations. That meant our donor would have to drive or fly to Jacksonville on Friday, have her plasma collected, spend two nights in a motel, donate again on Sunday, and return home. Doing this every weekend would get old in a hurry, but we had no other choice. Also, sooner or later I would have to travel with some of the donors or personally drive them there. And it happened very soon. I had to drive a new donor to Jax one weekend, so she could get her medical exam and begin donating. It was on that trip that Bill Page made a proposal that I never saw coming.

He said, "John, how would you like to open a plasma center in Fayetteville?" That was a dream I had had for a long time, but I didn't have the know how or the resources to do so. I said, "You've got to be kidding. I wouldn't know where to start, and besides, I don't have the money it would take to do that." Apparently, he had it all figured out. He said, "Sure you do. You can have a center just like this one. We can finance it with your anti-C donor." He said we would be partners, and we would each have 50 percent of the stock in the business. His plan was something like this: first we would hire an attorney to form a corporation called "Antibody Search of North Carolina", then we would find a suitable location, rent it, and furnish it one month at a time. In the first month, we would make a nice reception area, including a waiting room, desk and phone, chair for screening potential donors and taking blood samples, get the equipment for a small lab, and the reagents needed for testing blood. Month number two we would furnish the donor room, and on subsequent months, the centrifuge room, doctor's office, refrigerator and freezer room, and my office. We also had to have a medical director, so I would need to look for a physician to fill that position. We would immediately start preparing the SOP (standard operating procedure) which would have to accompany our application for a license to the FDA. He said it would take four to six months to obtain a license. After the FDA approved our SOP, they would come and physically inspect our facility. At that time, we would have to be fully operational, including drawing donors. We could do everything without the license except sell and ship plasma. Therefore, we would have to continue drawing the big money donors in Jacksonville.

I said, "Bill this is a huge undertaking. I need time to think this over. I'll get back to you in a few days." Juanita and I began talking it over. We would be taking a big chance. What if it didn't work out? Our biggest concern was me giving up my job at Cape Fear Valley Hospital, where I had worked for 12 years and had already started building up retirement. I had already given up a ten-year military career. That one I didn't regret. Had I not done that, I wouldn't have my wonderful wife and little Kelly, who was now in pre-K at St. Luke's in Sanford. Juanita said, "Whatever you decide, I'm with you." I couldn't ask for more.

CHAPTER 16

Let's Go for It!

THE DECISION WAS made. In April 1978, I would say good-bye to 12 years and 2 months at Cape Fear Valley Hospital and would go in business with Bill Page of Jacksonville, Florida to open a highly specialized blood plasma center in Fayetteville, North Carolina. I had dreamed of this for the past six years, not necessarily with a partner, but this could very well be my only chance in life to make my dream a reality.

I contacted an attorney, Hank Whitman, and we put in an application to become incorporated as "Antibody Search of North Carolina". Bill and I would be equal partners. I found a suitable location on Owen Drive, just a quarter of a mile from the hospital. The building had once been a church. I made a comment that I couldn't go wrong setting up a business in a church. It was a large open room, but the owner said he would construct it to my specifications. I drew up a floor plan exactly as I wanted it, and work began. It was completed in about 30 days. I wanted to get my application in to the FDA as soon as possible, so I hired a secretary from the hospital lab, who was also a friend, to type my standard operation procedure manual, using the one from the Jacksonville center. All we had to do was change the name from Florida to North Carolina. Debbie was very efficient, and she had it done in a couple of days.

Now it was time to do a little shopping. Juanita and I went to a rental company where we rented furniture for the waiting room along with four desks; a small desk for the reception room, an executive desk for myself, one for the medical director, and a secretary's desk. We rented with the option to buy, which we did later. Then we contacted a medical supply company and purchased a "Vampire" chair for collecting blood samples, plus the equipment for our lab. We purchased a small refrigerator and contacted a pharmaceutical company for our blood typing serum and reagents for detecting and identifying antibodies. We were now in our second month.

To better help the reader understand what we were doing, let me give a brief lesson on antigens and antibodies. Everyone's red blood cells look the same, shaped like bi-concave discs, but just as with people, no two are alike, except in identical twins. You can't see them, but there are hundreds of antigens found on the surface of red blood cells. Most are unimportant, but some are very important. The most important being antigen "A" and antigen "B". These two antigens determine if a person is blood group A, B, O, or AB. A person who is blood group "A" has the "A" antigen on his red blood cells. A group "B" person has "B" **antigens** on his red cells. Group "AB" has both antigens on his red cells, and a group "O" has neither antigen. Antibodies are found in the plasma or liquid portion of the blood. Someone with group "A" blood always has anti-B antibodies, group "B" will always have anti-A antibodies, group "AB" has neither antibody, and group "O" has both anti-A and anti-B. Now you can see why you can't give group A blood to a group B patient. His anti-A antibodies would attack the group A red cells causing a severe reaction, which could even result in death. In an emergency situation, group O can be given to anyone because it has no antigens for the antibodies to attack. On the other hand, group AB is known as the universal recipient, because it has no antibodies to attack red cells. Anti-A and anti-B are known as regular antibodies because they are always present in the absence of the corresponding antigen. These are the only two regular antibodies.

The third most important antigen is the Rho (D) antigen. It is found on the red blood cells of 85% of the population, and those persons are classified as Rh-positive. The other 15% do not have the Rho (D) antigen and are said to be Rh-negative. There are no natural occurring anti-Rho (D) antibodies. It is not acceptable to give Rh-positive blood to a Rh-negative patient, because it could cause him to produce anti-Rh antibodies. That type of antibody is called an immune antibody, also known as an irregular antibody.

In our business we were only interested in the irregular or immune antibodies. There are only two ways they can occur. One is by a blood transfusion and the other is through pregnancy. Since more women become pregnant than persons who are transfused, we would expect to find most of our antibodies in women, and that was certainly the case. So far, all our donors were female. By far, the, most common of these irregular antibodies is the anti-Rh, hereafter called anti-D. If we could find 20 or 30 anti-D donors and perform plasmapheresis on them twice a week, it would be enough to pay the bills. Then, the rare donors would be all profit after paying the donor fees. It was time to go to work.

Now that we had the reception area and lab ready, we could begin testing potential donors. After having our phone installed, we ran an ad in the local paper. It read something like this:

WANTED

Women who have had multiple pregnancies
and persons who have received multiple blood
transfusions. Also, those with known antibodies.

The phone began to ring as soon as the paper was delivered. Juanita was taking the calls, answering questions, and setting up appointments for people to be tested. We hired Marijane Haley as a lab tech to do the antibody screens and identifications. Only a small percentage of those being tested would have an antibody, and we would keep them on file for donating as soon as we could get the donor room and centrifuge room equipped. We also had to have a large commercial refrigerator and freezer.

I didn't know a lot about Bill Page. He had been extremely generous and came across as having almost unlimited funds. We had flown first class, stayed in the executive suite at one of the finest hotels in Atlantic Beach, and they wined and dined us at a fine restaurant. He had a very nice plasma center. He drove a new Cadillac, and his wife drove a new Lincoln. His family all worked at the center: his wife Joy, his son, his son's girlfriend, and his adopted son Mack. Only Tony, the vice president, was an outsider. Beyond that, I knew very little about Bill Page but was about to learn a lot more.

He called one day to let me know that the American Association of Blood Banks would be holding its annual convention in New Orleans in about two weeks. I already knew that, and Juanita and I had talked about going, even before I left the hospital. We had not been to a national meeting since Washington, DC in 1972. Bill said he wanted us to go, because we could meet many potential buyers. That sounded reasonable, so we began to make plans for the trip. Marijane could handle things while we were gone.

Arriving at the convention site, I found Bill at the bar drinking Bacardi and Coke and eating raw oysters on the half shell. He told me that he brought the entire family with him and that they would be going out to eat and wanted Juanita and me to join them.

During our conversation at dinner, we learned that he had gone out and purchased two new vans just for this trip. I didn't like the way that sounded. The big surprise came when he asked me to pay the entire bill for our meal. He said the hotel wouldn't take his credit card, that they only took cash, and he had used all his cash paying for their rooms. I thought all hotels took credit cards. We had ample cash for us but not for a whole army, but nevertheless, I paid the bill. Then he wanted to ride down to the French Quarter. I was wondering why, if he didn't have any money. Anyway, we went. We walked Bourbon Street and went in and out of every bar on the street without ever stopping or spending a dime.

Being broke, they apparently left and went home the following morning, because we never saw them again.

The following morning, I met a Mr. Vincent Novack from Columbus, Ohio. He was a broker for rare antibodies, and he told me he had great connections with all the European buyers, more specifically with those in Germany and Switzerland. I learned that there were only four countries in the world that manufactured blood typing serum: the two European countries, the United States, and Canada. Mr. Novack and I exchanged addresses and phone numbers, and I promised to send samples to him as soon as I received my FDA license.

Juanita had been sleeping in that morning, but when I returned to our room, she was ready to go. We decided to take a cruise on the

Mississippi River. We boarded a cruise boat and cruised up the river a way and returning, we left the Mississippi and went through a lock and onto a canal where we had an enjoyable trip through the bayou country. Returning, the captain was having a hard time docking the boat. I think he was embarrassed, and he became rude and discourteous to the passengers, saying we were like a bunch of cattle. That was totally uncalled for. We were only lining up to get off the boat.

There were several restaurants in our hotel, and boy, did we pick the wrong one for dinner that evening. There were no menus, so we had no idea about the prices. We sure found out when we got our bill. It took almost all our money to get out of that place. Apparently, we weren't the only ones to be fooled. As we were leaving, we saw another couple counting pennies, trying to scrape up enough money to pay their bill.

The remainder of our trip, we had to eat at a hole in the wall, that we called "Takie Outie", that served oriental food. We laughed as we would walk down the street eating teriyaki on a stick. As we headed home, we couldn't help being concerned about Bill Page and wondering if he would be able to send us money to continue our business.

On Monday morning, I called him and told him we needed $2,000. He said he would send it, and we finally received it on Friday. We had reached a conclusion that he wasn't as well off as we thought, and we wondered how much longer we could keep going.

Bill Page called and told me that he had taken on a couple of minor investors in his Florida business, and they had put $10,000 into his business. I knew that wouldn't last long the way he was spending money. Then I got a letter from one of the investors, who was a young attorney, asking for my personal financial statement, saying he needed to have more borrowing power for the business. I thought, "What a joke! This clown must be crazy if he thinks he's getting my personal financial statement." All he wanted to do was borrow money on my property, so he could recover the money he had given Bill Page. I wrote him a letter telling him that his request was completely out of line. Boy was he hot! He told Bill Page that he had better straighten me out. Bill called me laughing and said that no one had ever dared to tell this guy he was out of line. I never heard another word about it, and I'm pretty sure he lost his investment. Our anti-C donor was temporarily not selling, because the pharmaceutical companies had purchased all they needed for the moment. We desperately needed another good donor to keep us going. Then another miracle happened.

We located an anti-e donor in Greenville, South Carolina. I drove to Greenville to obtain a blood sample and to offer her a price feasible for her to donate. We came to an agreement: she and her husband would drive across the state to meet me at a designated spot on I-95, and I would take them on to Jacksonville to donate.

When I called Bill Page to tell him the good news, he was already in a meeting with his partners, discussing closing down his business. With the news of my new donor, they agreed to keep the business open. She donated about a dozen times, and we were able to sell about $40,000 worth of her plasma. This would keep us going for a few more weeks.

In the meantime, we heard from the FDA on our application. We had to re-submit a small portion of our SOP because of a change in regulations. The federal government never gets in a hurry, so we knew that our application would be held up for a couple more months.

We still didn't have a medical director for our new business, and that director would have to be a medical doctor. At that time, there were only 25 or 30 doctors in Fayetteville, and I started going over the list to try to decide who might work with us. I started with my old boss at the hospital, a pathologist. He told me, "John, I haven't done a physical since medical school and I don't feel comfortable doing one." I said, "For heaven sake doc, I could do the simple exam that we require, I just don't have M.D. after my name. He still wouldn't take the job.

I decided to go and speak to Dr. Howard Goodwin. I had known him for a long time, and I knew he would make a great medical director for us if he would take the job. He was receptive enough but said his other duties wouldn't allow him time to do it. I asked if he might recommend someone. He thought for a minute and said, "Yes, go talk with Dr. Linda Jackson." I said, "Do you really think she would do it?" He answered, "She'll either take the job or throw you out of her office."

I called Bill Page and told him I needed help. Juanita and I had determined by now that Bill Page was a pretty good con man, so I asked him to come up to Fayetteville and help me hire a doctor. He agreed, and we made a trip over to see Dr. Jackson. Doctor Goodwin had been right. She threw us out of her office without even listening to us.

Bill said. "We've got to hire a doctor. Keep trying and pay as much as you have to in order to get one." My next stop was at a hematologist's office. Dr. Meadows seemed interested, and I offered him $1000 per month for working one afternoon per week. He said, "Make it $1500, and I'll take the job. That was an excessive amount, but I had to have a medical director to operate my business. We put him to work right away doing physicals on all our potential donors. Dr. Meadows was not holding up his end of our agreement. His hours were 1 PM till 5 PM every Thursday. Seemed like he was always taking care of personal business and always showing up late, sometimes as late as 3 PM.

Our business was equipped except for the donor room, centrifuge room, and refrigerator room. We had placed an order with a company in Orlando, FL to make our four donor chairs. I made a trip to Orlando, rented a U-Haul trailer, and brought the chairs back. They were beautiful, turquoise leather with closed-in storage space beneath. Two trips to Jacksonville and I had the centrifuge, refrigerator, and freezer. Now all we needed was our FDA license. Then bad news struck again.

We were running out of money, and I couldn't reach Bill Page. I knew his CPA was Bob Prince, so I gave him a call and asked what was going on. He said, "Do you really want the truth?" I said, "I absolutely do." Then he gave me the news. He said, "Bill Page is gone. Shut down. Out of business. He's trying to find a buyer for the business, but I doubt he'll be able to. He'll probably be there about another week."

I felt like my heart sunk to my feet. How could this happen to us. We had worked so hard and spent so much money. The FDA inspector was scheduled to be here next week which meant that our license was only about a month away. Now we were broke, our partner was out of business, and we had no place to draw our donors and ship plasma. I hated to give the news to Juanita, but I had to. I said, "Baby, it looks like we're doomed this time. It will take another miracle to save us, and I don't see that happening. We're at the end of the rope."

That weekend we had planned to go to Georgia for a visit. My son Harvey, now i6 and in the 11th grade had gone out for football, and he had made the starting line-up as the defensive right tackle. We wanted to see him play. Harvey played for Baker High in Columbus, a 4-A school. I'm not sure but I believe they were playing arch-rival Jordan High that Friday night. Harvey played a great game. At 275 pounds, the backs didn't run over his position. The game ended in a tie. Then the officials made a ruling I had never heard of before. They said that in overtime, each team would get the ball once. If no one scored, the team gaining the most yards on that possession would be declared the winner. Harvey's team lost because the other team gained one yard more than they did. Very strange ruling.

That next day, at my parents' home, Harvey said, "Daddy, I bet I can outrun you in a 40-yard dash." I said, "I doubt that." Well, we measured off 40 yards, and my brother Jimmy said, "Ready! Set! Go!" We took off and boy was he fast, especially for his size. At age 39, I won but only by a couple of feet. I decided right then that that would be my last foot race. We had a nice visit with the kids. Wendy was in the 8th grade. We had started calling her Wendy when she stayed with us during the summer, and her mother called her Echo. Must have been a little confusing to her.

During his senior year, Harvey decided not to play football, but instead went out for track and field. He was by far the best shot-put thrower at Baker High. He worked very hard, every day, especially on technique, and he was throwing consistently at a distance of 55 to 57 feet. He went on to win the regional championship at Warner Robins, GA that year. Unfortunately, the pressure got to him at the State Championships, and he did not perform well.

Kelly had started to school that fall in the first grade. We had put her in a private school in Fayetteville, so we could take her to school each morning as we went to work and then pick her up in the afternoon, and she could stay with us in the plasma center.

That Monday morning, we dropped her off at the usual time at Haynie School, then proceeded to the office. It was gloom and doom that morning, not just for us, but for our employee, Marijane, who also depended on a job. The door opened, and a young man walked in. We recognized him as Jeff Schmidt, a sales rep from one of the pharmaceutical companies. We were thinking, "He's in the wrong place to make a sale today." But he wasn't there to make a sale. He said, "I was at the blood bank at Rocky Point Hospital last week and overheard them talking about a very unusual antibody they had found. I didn't want to get nosy, but I looked over their shoulder and got the name. It was an anti-e (little e) and it belonged to a patient named Mary Vick. That's all the information I could get." We normally would have been jumping with joy, but we had no idea how to get up with this person, and even if we did it might be too late to save us. It was all we had, and it might be worth a try. It would be useless to contact the blood bank and ask for information. I had to think of something else. Then I devised a plan. With a little luck, it might work.

I got on the phone to Rocky Point Hospital. "Rocky Point Hospital. How may I direct your call?" I said, "Medical records, please." Then, "Medical records. How may I help you?" I said, "This is Doctor Logan at Duke Medical Center. I am trying to locate one of my patients. I just received some new lab findings on her, and she was discharged from our hospital yesterday. Apparently, the phone number I have is incorrect, and I can't reach her. I know it's not your policy to give out that kind of information, but this is of utmost importance." She said, "And this is Dr. Logan at Duke?" I said, "It is." She said, "And what's the patient's name?" I said, "Mary Vick." "One minute please." She came back and gave me the phone number. My plan had worked. I told Jeff that if anything good came of this, he would be compensated.

I dialed the number for Mary Vick. She answered, and I told her who I was and what I wanted, but I was having trouble getting through to her, so I asked if I could drive up and talk with her. She agreed, so that evening Juanita and I drove to a little town about ten miles east of Rocky Point. I did not like the neighborhood I was driving into. It was not a place I would normally visit. We found a run-down house at the address and I knocked on the door. A middle-aged black lady came to the door. "Mrs. Vick?", I asked. She nodded, and I told her who we were and that I had talked with her earlier. When we entered the room, there were 10 or 12 people sitting around the room staring at us. They sat with their arms crossed over their chests, and no one so much as smiled. I explained to Mary that she had a very rare antibody and that it could be valuable to her. She said, "I thought you were going to tell be that I had something that was going to kill me." She agreed to let me take some blood samples, and I told her I would contact her as soon as

I got the results.

Mary's antibody was as strong and pure as Jeff had said it was. I called Bill Page and told him what I had. He told me he was trying to sell his center, and this might be just what he needed. As it turned out, it was.

The following day he called me back and told me that because of my antibody, he had been successful in selling his business, but that wasn't all. He had sold his interest in my business as well.

My new partner, Bud Johnston, called me and said he wanted to meet with me as soon as possible. He and his son Larry were there the next day. To my surprise, Bud handed me a check for $5000. Another miracle had happened. Now I felt like we were home free. Bud and Larry liked what they saw and said they looked forward to a good business relationship.

Later that week, I took Mary Vick to the airport, and we flew to Jacksonville for her medical exam and her first plasma donation. This was her first flight, and she had been a little apprehensive about it. On our return flight, we ran into some turbulence, and she became frightened. Back on the ground, she told me that this would be her last flight. That meant I would have to drive her to Jacksonville for future donations.

The following week we had our FDA inspection. It went very well, and we were told that we should receive our license in about two weeks. It couldn't come soon enough. I was tired of all the trips I had been making to Florida.

The coming weekend I would have to drive Mary Vick back to Jacksonville on Friday and stay until Sunday. Hopefully, this would be my last trip for a while. I went to bed early that Thursday, arose at 2 AM, drove the two-hour trip which was 100 miles north of Fayetteville. I picked up Mary, and her daughter Donnie around 4 AM, and we began our nine-hour drive south to Jacksonville, arriving around 1 PM. We completed her plasmapheresis at 2:30 PM, and I got them checked into a motel. We were all exhausted at that point.

Bud Johnston invited me to his home for dinner that evening. He had a very nice place located in a gated community, with his house right by the golf course. The house was small, but well furnished. The most impressive thing to me was the dining room. It was very small, with one of the walls being a mirror. That gave the room the appearance of being twice as large. We had an enjoyable evening, and Bud said that his son Larry and his wife wanted us to stop by their place for brunch on Saturday morning. Larry and his wife lived in an upscale neighborhood. They had a very nice home with a swimming pool in the back yard. Eggs Benedict was served for brunch along with orange juice/champagne cocktails. My new partners had made a good impression on me, and I felt sure that we would have a good relationship.

We completed Mary's second plasmapheresis at 11 AM on Sunday. As we headed home, I could tell that she was one happy woman. She had $1000 cash in her pocket. I don't think she had ever had that much money at one time. Donating twice a week, she could potentially earn $50,000 per year. She had trouble understanding how her plasma could be so valuable. Mary was 56 years old, and I told her she had most likely been walking around with gold in her veins for the last 30 years. I told her that she probably developed it after her children were born. She said, "Lord, I wish I had known about this sooner."

We pulled over somewhere in South Georgia and went into a fast food restaurant for lunch. You should have seen the people staring at us. They weren't accustomed to seeing a young white man walk in with two black women. I'm sure they thought I was with my wife and mother-in-law. I think it bothered Mary most of all, because the next time we stopped, she said, "Why don't you go in and just bring us something back." I couldn't help but laugh, and I said, "Sure, not a problem."

In November, we finally received our FDA license. It had taken eight months, twice as long as expected, and it had cost us approximately $100,000. The nice thing was that we had paid for everything with our donors, except for the $5,000 from Bud Johnston. We did, however, owe the medical director, Dr. Meadows four months of pay, which was $6,000. I had not been happy with his performance. He had never come to work on time, always keeping our donors waiting. When Bud found out what he was charging us, he said, "This guy has to go!" He would soon be gone.

The same day we received our license, we had two shipments of plasma go out. We would no longer have to take donors to Jacksonville, and we would now have our weekends off. Because of having to work weekends, we had hardly had a chance to attend church for the past 8 months. Now we could start going again.

In December, we received two checks in the mail on the same day for the plasma we had shipped the day we got our license: one for $2,000 and one for $6,000. Now we could have a Merry Christmas and look forward to a great year in 1979.

I started the new year looking for a new medical director. Then it dawned on me. Maybe I could hire one of the resident doctors from FAHEC (Fayetteville Area Health Education Center). After all, they had all graduated from the Duke University School of Medicine, and they all had M.D. after their names. They were seeing lots of patients at FAHEC, but they weren't being paid. They just might appreciate a little job where they could pick up a few bucks. I went and talked with the director of FAHEC and got permission to speak with the residents. The director even recommended one of them. Betty Braddock was having lunch when I knocked on her door. I told her what I needed, which was to stop by our center at 1 PM each Thursday and perform the exams we needed and to do a three-month review of the donors' charts. I offered her $100 per month plus $25 extra for each exam she performed. She didn't even hesitate, saying, "When do I start?"

I sent Dr. Meadows a notice that he was fired, because he had not performed as he had agreed. He wasn't at all happy about being fired, and he asked if I would stop by his office and talk with him. I agreed, and the first thing he did was remind me that I owed him $6000. Then he said, "Do you agree that you owe me that money? Speak up so I can hear you." I knew right then that he was recording our conversation. So, I told him loud and clear, "No sir, I don't feel like I owe you that much money." He said, "Then, why not?" I said, "Our agreement was that you would be at our center from 1 PM till 5 PM each Thursday. You have never been on time, and I didn't appreciate you keeping my donors waiting, sometimes as long as two hours. He said, "Do you have another doctor?" I said, "I certainly do." He said, "Well, how much are you paying him?" I told him, "$100 per month." He said. "I don't be-lieve you." I said, "Then our conversation is over", and I got up to walk out. As I was leaving, I heard him say, "I'll sue you!"

Sometime in January we learned that Bud Johnston was closing the plasma center in Jacksonville. Apparently, he had sunk a lot of money in the business, and it still wasn't able to survive. I think the real problem was that they didn't have any good donors as we did. They had a few anti-D donors, but they don't produce much income. It would appear that they only survived for the past year because of our donors.

Bud Johnston was a business man, but he knew absolutely nothing about the antibody business. He had some type of automotive business and had done quite well. He was in completely new territory now. So, he called me and said that we had to find ways to cut costs. To do that, Juanita and I stopped drawing a salary and began drawing unemployment. We knew that couldn't last too long, because the unemployment office would find us another job sooner or later, and we didn't want that. Only Marijane was drawing a salary.

Although we didn't have any current orders for our anti-C (Big C) donor, May Gibbons, we were still drawing her occasionally, because we knew that sooner or later, we would get an order. She was scheduled to come in and donate on a Tuesday afternoon at 1 PM. She didn't show up, and we couldn't reach her on the phone. She never showed up the entire afternoon. That wasn't like her. When we couldn't reach her the following morning, we knew something was wrong. Juanita and I decided to pay her a visit. When we arrived at her home, we got no answer at the door. Juanita looked through a window and said, "You're not going to believe this. The house is empty." May Gibbons had moved out, and the bad thing was, she had taken the car. We had bought a new Mercury Cougher XR-7 for her to drive as long as she was a donor. The car belonged to the corporation, and we had the title. We had no idea where she was. It would take a detective to find her, and if we couldn't afford to pay ourselves, we surely couldn't afford a detective. I would have to do some serious thinking.

I didn't even have a set of keys to the car. Then I remembered. There had been a little metal tag on the key ring with a number stamped on it. If I could find those tags, I just might be able to get a new set of keys made. I looked in the packet where I kept the title, bill of sale, and some other papers that came with the car. Bingo! There were the little metal tags!

I drove over to the Mercury Dealership and gave them the story of how I had lost both sets of keys to my car and asked if they could possibly make me a new set. The clerk said, "Not a problem." Ten minutes later I had two new sets of keys. But this was only step one. I still had to find the car, and that wouldn't be easy. Then I remembered. The phone was still ringing at their house. They would be getting another phone bill, and there just might be something in it to indicate where they went. I had to intercept that bill, but how? We went back to the house and checked the mailbox. There was no mail. They had probably left a forwarding address, and if so, I'd never see that phone bill, and I doubted if the post office would give me their address. Then a plan came to me. I went to the phone company. I said, "I'm Ron Gibbons, and I'd like to have my phone disconnected because I'm moving out of town. Please send me a final bill to my workplace. Send it to Ron Gibbons, c/o Antibody Search of North Carolina," The lady said, "Thanks for stopping by Mr. Gibbons. We'll get that bill out in a few days." I told Bud Johnston what had happened. He said, "You find that car. I'll go get it, and we'll sell it."

A couple of days later I received a letter from a Fayetteville attorney. Dr. Meadows was suing us for $6000. I didn't have time to fool with this, so I gave the letter to my corporate attorney and told him to handle it. A few days later he called me and said he had settled with Dr. Meadows' attorney. He said, "Send me a check for $1500 and it's over." I couldn't have been more pleased.

Two weeks passed, and we finally received a phone bill addressed to Ron Gibbons. Juanita and Marijane gathered around me as I opened it. On the bill there were a half dozen calls to Tucson, Arizona on the day before May disappeared. She was at that number, or someone at that number knew where she was. How could we find out? Then Marijane said, "I've got an idea." I handed her the phone bill and she headed up to the front desk. A few minutes later she came back, handed me a piece of paper and said, "Here's her address." " How did you do it, Marijane", I asked. She said, "I pretended to be from the phone company and said I was updating records, and they fell for it." I said, "Great job, Marijane. Thanks!"

I was immediately on the phone with Bud Johnston. "We found

her", I said. He told me to overnight the keys to him, and he would send someone to pick it up. May Gibbons was living in Houston, Texas. Bud bought a one-way ticket to Houston and sent a guy to get the car. He landed in Houston and took a cab to the address. The car was sitting in the driveway. Then this idiot got cold feet and backed out. He then took a bus back to Jacksonville. Talk about mad, Bud was hot under the collar. I couldn't believe it when he told me what happened. I said, "what are we going to do Bud?" He said, "I'm going after the damn thing myself!" And that's exactly what he did. He and his son Larry were on the next flight to Houston. It was 9 PM when the cab dropped them off at the address. Bud waited out at the street while Larry walked to the car. He saw several people setting around a table laughing and talking. He started the car and backed out to the street without turning on the lights. He and Bud drove away.

By the time May realized the car was gone, Bud and Larry were rolling down I-10, already in the Florida Panhandle. I wish I could have seen May's reaction. She got on the phone to the Houston Police Department and reported her car stolen. Then she called me and asked if I was the one who stole her car. I said, "May, I think you've got that backwards. You stole our car. That was your car to drive as long as you donated plasma for us. You had no authority to take that car when you moved away." She said, "I'll have you arrested!" I said, "OK, best of luck", and hung up.

Around the middle of the afternoon, I received a call from the Houston, Texas Police Department. "This is officer (I don't remember his name). We had a report of a stolen vehicle, and your name was given to us. Can you help us clear this up?" I said, "The vehicle in question is a corporate vehicle. The title is in our name. Mrs. Gibbons was authorized to keep and drive the vehicle as long as she worked for us, but she had no authority to take it to Texas, so we had to re-possess it." He said, "I figured it was something like that. Thanks for your help." This matter was closed.

The unemployment office called and said they had found me a job. I said, "Funny thing, I was about to call you and tell you that my old boss had called Juanita and me back to work. She said, "Well, I'm glad to hear that." When I told Bud Johnston that Juanita and I had to get back on the payroll, he was not pleased. He said, "We can't afford to pay three employees up there. I suggest you lay off Marijane." That was one of the most difficult things I ever had to do. She and I had worked together at the hospital, and I had brought her here. Not only was she a great worker and an asset to our business, she was also a good friend. Now I had to fire her. I know she found another job quickly and worked there until retirement, but I have always felt bad about what happened. We never spoke again afterwards.

Our business was doing OK, but not making money fast enough to please Bud Johnston, and he was becoming a nuisance. He was calling every day and wanted a report of everything we did, even who called. That was bad enough, but then he started calling on weekends. If I wasn't home, he would let the phone ring for hours until I answered. Then he started coming up with ideas that I thought were stupid. This continued through 1979, 1980, and into 1981. Then he came up with an idea that was absurd. He wanted Juanita and I to sell our home in North Carolina and move to Jacksonville and also move our business there. Did he really think our donors would drive 400 miles to donate? It was a crazy idea and I told him so. That was when he broke ties with me. He wanted out of the business. He began looking for someone to buy his interest in our business. He found a buyer in the person of Vincent Novack of Columbus, Ohio. Vincent called me and told me his plan to buy out Bud, but under one condition. He wanted me to give him one share of my stock, so he would have 51 percent. Without thinking, I initially told him I would, just to get away from Bud. When I told Juanita, she said, "Don't you do that! If he has 51 percent, you'll be nothing more than an employee. She was right.

The first thing I did the following morning was call Vincent Novack. I told him that I had had second thoughts and would not let him have the one share of my stock that he wanted. He was furious. He said, "Then I won't buy out Bud Johnston, and you'll be out of business." I said, "Really?" He said, "Bud Johnston said if he couldn't find a buyer, he was going to shut down his business in Fayetteville." I said, "Wow, I hadn't heard that." Vincent hung up but called back a few minutes later and wanted to know if there was any way to salvage this deal. I told him there was not a chance.

I learned that Bud had said that if he couldn't sell out, he would close me down and have an auction of the contents of the business and turn in the FDA license. It was time for me to speak with the corporate attorney.

When I met with Mr. Whitman, my attorney, he asked me what I wanted to do. I told him that ideally, I would like to keep my business open, because it was still making a profit. I said, "I just want Bud Johnston out of my life." Mr. Whitman came up with a plan. He said we would hold a meeting at his office to determine the future of the business. Juanita and I, the only officers of the corporation, along with Bud and Larry Johnston would attend. The plan was to hold an auction and I would buy everything, then re-open the business under a new name. I needed someone to do the bidding for me. That way, Bud wouldn't know what was going on. I liked his plan, but there were problems facing me. First of all, we would be dissolving the current corporation, "Antibody Search of North Carolina" and I would have to form a new corporation. Could this be done and keep my FDA license, or would I have to start over from scratch? I didn't know, but I would find out. The other problem was money. Would I be able to come up with enough money to buy everything? Unknowing to Bud, Juanita and I had put aside $13,000 over the past three years. It might be enough if there weren't too many bidders running up the price.

A week later we were at Mr. Whitman's office for the corporate meeting. As president, I called the meeting to order and after saying a few words and passing out a financial statement, I said, "We are here today to determine the future of this corporation. Since Mr. Johnston has been unable to sell his share of the business, he has suggested that we hold an auction. We will use the proceeds to pay what liabilities we have, then split whatever profit is left, if any, among the shareholders." The Johnstons were busy going over the financial statement. They didn't like the fact that I was owed some back pay, and they strongly objected. So, I said, "If you find that to be a problem, scratch it off. I'll forfeit that pay." I wanted to get this thing settled. That seemed to have pleased them, and it was decided that I would contact an auction company and set up the auction as soon as possible. The meeting was adjourned.

I contacted the Jones Auction Company, and we were able to

schedule an auction in three weeks. My next step was to contact the FDA. I called FDA Headquarters in Silver Spring, Maryland and got the chief inspector of plasma centers on the phone. Luckily, he was the same person who had done our initial inspection three years earlier. I told him who I was and where I was from. He said, "Sure, I remember you. You had the nice facility in North Carolina." I said, "Bob, I'm making a slight change down here. I'm buying out my partner, and I want to change the name of the company. However, there will be no changes in location, personnel, manufacturing procedure, or the standard operating procedure. Can you possibly issue us a new license in the name of the new company without us having to start all over again?" I held my breath as he thought for a minute, then said, "Give me the new name of your company and let me know what day you want it to go in effect, and I'll get it delivered to you that day." This was indeed another miracle. I learned later that he had never done this for anyone before.

We were driving a 1980 Mercury Cougar XR-7 and since it belonged to the corporation, we had to sell it. We ran an ad in the local paper, and a couple of days later it was gone. There was just one more hurdle to cross, and that was the auction. I had prepared an itemized list of the contents of our business and provided it to the auction company, so they could distribute it to all the potential buyers. I began to get calls from other centers around the country concerning the auction. I told them I was hoping to buy everything back and try to remain in business.

There was only one person in the world that I trusted to do the bidding for me, and that was my brother, Don. Don was a chemical engineer with Firestone and he had a brilliant mind. He had recently put a suggestion into the suggestion box at work. From what he told me, I thought it was a relatively simple suggestion, but Firestone jumped all over it and paid Don the maximum suggestion award of $25,000. His suggestion saved the company more than $250,000 on a proposed project. Don agreed to be there for the auction.

Mr. Whitman had already got us incorporated as "Antibody Corporation of America", and we had opened a new bank account in that name and deposited $12,000. Everything was set for the auction.

The auction would begin at 10 AM. It was late in the summer, and

245

it was extremely hot that day. Bud and Larry Johnston were there early checking things over and looking over the list of items being auctioned As 10 AM drew near, a few doctors came in, and several onlookers from surrounding businesses were there. Bud made the comment to me that we had no buyers. He apparently was very concerned. My brother Don was nowhere to be seen. We had him waiting out back in the car. Our plan was that Juanita would motion for him to come in after the auction started so that Bud wouldn't have time to question him.

The auction began in the waiting room. We had a sofa, chair, tables lamps, two nice artificial plants, a decorative mirror, and a couple of pictures. I would do the bidding here, and then Don would take over The auctioneer asked for a $200 starting bid, and no one would open. I went to $100, $50.00 and still no bids. Then the Auctioneer said, "John, you'll go $35, won't you?" I said, "Yeah, I guess I can use this stuff at home." So, I bought the whole room for $35. I couldn't believe it, and neither could the others. Some of them ran next door to tell people how cheap everything was going. At that moment Don showed up. He bought everything in Juanita's reception area and the laboratory for almost nothing. It was looking good at this point. If it continued this way, we were home free. In the donor room, Don bought the four chairs at a good price. I had given Don an itemized list with the maximum price he should pay. So far, everything was going for much less. We had a very nice emergency medical chest in the donor rom which I knew some of the doctors were after. I told Don to make sure he got that kit, because I didn't want to operate the business without it, and it would take a while to replace it. One of the doctors ran the price up pretty high, but Don wouldn't let him have it. That left the doctor shaking his head. Then we had a group of hemostats and surgical scissors that the doctor paid twice their value. I had to motion to Don to stop bidding on that lot. We replaced them the next day for about half what the doctor paid.

At about the halfway point of the auction, Bud Johnston walked over to me and said, "Who is that doing all the buying?" I said, "My brother." He said, "I thought so." I saw him walk over to Larry and tell him. They were puzzled. Why would my brother want this place? After all, we wouldn't have a license and it would take months to get a new one. Little did he know of the arrangement I had made with the FDA.

There were only three items Don didn't get: a trash can, a picture that I didn't want anyway, and a spare motor for the centrifuge. Bud had tried to run up the bid, and Don let him have it. At the end of the auction, Bud let us have that motor anyway.

When it was all over, we had bought the entire business for about $8000. After we paid the auction company and other outstanding bills, Bud and I split the $2000 that was left. Then Bud made me an offer. He said, "Give me a thousand dollars and you can keep the old license. That way, you won't have to apply for a new one. The FDA won't know the difference." I almost laughed, but I kept my composure and said, "Let me think about it."

It was over! It was a miracle, a dream come true. Juanita and I had our own business now, and I knew we would do well. Now it was time to celebrate. My youngest brother, Jimmy had made the trip with Don. I knew they both liked seafood, so did Juanita, myself, and Kelly, who was almost 9 years old now. I would have a seafood feast like they had never had before. I had learned about "real" seafood from a friend from New England, who was also a donor.

I went shopping at Kroger, as they had the best seafood department in town. I purchased five live lobsters, steamer clams, and colossal shrimp. When I asked for three pounds of Alaskan King Crab legs, the girl said, "Sir, they are $29 per pound." I said, Ma'am, I can afford 'em today!" We had a wonderful evening. It was a celebration I will always remember!

CHAPTER 17

This is Our Business Now!

"ANTIBODY CORPORATION OF America". Our business was small, but we had a big name that also sounded impressive. It was hard to believe we had pulled this off, unbeknown to anyone else. We would work hard to make our business a success.

When the postman stopped by on our first day of business, he delivered our new FDA license, just as we had been promised. We proudly placed in on the wall where the old license had been. We didn't have any donors scheduled for that day, so we took the afternoon off to shop for a new car. We found one we really liked at Lafayette Ford. It was a 1982 Thunderbird with all the options we wanted. We made a down payment and were ready to ride.

The following day, we began scheduling our anti-D donors. We had about 20 or so that were active. Drawing them twice weekly would produce about 100 liters of plasma per month. That would bring in about $8500, enough to pay most of our expenses.

There were two uses for anti-D. One was for anti-Rho (D) typing serum for determining one's Rh factor, and the other was for the manufacture of RhoGAM, a product used for the prevention of anti-D antibodies in Rh negative mothers who had delivered Rh positive babies. The sole manufacture of this product in the United States was Ortho Diagnostics, to whom we sold most of our plasma, and there was a smaller company in Nova Scotia, Canada that also bought from us.

In addition to the anti-D donors, we had donors with anti-c (little-c), three with anti-E (big-E), anti-e (little-e), saline anti-D, anti-JKa, anti-Kell, anti-Lewis-A, and Anti-Lewis-B. We would call all the donors in for a single donation, so we could get samples to all the manufacturers who purchased our products. We would also send samples to all the brokers who primarily did business overseas.

The majority of our donors had been with us for two or three years, and since they donated frequently, we had almost become like one big happy family. We were very close friends with some of them. One such couple was Ray and Kaye. They were from Boston and had come to Fayetteville by way of the Army as so many of the residents of this city had done. Ray was in the auto sound system business with a couple of partners. They had two little girls: Lori, and Shari. Although they were several years younger than us, it didn't seem to matter to them, and we developed a very close friendship. It started by them inviting us to dinner. Ray was big on "real" seafood, and he would always bring in things like Alaskan King Crab legs and/or steamer clams. He taught me more about seafood than I had learned in my entire life.

Juanita was turning 40 on May 1, and she had never had a birthday party. Kaye wanted to change that, so she began planning a big surprise celebration for her. It would be on a Saturday evening, and she would invite us over for a spaghetti dinner.

Juanita's mother and stepfather came on Friday afternoon to spend the weekend with us. I had told them about the party, and Juanita's mother was especially looking forward to going. Ray and his family had also stopped by that Friday evening. As we were all sitting around the table talking, Bill, the stepfather, suddenly said to his wife, "Are you going to that party tomorrow night?" Juanita's mother gave him a dirty look and said, "What are you talking about?" He said, "You know, that surprise birthday party for Juanita." Kaye and I couldn't believe what we were hearing. She looked at me, then got up and walked back to the bedroom. I followed her a few minutes later. She was furious and said, "Can you believe this crap!" I said, "No, I can't!" I told her I would come and help her with the final preparations the next morning.

Juanita never mentioned what Bill had said, but I knew she must have heard him. Anyway, after breakfast on Saturday morning, I told her I had to leave for a little while to take care of some business. She didn't much like me leaving her alone with the company, but she said, "OK."

By mid-afternoon, Kaye and I had finished with all the decorating and other preparations for Juanita's party. When I returned home, Juanita was really upset with me because I had left her alone to entertain her mother and Bill. Had she known I was with Kaye all day, she would have been even more upset. Kaye wanted us there for dinner at 7 PM, so we left around 6:15 so we would have plenty of time to get there. About 20 guests had been invited, and most of them were friends from our bowling league. They had parked their cars away from the house, so everything looked normal. Juanita rang the doorbell, and when the door was opened, everyone shouted, "Surprise!" And she was surprised, more so than I had ever seen her. Her first birthday party was a huge success. Till this day, she denies having heard Bill ask about her party that Friday night, and I believe her. That's one reason we've been together for almost 50 years. We've always been honest with each other.

We began sending samples of all our rare antibodies to all our potential buyers. Several of them called saying, "We were told you were out of business." I said, "Hardly, we're just getting started." And start it did! We began getting orders right away for our products. Things were looking very good for our new business.

We had just the right amount of work to keep the two of us busy. We were able to maintain a business bank account of around $20,000 and we decided on a salary of $800 per week for me and $600 for Juanita. Depending on our sales, occasionally we would get a bonus of $1000 to $5000. Together we earned more than $100,000 that first year. We had never had that kind of money before, and we were enjoying it. I was especially happy for Juanita because she loved pretty clothes, and now she could shop any time she pleased. And shop she did! She didn't spend all her money on clothes. She also saved money, opening an IRA and adding money to it on a regular basis. I was enjoying my extra money also. In addition to opening an IRA, I began investing in coins for my collection. I had been interested in coin collecting since my grandmother had given me some Indian Head Cents when I was a small child. I had never bought a coin until 1979 when I bought a Flying Eagle Cent and a Three Cent Nickel at a little shop in Plains, GA while Jimmy Carter was president. Now I was working to complete many sets of coins. By 1984, I had all the silver dollars from 1878 to date, all the half dollars, quarters, and dimes from 1892, except for five of the quarters. I also had all the nickels from 1883, and all the cents from 1856, including the very rare 1856 Flying Eagle Cent. My collection did not contain junk coins. They were all of high-quality. My complete collection was valued at around $100,000. I also had a nice collection of baseball cards. I put together a complete set of Topps cards from 1954, 1955, and 1956. Those were some of my teenage years when I had such a great interest in baseball. The Beckett price guide showed my collection was worth around $20,000, but I was to find out later that baseball cards were not a good investment.

We remembered Jeff Schmidt. Jeff was the sales rep who had given us the lead on Mary Vick, the anti-e donor from Rocky Point. We had promised to compensate him if anything good transpired. It had actually saved our business. We mailed Jeff a check for $2000 for what he had done for us. He sent us a thank-you letter, expressing his appreciation and saying how both he and his wife were overwhelmed.

In 1982, we enrolled Kelly in the 5th grade at the Fayetteville Academy, a college preparatory school. It was expensive, but we wanted the best for her. She had attended Haynie School her first four years. It was an OK school, but far behind the Academy in learning. The 5th grade was very tough for her, because she had so much catching up to do. I was up with her almost every night helping with her homework. By the 6th grade, she had caught up and we didn't have to help with homework except for some of her projects.

In 1984, we decided it was time for a new car. We would trade the Thunderbird for something with a little more class. We started out by looking at Lincoln Town Cars. We found one that we really liked. It was loaded. We also knew what we were willing to pay. The sales manager was not meeting our price, so we began threatening to leave and check out the Cadillacs. He did not want us to leave, so he finally came down to our price of $18,000.

Juanita and I had made many trips to Florida over the past few years, and we had made a trip to New Orleans, but other than that, we hadn't had a real vacation in a long time. So, we decided to take a few days off, just the two of us, and go on a cruise to the Bahamas. This would be our honeymoon trip that we didn't get to take following our wedding. We sailed out of Miami and headed for Nassau. Sailing was very smooth, nothing like the trips across the Atlantic on the naval transport ships. The ship's casino was a new experience for us. We had never been to a casino. I played the slots, but not being a gambler, I would stop every time I got ahead. I think Juanita was a little more of a gambler than me, and she really had fun. At Nassau, we left the ship for a day. We took the horse and buggy ride around the city, saw a great show at the hotel and casino, and did some shopping. Back on the ship, we sailed to Freeport, a more modernized city on another island. There we visited the casino and enjoyed visiting the many shops in the city. There was also great entertainment on the ship, and the food was unbelievable. We thoroughly enjoyed ourselves on our well-deserved vacation.

We decided to expand our operation, so we began drawing some anti-A and anti-B donors. We would ship this material to Ortho Diagnostics monthly. We would take on 15 to 20 new donors, and this required us to hire an additional employee.

Both Juanita and I had been bowling in a league for the past several years. We bowled together in a mixed league, and I bowled in a men's league. Juanita bowled in a women's league and while she was bowling, I began taking our daughter Kelly to the skating rink, which was next door to the bowling alley. Kelly had never skated before, but she improved every week, and by the time Juanita's league ended, she was skating pretty well. We held hands much of the time when we skated, and one night we were awarded "best couple on the floor." We were definitely not the best skaters, but we were regulars, and I think they appreciated our effort.

Kelly was now 12 years old, and I wanted her to begin participating in sports as I had done. We put up a basketball goal at the end of the garage, and I began teaching her how to do lay-ups and jump shots. I was now 45 years old, and those lay-ups were hard on me, but we got it done. I had her doing jump shots like a boy; that is, jump high in the air, hesitate, then shoot. Most girls do jump shots by jumping and shooting at the same time. I had talked to Mrs. McLaurin, the varsity coach, and told her I was teaching Kelly to do jump shots. When she saw Kelly shooting, she was so impressed that she had her demonstrate for her varsity girls. This was somewhat intimidating for Kelly.

Harvey had graduated from Baker High in 1980. At his graduation, he introduced me to his best friend, Jimmy Mailman. Harvey said, "Rain or shine, he delivers." By this time Harvey was a pretty good musician, playing both guitar and electric bass. He joined the Peters family music group, called "Mama's Dream", where he played bass for about 2 1/2 years. Juanita and I had the pleasure of seeing them perform once in Columbus. They were an excellent group.

Around 1984, Juanita and I joined the TBA (Tournament Bowlers Association), an amateur association founded and operated by professional bowler, Bill Allen of Florida. We bowled in tournaments in North Carolina, South Carolina, Georgia, and Florida. In one of the tournaments in Fayetteville, I qualified in the top 12. In a professional style format, I had to bowl a match against each of the other 11 bowlers. I averaged over 200 for those 11 games and was in first place. In the 12th and final game, against the guy in second place, it was very close. Going into the 10th frame, I needed a spare to win the tournament. I did not want to leave a 10-pin, so I deliberately aimed for the Brooklyn side. It was a perfect hit, but I left the 7-pin. I got too careful and slowed the ball down on my attempt to make it, and the ball broke into the gutter just as it got to the pin. Instead of winning the tournament, that dropped me to 3rd place, and instead of winning $1500, I only won $400. It was the most agonizing defeat I have ever suffered.

1984 was a very busy year. Our business was continuing to do well, and I had also invested a lot of money in my coin collection. I decided I would become a part-time coin dealer. I called the business "John Wills Rare Coins." I decided to do my first show that year in Lumberton, NC, and Kelly would be my assistant. We had a lot of fun, and I believe we sold about $430 worth of coins. That was my first of many shows to come. I was also elected president of the Cape Fear Coin Club where I would serve in that office for the next 14 years. I was also the club auctioneer and the bourse chairman for all our local coin shows. Almost every weekend we were either at a bowling tournament or a coin show.

During this time the "Urban Cowboy" craze was going around, and our friends Ray and Kaye were caught up in it. It didn't matter that they were from Massachusetts; they both had and wore their cowboy boots and hats. There was a club near their home that featured a mechanical bull, and they frequented that club at least once or twice a week. They usually invited us, and we would go with them when we could. They would enter the bull riding contest. Kaye was actually a better rider than Ray, and she would usually be in the top two or three places. There was no way Juanita and I were going to attempt riding that thing.

We would invite them to go with us to coin shows or bowling tournaments, but Ray was always working on Saturdays. Sometime Kaye and the girls would go with us, and Ray would join us on Saturday night after he got off work. On one trip to a coin show in Charlotte when it was just Kaye and the girls, we were out by the swimming pool on Saturday afternoon. Our daughter Kelly who was around 12 years old, was playing with 4-year Shari and 2-year Lori in the shallow end. Kaye, Juanita, and I were sitting nearby to keep an eye on them. For some reason, Kaye went back to her room. She had taken the girls out of the water while she was gone. Suddenly Shari came up to Juanita and said, "Lori's in the water." Neither of us realized what she said. Then she repeated it, and Juanita realized it this time. She jumped to her feet, rushed to the edge of the pool, jumped in and pulled the little girl from the water. She handed her to me, shouting, "Do something!" Her eyes were rolling back, and she was gasping for breath. Her pulse was strong. I laid her on a towel, and she began to recover. Meanwhile, Kelly went to get Kaye, telling her that Lori was about to drown, or something like that. Kaye came running from the room, vaulted over a 4-foot fence, shouting, "My Baby! My Baby!" Juanita said, "She's OK, Kaye. She's OK." And she was OK. Thank God Juanita heard Shari and reacted as she did. In another minute or two, it would have been a great tragedy. Later that year, Juanita pulled a drowning boy from a pool in Florida, quite a feat for someone who can't even swim.

My daughter, Wendy, graduated from high school in 1983. Shortly thereafter, she enlisted in the Air Force where she spent a couple of years. She was married in 1985 and gave birth to my first grandchild, Nichole, in 1986. Unfortunately, her marriage did not last.

Nichole has two children, Kahlen and Jackson, my only great-grandchildren. She and her family reside in Columbus, GA.

Wendy is currently married to Nick Kronberg, a truck driver from White Bear Lake, MN. They reside in Cusseta, GA, next door to Harvey and Shirley. Wendy now manages the cafeteria at the local high school.

My son Harvey, began driving a truck cross-country in 1984. A few years later he met Shirley Swarm, from the State of New York, who was his co-driver for a period of time. A romantic relationship eventually developed, and they were married in 1988. It was during this period of time when they were driving together that Harvey learned to play banjo, mandolin, and fiddle. He would practice in the sleeper while Shirley drove. A few years later, Harvey became an excellent lead guitar player. He played lead guitar in a traditional country music band called "Legends Only" for several years. Their highlight performance was playing at the world-famous Tootsie's Orchid Lounge in Nashville, TN. He currently performs gospel music with two of his friends, entertaining at many churches around the area. Harvey and Shirley have two daughters, Jennifer and Shelby. Jennifer graduated from Georgia Southwestern University in Americus, GA. She later received her master's degree and is now working on her doctorate. She teaches special education at a high school in Manchester, GA. She married Chris Bussey, and they reside in Columbus, GA. Shelby graduated from Troy University in Troy, AL. She is a social worker and currently works for an organization for battered women in Phoenix City, AL. She married Kasey Stanton, and they reside in Cusseta, GA.

Meanwhile back at our plasma center, everything was going smoothly. It was difficult to procure any new donors with rare antibodies, although we did pick up a new anti-C donor from the local hospital blood bank. The supervisor was a previous student of mine, and he was willing to work with us. For his efforts we took him and his wife out to dinner and presented them with a finder's fee of $2000. We visited all the hospitals within 50 miles of Fayetteville, but it was difficult to get information from the blood bank personnel.

Kelly was now in the 7th grade. We would drop her off at the academy every morning, and one of us would pick her up in the afternoon and bring her back to the center. She loved to hang out in my office. I had a large map of the United States on my wall with pins showing the location of our buyers and out-o-town donors. We had one donor in Santa Barbara, California. She had lived in Fayetteville while her husband was in the army, but then moved back to California. She had a good quality anti-E antibody, so we would fly her to Fayetteville every two weeks for a couple of donations.

Kelly loved to study the map. By now she knew the capital of every state and the location of every state. Sometimes I would play a little game with her. She would stand a few feet from the map, and I would have her to close her eyes and put her finger on a certain state. She was usually right on it or very close. Also, while in the 7th grade, she had to make a science project. We decided on something she could work on in the plasma center. She would determine the blood types of 100 people and see how the percentage of each blood type compared to the national average. In her project, she illustrated how blood typing was done. It was a very professional and beautiful display. She was awarded first place at her school and received an invitation to enter her exhibit at a Southeast Regional Exhibition at Pembroke State University in Pembroke, NC. There she was awarded 2nd Place.

1984 was a very busy year for all of us. Kelly was a starting guard on the Junior Varsity Basketball Team. Juanita and I always tried to support her by attending her games. The most memorable game was a home game against Cape Fear Academy. We were losing by one point with about 10 seconds to go. Kelly attempted a jump shot but was fouled on the play and was awarded two free-throws. She banked in the first shot for a tie and hit nothing but net on her second shot to win the game.

On a Saturday morning in 1986, I received a call from Mary Davis. Mary was the mother of my sister-in-law, Carolyn. Her words were, "Johnny, if you ever want to see your mother alive again, you should come immediately." We packed up and headed for Georgia. Mama was in the hospital in Dawson, GA, if you could even call it a hospital. It was the same place that turned my Dad away in 1977 when he so desperately needed emergency care after his accident. Mama was in a coma when we arrived. Her doctor was some foreign doctor that probably bought his credentials instead of going to med school. I asked him for her diagnosis, and he said she had a stroke. I asked him what part of her body it affected, and he said it affected her brain. When my brother Don arrived a short time later, he said, "We've got to get her out of here and to a better place." She was transferred to a hospital in Albany, GA. The doctor there ordered blood work, and the results showed that her electrolytes were terribly out of balance: the electrolytes being her sodium, potassium, and chlorides. He immediately began to take steps to correct this, but it was apparently too late. She remained in a coma. We stayed at the hospital with her along with other family members for several days. Once, when Jimmy and I were in the room, we began talking to her, and suddenly Jimmy said, "Look, she's got tears in her eyes." That led us to believe that she could hear us but was unable to respond. It became apparent that she wasn't going to recover. The doctor said it could go on like this for a long time. Juanita and I had to return home. A few days later my brother Melvin called to say she was gone. She was 76 years old. Mama was a very good woman but had an extremely hard life. Caring for my retarded brother was a full-time job alone, and Mama always prayed that she would outlive Jerry, because she knew that no one else would ever care for him the way she did. That prayer was not answered. Jerry was 52 at that time. He died in a nursing home about ten years later after falling out of bed and breaking his hip.

Juanita's father was Clarence Edwards. He and Juanita's mother were divorced, and he boarded with a lady in Walkertown, NC. The first time I met him, he wasn't so sure about me and didn't have much to say, but as he got to know me, we developed a great relationship. He called me "John Boy" and he would have done anything for me as I would for him. That was very much unlike his relationship with Juanita's first husband.

Clarence was the old-fashioned type. They had an old fashioned well for drawing water, an outdoor toilet, and cooked on a wood-burning stove. We would visit him fairly often. At age 74, he was in great physical condition, but suddenly he began to have some medical problems and was diagnosed with colon cancer. The cancer had already spread to his liver. Initially, the doctors were not going to operate on him but then changed their mind, and surgery was performed. As his condition worsened, we brought him to our home to care for him, but eventually he went to a cancer center where he passed away in February 1987. He was taken to Virginia to be laid to rest with other family members.

Juanita went to Virginia a couple of days ahead of Kelly and me. On the day of the funeral, we left home early in the '84 Lincoln. We stopped in Greensboro for a break, and as we started the car, the timing chain broke, leaving us stranded. We called a tow truck to take us to the Lincoln dealership. We weren't sure how we were going to get to Virginia, but we made a quick decision to trade cars. As we arrived at the dealership, we asked to speak to a sales rep. He showed us the Town Cars in stock. There weren't many, but we found a burgundy one that we liked and began to negotiate. Our car had 98,000 miles on it, and I don't recall what they allowed us on a trade. We called my personal banker back in Fayetteville, and she spoke to the finance manager. She told him to put us in the car, and she would mail him a check. Within minutes, we were in our new car and on the road to Virginia.

In 1987, Juanita and Kelly wanted a swimming pool. I told them that it took a lot of work to maintain a pool. They said, "Oh please, we'll help take care of it", so I let them talk me into getting one. If I got a pool, I wanted an in-ground one, so we contracted a pool company to begin work. It was finally completed around the end of August, so we still had a little time to use it before it got too cold. Problem was, we had to fill it with water first. I decided to fill it from the well which was probably not a smart idea. Pumping 20,000 gallons of water from your well takes a long time, especially when your pump breaks down three times in the process. We finally got it full, and it was ready to use by September. My brother Melvin, and his wife Faye, came for a visit that first weekend the pool was open. I insisted that Melvin go swimming with me. After all, it only seemed appropriate. He was the one who insisted that I learn to swim back in 1951. He got in the pool but didn't stay long, saying, " This is the coldest water I've ever been in." I think the water temperature was 77 degrees. It never got over 78 degrees that year, so we didn't get much use from it. However, over the years it has given a lot of pleasure to us. By the way, I'm the one who has maintained it over the years.

As I mentioned earlier, I wanted my daughter Kelly to participate in sports, so in addition to basketball, I began working with her in softball. I spent a lot of time teaching her to hit, and it paid off for her. As petite as she was, she became a power hitter, and as a starter on the team as shortstop, she was always the clean-up batter or the lead-off batter. It gave me a great deal of pride and pleasure to watch her play.

Kelly was also a great volleyball player. Funny thing, I never worked with her at all, and that turned out to be her best sport. She made the all-conference team in her senior year.

When Kelly was in the 7th grade she joined the Cape Fear Coin Club as a junior member. She was very active, going to all the meetings with me and to many coin shows. She had two exhibits that she put on display at shows which had competitive exhibits, and she won many awards, sometimes finishing 1st and 2nd. One display was called "*The Toning of Silver*" and another called "*The History of North Carolina as illustrated by Coins, Tokens, and Medals.*" That one was made as a North Carolina History project. It won 1st place at her school and was put on display at the Cumberland County Courthouse for a month. The American Numismatic Association held its winter convention in Charlotte, NC that year, and we decided to enter her exhibit. We were thrilled when they announced that she had won the "People's Choice" award. That year, I also nominated Kelly for the "Young Numismatist of the Year", and she won that award also. She was now a teenager, and unfortunately, she began to lose interest in coins. She began to take an interest in other things like, well maybe, boys.

We took a little three-day cruise when Kelly was in high school. We didn't make any stops on that cruise, just made a big circle in the Atlantic and came back. We had a great time as there were lots of entertainment, games, and great food. Early one morning while Juanita and Kelly were sleeping in, I went out on deck where a group of people were shooting skeet. The ship's captain was there shooting. I don't think he ever missed. I tried my hand at it, and I think I only had one hit, but it was still fun.

Juanita's brother, Robert, worked in the oil fields of Libya for a couple of years. He was out in the hot desert, but the pay was good, and when he came home, he had a pocket full of cash. He put some of that cash to good use when the 29-acre farm where his mother and step-father lived, was put up for sale by auction. Robert was fortunate enough to have the winning bid and pay cash for it.

One weekend while we were visiting Juanita's family in Virginia, Bill, Juanita's step-father, mentioned that he would like to sell his truck, a 1979 Chevy Cheyenne. It was bright yellow, with a short-bed and 4-wheel drive. He made us an offer we couldn't refuse, so we bought it. A truck always came in handy when you lived in the country as we did. Juanita put it to good use one day when she went and bought a load of lumber and asked me to build a deck on the back of the house. That was around 1987, just before we put in the swimming pool. I had never built a deck before, but I got to work, and it turned out to be a pretty nice deck. After 30 years, it's still in decent shape.

A year after returning from Libya, Robert, along with Juanita's mother and step-father were visiting, when Robert mentioned he didn't have a job. I kind of jokingly told him I would hire him as a handy-man. He said, "what's the pay?" I told him, "Room and board plus $100 per week and I'll keep the cooler full of beer." He said, "I can't turn that down." I had to back off of the beer thing, because he could put away some beer. Anyway, he moved in with us, and we put him to work. He cleared the brush from along the road frontage, then built a nice ranch type fence along the entire frontage and part way down one side. He also built a nice pier at the pond. One day he made us an offer we couldn't refuse. He didn't have a vehicle, so he offered us the 29-acre farm in Virginia for our Chevy Cheyenne pick-up. Several months later he got a DWI and was facing some real trouble. We ended up buying the truck back, and he moved to Arkansas. We kept the truck for about 15 years before finally selling it.

Shortly after my son Harvey and Shirley married, they came to visit us for a weekend. They brought with them their beloved pet, a Basset Hound. We didn't want the dog in the house because of our cats, so they put it in the fenced-in area around the pool. After finishing dinner that Friday night, I walked outside and noticed the dog floundering in the pool. He was definitely in serious trouble. I rushed back inside and said, "Harvey, your dog is in trouble!" He and Shirley rushed out, and by now the dog was motionless in the water. Harvey pulled the lifeless animal from the pool and laid it on its side. It was not breathing. Shirley said, "Daddy, should I give it mouth-to-mouth?" I had not even thought of that, but I said, "Sure, if you don't mind doing it." She opened the dog's mouth as wide as possible and placed her mouth into the dog's throat. Pinching off the dog's nostrils with her left hand, she began pushing air into the dog's lungs. Within a minute the dog was breathing on its own, and it soon began to recover.

Meanwhile, Juanita was calling a vet. We don't know how she did it, but somehow, she got her sister Jewell on the phone. Not recognizing

Jewell's voice, she told the "vet" what had happened and that we had given the dog mouth -to-mouth resuscitation. The "vet" said, "You've got to be kidding!" Juanita was thinking, "What kind of vet is this?" Then Juanita said, "What should we do?" The "vet" said, "Have you tried pumping his tail?" Juanita's reply was, "What?" Then the "vet' said, "Juanita, this is Jewell. Are you drunk or something?" We all had a good laugh from that conversation. Then Juanita got a real vet on the phone who said we had done the right thing, but that the dog should have a round of antibiotics to prevent a possible infection from water in the lungs. The animal made a full recovery, but without Shirley's quick thinking and professional-like action, there's no doubt in my mind about the dog's fate. If anyone in our family ever needs mouth-to-mouth resuscitation, I hope Shirley is around.

We had bought Juanita a new Mustang convertible in 1984. That car had 4-on-the-floor and it was fun for her to drive except when she had to stop on a hill at a traffic light. She was always afraid of rolling into the car behind her. We had sold her 1966 pony car to her ex-husband. That was the last of seven fastback Mustangs we had owned. Then we traded the 1984 for a new 1987 convertible Mustang with an automatic transmission. That one suited her a lot better.

When Kelly was 15, I began teaching her to drive. She learned in the old yellow pick-up. We started out by driving in a big circle around the field. Afterwards, we began taking five or six-mile trips around some of the backroads. The day she turned 16, she was ready to get her license. She was still 16 when she began her senior year of high school, turning 17 on November 4. Just like her mother, she was a beautiful young lady, and we couldn't have asked for a better daughter. That fall, we presented her with a graduation present, a 1990 candy apple red Mustang GT convertible with a white top and white interior. That way, she had her own car to drive to school each day just as all the other seniors did. During that final year, Kelly applied for enrollment at the University of North Carolina at Chapel Hill, along with applications to several other universities. We were all pleased when she was accepted to UNC, Chapel Hill.

My lovely wife seemed to get more beautiful with age. She was one classy woman. One day while I was in Sanford, I spotted a car on a lot that looked like it would fit Juanita. It was a 1988 Mercedes 560-SL sports car. It was white with a hard removable top and a black convertible top. I think the mileage was around 9,000. The car was expensive, and I really didn't want to buy it, so I decided to lease it for 3 years. By then she would probably be ready for something else anyway. We started the proceedings for the lease. They wanted to make sure I had insurance. I presented them with proof of insurance, but it didn't satisfy them. They wanted the required $300,000 in North Carolina to be raised to one million. I thought all was set for the signing of the lease, but then they started questioning my income. I said, "Look, if I couldn't afford it, I wouldn't be trying to lease it." They said, "We want to see proof that you earn $60,000 per year." I said, "$60,000? I haven't earned that piddly-ass amount in over 10 years." I showed them my tax return where I had earned $124,000 that last year. I said, "If you jerk me around anymore this deal is off."

The 560-SL was the perfect car for Juanita. She was the "Lady in the white Mercedes". She sure turned a lot of heads. I guess I was a little jealous. I had to have a new car also, so I traded the 1987 Town Car for a new 1989 model. Now, all three of us had a new car. For Christmas that year, we all got cell phones for our cars. Few people had them at that time because they were so expensive.

Juanita and I were not wealthy, but since we had taken control of our business in 1981, our lives had changed. We had more money than ever before; we had fine cars, Juanita had fine clothes and jewelry, I had a fabulous coin collection and sport card collection, we had IRAs, our 36 acres of land was paid for, we had 29 acres of land with a house and barn in the Blue Ridge Mountains of Virginia that was paid for, and we only owed about $6,000 on our home. We were in great shape and we were having fun, maybe too much fun. In the early years of our marriage, we had a very difficult time, but we went to church whenever we could, and we were thankful to be blessed with what we had. Now, we had about everything we wanted, but we hadn't been to church for years. Our Sundays were spent at coin shows, bowling tournaments, or off on a trip somewhere. We also did a lot of partying with our friends.

In early 1990 we got some bad news. Researchers in England were having great success in cloning rare blood group antibodies in goats. It was predicted that in a relatively short time these monoclonal antibodies would be replacing the rare donors such as we were drawing.

We made the decision to sell our business while it was still profitable. We had an advertising agency come and produce a video of the business and advertise it for us. That only produced one person of interest, but he backed out because he didn't feel he knew enough about it to become involved. I contacted our old friend, Vincent Novack, up in Columbus, Ohio. He previously had a great interest in buying into the business back in 1981, but since I wouldn't let him have a controlling interest, he backed out. Now he was very interested. All we had to do was work out the details.

We presented Vincent with a cash price for the business. There were, however, two items we wanted to keep. We had just traded the 1989 Lincoln for a 1990 model, and it was paid for. We wanted to keep that car as well as a storage building that the corporation owned. We would deduct the value of those two items from the cash price. Juanita could keep her Mercedes because it was a personal lease rather than through the corporation. One of Vincent's main concerns was finding someone to manage the business. Looking back, I would have been smart to have stayed and managed it for him, but at the time I wanted out of the business. I did, however, agree to take on the role of an advisor for six months at a salary of $5,000 per month.

At that time, we had two employees other than Juanita and me: Michele Kahn and Cindy Fairfield. Michele had been with us for a long time, and although she was only in her mid-20s, she was a hard worker, very smart, and knew the business well. I highly recommended her for the job of manager. I told Vincent to call her at home and talk with her. He called that evening and asked to speak with Michele. Her husband, thinking it was a friend of his said, "Get the hell out of town." Vincent said, "Pardon me?" The husband said, "You heard me. I said, get the hell out of town!" Vincent, thinking he had the wrong number, hung up. I believe he did call back later and speak with Michele, but I don't know what was said.

Cindy Fairfield had been a donor for a long time but had worked as an employee for maybe a month. She knew very little about running the business, but because she was older, mid 40s, Vincent hired her at a salary she had never dreamed of having. Very big mistake!

In late spring of 1990, Vincent Novack made the trip to Fayetteville. We sat down with the attorney, signed all the necessary paperwork, and received our payment for the business. Vincent was now the new owner of Antibody Corporation of America, the business we had worked so hard to build up and the business that had given us the American Dream for the past nine years. It was kind of sad to see it go, but I had already made plans for a new venture and was looking forward to getting started.

CHAPTER **18**

Starting a New Business

OVER THE PAST few years, I had accumulated an inventory of coins, mostly in my personal collection, that was valued at over $100,000, and I had been doing coin shows since 1984. I had developed a good knowledge of coins and had a good reputation among both dealers and collectors in North Carolina and surrounding states. I had already rented the upstairs portion of the building we were in. This would be our new workplace.

Dealing in coins can be a very dangerous business. Therefore, I did not want a walk-in type retail coin shop. I wanted to have an office where I would have a place to purchase coins and to see customers by appointment.

The name of my business was "John Wills Rare Coins", but the sign outside read "John Wills R.C., Numismatic investments." The average person would not know what that meant, and that was the idea. I would also continue to do coin shows on the weekends, maybe even work some of the larger and major shows.

Juanita would also have her own little business. She had invested a few thousand in gold and silver jewelry. Her business was called "Jan's Gems." We were both in the same office, and we each had a showcase displaying some of our material. We had a very nice set-up. Our office was large, with a sofa and chair in the waiting area, and we each had our own desk. One of the first things we did was put an ad in the newspaper and in the phone book. We were ready for business.

The newspaper ad did not produce many customers, but the phone book ad did well. That's where people go if they're looking for a coin dealer. As soon as the new phone book was out, our phone began ringing. I bought some very nice coin collections, one in particular that I paid $25,000 for. There was a lot of room for profit in that collection.

Juanita and I made two major trips that year. We went to the American Numismatic Association convention in Seattle, WA and to a major show in Long Beach, CA. Both trips were a combination of business and pleasure, probably more pleasure than business. We had two families in Seattle that we had been good friends with, and they both offered to let us stay with them, which we did. There were Bobby and Betty Melton, my friends I had known from Germany, who had been stationed at Ft. Bragg. He had helped me get that assignment to the Green Berets. Marlene and Perry Bartram, that I had known from my time at Cape Fear Valley Hospital also lived in the Seattle area. We spent much of our time with them.

I took lots of coins to sell to dealers at the show, and while I was doing that, Marlene was entertaining Juanita by showing her around Seattle. Perry's parents were also very hospitable. They took us on a day's trip to Mt. St. Helens, the volcano that had erupted so violently back in 1980. It was totally unbelievable to see the damage it had caused. Marlene and Perry also had a nice little pond on their property that was stocked with rainbow trout. That was the first time I had ever done any fly fishing. I caught two rainbows and cooked them for breakfast the following morning. I said, "It sure would be nice to have some grits with these." To my surprise, Marlene brought out a box. I just couldn't believe someone in the state of Washington would have grits!

The weather was cloudy the entire time we were there, and we couldn't see the summit of Mt. Rainier, but as we departed SEATAC airport, the pilot flew right by the summit, giving us an awesome view. I'll always have great memories of that trip.

I sold several thousand dollars' worth of coins at both the Seattle and Long Beach Coin Shows. Unfortunately, we didn't have any friends in the Long Beach or Los Angeles area, so we stayed at a motel in Long Beach. We rented a car at the LAX airport, so we could come and go as we pleased, despite the massive amount of traffic on the freeways. We visited the waterfront at Long Beach and took a tour of the historic

Queen Mary Hotel as well as the famous Spruce Goose, a massive wooden plane built by the Howard Hughes Aircraft Company for transporting troops across the ocean during World War II. However, it was never used because the war ended before the plane was completed. The highlight of our trip was our visit to Hollywood. We enjoyed seeing the "Walk Of Fame" along Hollywood Boulevard and visiting some of the shops along Rodeo Drive. Of course, we had to take a ride up Mulholland Drive to the top of the hill where we got an awesome view of the city below. A visit to Universal Studios was also very entertaining.

A lot happened in 1990 after we sold our business. Kelly graduated from the Fayetteville Academy and moved into Granville Towers in Chapel Hill that fall to begin classes at the University of North Carolina.

We also made some additions to the house that year. The master bedroom was enlarged, and we both got walk-in closets. Central heat and air were also installed. Our single carport was made into a two-car garage. We also had a barn built, large enough to park the truck and tractor. All those additions cost twice as much as the house had cost back in 1966.

In honor of Kelly's graduation, our "retirement" from the antibody business, and as a "house warming", we had a big pool party in June with many friends and family members attending. 1990 had been a great year. We got so much done that we had wanted to do for a long time.

The party was about to be over. In early 1991 we got bad news, really bad. We learned that we owed a large sum of money to the IRS, more money than we had. We had spent a very large sum of money doing all the things we did in 1990, and there wasn't enough left to pay the taxes due. I thought we had already taken care of that. How could this be? Maybe it was stupidity on my part, but we were paying an accountant to take care of those things. He had not kept us informed properly. I panicked. Without considering all the possible options, I refinanced our home in order to pay the tax bill. That was a huge mistake, a mistake that I would never recover from.

Over the past 10 years, we had earned over $100,000 per year, and we had developed a lifestyle that we could no longer sustain. Under normal circumstances, the coin business would have been pretty good, but it couldn't produce the kind of income we had grown accustomed to. Things went from bad to worse. Our monthly bills exceeded our income, and we were still paying for Juanita's Mercedes until the end of the year, and that alone was around $1,000 per month. We had to make some tough decisions. Juanita would look for a job. I began to sell off coins from my personal collection, then it was my sports cards, and my guns. Problem was, those things wouldn't last forever. I was doing a coin show almost every weekend, and I was traveling as far as Orlando, Atlanta, Roanoke, VA, Knoxville, TN, Baltimore, and Cherry Hill, NJ. We were keeping up with the bills, but my inventory was rapidly being depleted. Juanita took a tele-marketing job with the minor league baseball team, the Fayetteville Generals. She was good at the job: nice voice, excellent on the phone, but selling season tickets wasn't easy. Working on commission, there were days when she received no pay.

Sometime in 1991, I was called out of a coin club meeting by the police and told that my daughter had been in an auto accident and had been taken to the hospital. He didn't know her condition. As I headed out, I was praying that she was OK. Minutes later, my wife called me in the car to let me know she was, in fact, OK. A car had pulled out in front of her and her boyfriend, and they had broadsided it. Thank God we had stressed the importance of wearing a seat belt, or otherwise, she would have likely been thrown through the windshield.

Juanita only stayed with the tele-marketing job for two months. She then took a job with Wal-Mart, working in ladies' clothing and as a cashier when needed. She was a very classy lady, and after six months they wanted to put her in the cash office. Problem was, they didn't want to take time to train her properly. We went to Virginia for the weekend, and Juanita worried about that job all weekend long. She was to start the new position on Monday. She was about to have a nervous breakdown. I said, "Baby, you don't have to do this." She said, "What can I do?" I said, "Quit, and come and help me until you can find something else." That's exactly what she did. She wrote out her resignation on our way back from Virginia. We stopped at Wal-Mart, and she walked in and handed them her resignation. They said, "You've got to be kidding?" She said, "I don't think so", as she walked out the door. I don't think I had ever seen her so happy.

She helped me for a short time and then found a job with Belk, working in cosmetics. By now, we had turned in Juanita's Mercedes and she was driving the old yellow truck to work. I felt so bad for her. We were having it so tough, and it wasn't about to get any better any time soon. I knew that she really loved me to go through what she was going through, or else, she would have been gone.

One day we got some surprising news. Our old business, Antibody Corporation of America, was closing down. Vincent Novack had failed an FDA inspection and apparently, not taking it seriously, had been shut down. What a shame. Two years ago, we had left such a great business.

Each year the rent on my office kept getting higher and higher. In early 1994, I moved into a small office in one of the large bank buildings. In May of '94, Kelly was about to graduate from college. We had been unable to pay her tuition in her senior year, and she had to take out a student loan. She graduated with a degree in elementary education.

A few days after graduation, Kelly was sitting in my office making calls to find a teaching job. She wasn't having much luck initially, but then she decided to call Ft. Bragg Schools. She got Dr. Jeter, principal at Holbrook school, on the phone. That call would end up giving her a career that she never dreamed of. He told her that as a rule, he never hired first year teachers but told her to come in for an interview. I suppose he liked what he saw, and she ended up getting a job. As of 2018, she has been working with the Department of Defense Schools for 24 years. She received her master's degree in 1998 from Fayetteville State University and has been one of the most outstanding teachers at Ft. Bragg, being awarded "Teacher of the Year" in 2016.

Bad news came our way again. We got the word that Juanita's mother, Helen, had a massive stroke. For some time, we had feared that might happen. A few years earlier, she had what we thought was a massive stroke while visiting at the home of her daughter Jewell. Juanita and I were there at the time. Responding quickly, Juanita called 911 and had an ambulance there within minutes. I accompanied her in the ambulance, and before we reached the hospital, she had begun to recover. The emergency room doctor diagnosed it as a TIA or mini-stroke, and by the next morning she was OK. We believe that she had several more minor TIAs over the next few years, and she also had a problem with high blood pressure.

But now, this was not a TIA. It was the "big one". Bill, her husband not knowing what to do, called his daughter instead of calling 911. It was hours before she got to the hospital. By then, it was too late. She would be paralyzed and unable to speak for the remainder of her life. She lived for three more years and passed away in a nursing home on her birthday in 1997 at the age of 82. Like Juanita's father, Helen was always so good to me. I called her Mama, and she treated me like a son. Juanita and her mother were very close. I know Juanita thinks of her every day, and she always will.

In 1995 my coin business was doing fairly well. I had expanded my business to become a PCGS (Professional Coin Grading Service) authorized dealer and had begun to buy and sell scrap gold. I was doing a local show at Fayetteville one weekend and had had a very good day on Saturday. At the end of the day, I was walking to my car along with a customer, carrying a small, empty lock box and my attaché case. In my case was a rare 1876 proof twenty cent piece that I had accepted from a customer to have certified and graded by PCGS. That coin alone was valued at around $3,500. In addition, there were several new purchases and a gold necklace valued at around $1,500. Normally, I was very alert when walking to my car and leaving a show, but this time, I was busy talking and not paying attention to my surroundings. Somewhere out there in the parking lot were two would-be thieves in an old blue beat-up Chevy pick-up, looking for an easy target. Seeing me put my case and the lock box in the trunk, they decided to follow me. Usually I would try to determine if I was being followed, but this time was different. As I headed up the freeway, my mind was on the new purchases I had made. I would stop by my office and package, label, and price them for the show on Sunday. Then as I approached the mall, my mind shifted to my wife, who was working at the Belk store. I drove right past the exit to my office, then decided to take the next exit and stop and see Juanita. As a rule, I didn't stop and leave my car unattended if there were valuables in it, but this time I did. I found a parking space on the end of the row, next to the Belk store. I walked in and before I even got to Juanita's department, I heard it on the intercom. License plate so-an-so, go to your car. I knew Immediately what had happened. The trunk was standing open, and a lady was nearby. "I saw it all", she said, "And, I got most of their license number."

That lady was a co-worker of Juanita, and she had just gotten off work and was walking to her car to go home. She agreed to wait for the police to arrive and give them a report. She said the old blue truck pulled up behind my car, and the passenger jumped out, took a tire tool, and pried open the trunk of my Lincoln. He grabbed my attaché case and the lock box, threw them in the bed of the truck, got in, and they drove away. She said that she was no more than 20 feet away, and that the man gave her a big smile as he was leaving. The police were going to dust my car for fingerprints, but the lady said the man was wearing gloves, so I told them to forget the fingerprints. She agreed to go to the station for a composite drawing.

North Carolina license plates have three letters, followed by four numerals. The lady got the numbers but said there were two small letters preceding the numbers. She was unable to get those letters. Some began to speculate that it was an out-of-state license plate. We didn't have enough to trace that plate. Then a couple of days later, I spotted a plate with two small letters preceding the numbers. The letters were "ID". That was a dealer plate. I learned that there were two types of dealer plates, "ID" for independent dealer and "FD" for franchised dealers. Now I had it narrowed down to two possibilities. I had a friend of mine in the sheriff's department to run a check on those two plates. The "FD" plate belonged to a new car dealership in Raleigh, NC and the "ID" plate belonged to a used car lot in Lumberton, NC. I suspected the latter was the most likely, since Lumberton was only about 35 miles away. I went to the investigator in Fayetteville and gave him my information. He told me to have the police in Lumberton look into it. So, I went to the Lumberton Police Department, and they said that since the crime was committed in Fayetteville, that the Fayetteville Police Department would have to investigate it, but that they would co-operate. It was unreal what a lack of interest anyone had in investigating my case. The Fayetteville Police finally called the used car dealer in Lumberton, and they said the license plate had been stolen about a month earlier. I was at a dead end, but I was not giving up yet. I felt sure that this guy was from Lumberton, or at least in that area. With the police all but having swept my case under the rug, I was on my own to try to find him. I realized I would never see my coins again. By now he would have sold the $5,000 worth of goods for little to nothing, to a pawn shop. All I had now was a composite drawing of this guy, and I knew he drove and old blue Chevy pick-up. Then I remembered. I had a friend in the coin club who lived in Lumberton, and he operated a pool hall. He might have seen this guy or at least be able to offer some assistance.

I walked into the pool hall and said, "Charles, I need your help in finding this guy." He studied the drawing and said, "I don't recognize him." I told him about the blue pick-up, and he said, "Let's take a ride. Maybe we can find it." We drove all around town and finally down a dead-end street, in a neighborhood that I didn't feel comfortable to be in. Suddenly, he said, "Stop." We were in front of a run-down house with a man standing on the porch with no shirt. Charles said, "Bunkie, have you seen an old blue Chevy pick-up around this area lately?" Apparently, Charles knew Bunkie from the pool room. Bunkie replied, "It's been a couple of months, but he would park at the end of the street and sit there for hours. I think he was doing drugs." That was as close as I ever got, but I continued to pass out some of the composite drawing with hope that someone might see him.

In the meantime, I had to scrape up $3,500 for the customer's coin I had lost. That hurt. The customer did take some coins from my inventory, so I didn't have to pay it all in cash.

Two or three months went by. I was awakened by the ringing of the telephone. As I got out of bed, I noticed the time was a little after 2 AM. I thought, "Who could be calling this time of night?" When I answered, a voice on the other end said, "Do you remember that guy that broke into your car and stole your coins?" My answer was, "How could I ever forget?" The voice said, "He'll never do it again." I said, "What do you mean?" His answer was, "Not unless he comes out from under six feet of dirt." I said, "Maybe I better not ask any more questions." He said, "I'm not going to tell you anything else, except that he was from Maxton, NC, and let's just say he was involved In a robbery that went bad, and someone blew his sorry ass away." End of the call. I knew who the caller was but never acknowledged it. He had been a plasma donor for us, and he had also purchased coins from me on several occasions.

We had developed a reasonable friendship over the years. I saw him on many occasions after that, but neither of us ever mentioned that phone conversation. What actually happened will always be a mystery to me. I can only speculate.

Bad luck was about to strike again. It was on a Monday afternoon near closing time. Four young men came to my office and said they wanted to sell some gold for their grandmother. At that time, gold had climbed to almost $2,000 per ounce, and a lot of people were selling their gold. They had a considerable amount, much of it broken or damaged but there were a few decent pieces. I began to sort it out as to whether it was 10K, 14K, or 18K, and then weighed it. The scrap gold value was somewhere around $1,000 dollars, so I purchased it with cash. Any time I purchased something that was nice or usable, I would save it for re-sale or offer it to Juanita. I believe there were five pieces I had saved. The rest I sold as scrap, and it went to the melting pot.

About two weeks later, I got a visit from two detectives, asking if I knew certain people. Some I did, and some I didn't. Then they told me there was a robbery and that they had arrested several suspects. The suspects had told them that they had sold me a large amount of gold for cash. They asked, "Have you bought any gold lately." I said, "Yes, would you lie to see it?" I showed them a bag of scrap gold that I had bought over the past few days and they said, "That's not it." I told them that I didn't keep large amounts of cash on hand. The detective said, "You wrote them a check, and we would like to see your checkbook." I said, "No problem." They didn't find what they were looking for, so they thanked me and left.

Another week or so went by, and the detectives came back. They told me that one of the suspects told them that I paid cash for the gold, and he was ready to take a lie detector test. I still had the five nice pieces, and I wanted the lady to have them back, so I confessed that I had bought the jewelry but did not know it was stolen. I told them to bring the lady in, and I would give her back what I had. They came back the next morning, and I handed over the five items I had. I told them that was all I had. They left, and later that afternoon the lady called me demanding to know where the rest was. When I told her it had gone to the melting pot, she got very angry, saying she was going to sue me and have my business. I said, "I'm sorry, but there's nothing more I can do for you." Had I known what was coming next, I would never have confessed or given her back those five pieces.

Apparently, she kept badgering the detectives until one of them charged me with receiving stolen property. That was a felony. I was told to go to the Law Enforcement Center and turn myself in, so they wouldn't have to handcuff me and haul me away. That I did, and I was treated with respect as I was fingerprinted and photographed. I was able to sign myself out, so I was able to avoid being locked up.

Back at my office I called an attorney. He said, "Write me a check for $200 and I'll get you out of this. I couldn't have been more pleased. When he came to pick up the check, he informed me that he didn't know I had been charged with a felony. Now his fee was $2,500. I had to borrow the money on a credit card. A court date was set for the following month. If I was convicted, I was facing possible jail time.

On the morning of my court date, the judge called my case. I said, "Your Honor, my attorney is not here to represent me." The judge continued my case until the following month. I was mad, very mad. I went straight to my attorney's office and gave him a piece of my mind. He assured me that it wouldn't happen again. I said, "It better not!"

I have mentioned my brother Don several times in my book, but it wouldn't be complete without saying a few more things about him. In early 1986, he left the Firestone plant at Albany, GA to take a job with a carbon black company in Borger, TX. He purchased a home in nearby Fritch and settled in with his wife Carolyn, and children Pam and Jason. Don and Carolyn are still residing there today. Over the years, Juanita and I have had the pleasure of visiting them several times. Fritch is located in the Texas Panhandle some 50 miles north of Amarillo. Lake Meredith is nearby and serves as a reservoir for the surrounding area.

When I think of Amarillo, I always think of the Big Texan, a famous restaurant located on Interstate 40. The restaurant features a 72-ounce steak that is offered for free if one can eat it within an hour along with the roll, salad, and potato. This thing looks like a big roast! I would never attempt to eat it, but each time we've been, someone was giving it a try. A number of people have accomplished this feat, although not while we were there. One of my favorite items on the menu is the special appetizer tray which features buffalo, jack rabbit, rattlesnake, and calf fries. Where I came from, calf fries were called mountain oysters. Need I say more? They also have a couple of guys playing fiddle and guitar, and they will come to your table and play you a country song for a tip. By the way, on our last visit the price of that steak was $39.95. I'm sure it's more by now. It's always a fun place to have dinner.

Another of our favorites was the Palo Duro Canyon National Park, the second largest canyon in America, just south of Amarillo. We visited the park on two occasions and enjoyed the drama, "Texas", which is located in an amphitheater within the canyon. The musical gives the history of the early settlers in the area.

Don and Carolyn's children now live in the Houston area. Pam, like Kelly, is a teacher. They have always been very close and are more like sisters than cousins. Pam and her husband, Chuck, who is also a teacher, have two boys, Alex and Grant. Jason has two sons from his first marriage, Keegan and Paxton. He is now married to his second wife, Marisa.

In 1996, Don's job took him to Akron, Ohio, a city just south of Cleveland. We had the pleasure of visiting them on Easter weekend in 1997. It had snowed the night before and was very cold. Our daughter Kelly was with us. I had never seen any of the great lakes, so, on Saturday we took a ride along the shore of Lake Erie, all the way to Erie, PA. I was amazed at the amount of ice in the lake. There were huge chunks of jagged ice that stretched out from the shore for at least half a mile. There was a strong, icy wind blowing from over the lake. It felt more like December than April.

By the time we returned to Cleveland, it was late afternoon and we decided to have dinner. I had seen an ad somewhere about a restaurant called Dick's Last Resort. I really liked the way the menu looked, so we decided to give it a try. The place was crowded, but we found a place to sit, on a bench at a long table. Glancing around, something caught my eye. Above the bar hung a nice assortment of ladies' panties and bras. I began to wonder about this place.

The waitress came to our table and said in a very hateful tone, "I'm going to read the menu one time, and you better listen! I am not going to repeat it!" No one said anything. We placed our order, and I said to

Kelly, "I don't know about this place." She agreed. We felt like getting up and leaving. Then the gentleman seated beside me said, "Have you been here before?" I said, "No, and I won't be coming back again." Then he said, "Let me tell you about this place. It's different." I thought, "You've got that right!" Then he said, "They deliberately try to be rude, and they want you to be rude back to them." I said, "OK, I'll play their little game." When the waitress came back, I said, "You know, for a Yankee Girl, you're not too bad." I got a great big smile out of her. From that point on, I was as rude as I could be, and she was loving it. I probably had more fun than anyone else that night. I have heard that there are a few more of those restaurants around the country, but I haven't visited another one, but yes, I would.

While I was waiting for my next court date, I did three things. First of all, I would discontinue buying scrap gold. Then I found someone to be a character witness. Finally, I was able to speak with one of the assistant District Attorneys, who just happened to be the daughter of one of my best friends. She told me that another assistant District Attorney had my case, and she couldn't help me. However, she did tell me something I was glad to hear. She said, "Even if you plead guilty and tell the judge you knew that the property was stolen, you will not go to jail. We barely have room for the violent criminals. The jail is full." That made me feel a little better, but I still had a felony hanging over me.

The next month I sat in the courtroom half a day with my witness, and my case was continued again. This went on month after month. It was agonizing. Finally, one day my attorney called me and said, "It's over." I said, "In what way?" He said, "The D.A. has dropped the charges." I was overjoyed. After all the bad things that were happening, something finally went my way. Maybe my friend's daughter had something to do with it. I'll never know.

I was about ready to get out of this business. I even took on a part time job working at a local convenience store. The pay was only $7.00 per hour and I was working about 20 hours per week. That was a tough job. I did it all: worked as a cashier, stocked shelves and the refrigerators, rented videos, filled LP gas tanks, mopped, waxed, and buffed floors, hauled off the trash, and anything else that needed to be done. After six months, I had had enough of that job, so I went back full time in my office. When I left the store, I was told by a man that hung out there a lot, "You're the best employee this store has ever had." That may well have been true.

Juanita and I really enjoyed bowling. In 1997, we joined NABI (National Amateur Bowling Institution). In one of the tournaments, Juanita qualified in the top five and in the stepladder finals, she worked her way to the championship game. That game was close, and in the 10th frame she got a headpin strike which forced her opponent to double in the 10th. He struck on the first shot, but on the second shot, he left the 10-pin on a pocket hit, giving Juanita the championship. She won $500 cash plus a championship jacket and an entry to bowl in the "Tournament of Champions" in Las Vegas, which I'll talk about later.

Our daughter Kelly had been dating since age 16 and a couple of years later had become engaged. The two of them were already looking at homes. The engagement eventually fell apart, and they went their separate ways. While in college, she had taken on a summer job at PD Quix, a fast food restaurant in Sanford, NC. One of the managers there, David Sears, had taken a liking to her, and they began a relationship. That relationship turned into an engagement, and they made plans to be married in 1996. Kelly always wanted to have a big, fancy wedding, and Juanita wanted that for her also. A wedding like that would be expensive, and we didn't have that kind of money anymore. Kelly agreed to share the cost of the wedding with her mother. To afford it, Juanita borrowed money on her life insurance policy. Juanita and Kelly rented one of the largest churches in Fayetteville for the wedding site and planned for a reception dinner at the Holiday Inn Bordeaux. It was a beautiful wedding with somewhere between 150 and 200 friends and family members attending. Everything went as planned, and it was certainly a day to remember.

David and Kelly bought a home in the country a few miles out of Sanford, where they lived for several years. Then around 2004, it was time for a bigger and nicer home, so they started looking for a piece of land on which to build that dream house. Unfortunately, buying land and building the home they wanted was going to be a little above their means, as the house alone would cost in the $500,000 range. Juanita and I had a suggestion. We would sell them 8 1/2 acres of land at a favorable price, so they could build the home they wanted. David was now the sole owner of PD Quix and had three stores, and Kelly had a good paying job with the Dept. of Defense Schools at Ft. Bragg, NC. They took us up on the offer and began making plans for their new home. Later, we sold them another 8 1/2 acres, so now they had 17 acres total. David began making improvements on the land by building a road through the swamp that ran through the center of the property and created trails and a field to plant food for wildlife. The place is a wildlife haven. Deer and wild turkey are abundant.

The house was completed somewhere around 2006, and it was beautiful, and I might add, large. There are four bedrooms and five bathrooms. There is a three-car garage on the end of the house and another three-car garage in a separate building with a billiards and trophy room upstairs.

It seems that anymore, very few marriages last, and theirs would be no exception.

After being married for 10 years or so, they began having marital problems and were eventually divorced, but not before their son, Blake, was born in 2008. The two of them share custody, and both are very good parents. It would appear as if Kelly and David are getting along better now than when they were married.

Kelly now lives in beautiful Carolina Lakes, a gated community located only about five miles from us. I don't think she's ever been happier in her life. David, of course, lives in the "big" house which is only about 200 yards away from us.

As I write this book, Blake is 10 years old and a wonderful grandson. He attends a Christian School in Sanford and is a good student. He plays baseball and basketball with basketball being his favorite. His father is teaching him to hunt, and just this year, he killed his first turkey, a 20-pound gobbler. Juanita and I see him on a regular basis, and we also take him to school three days a week. His other grandmother takes him the other two days.

Meanwhile, Juanita had been working at Belk for two years. One day I went to the hospital blood bank to donate a pint of blood. While there, the supervisor told me he was looking for an employee to work in the donor room. I asked if he would consider hiring Juanita, because she had years of experience and liked that kind of work. He told me to send her in for an interview. She got the job and was happy to be working in the blood bank again.

In the fall of 1997, Juanita and I decided to take a vacation. We would go to Las Vegas for a few days, and while there, she would bowl in the "Tournament of Champions". We took a flight out of Raleigh. After arriving in Vegas, we checked into our hotel, and after having dinner, we decided to go down to the casino, the first time we had been in one since our cruise to the Bahamas. We didn't have a lot of money, especially to waste on gambling, but we each got a roll of quarters to play the slots. I put five or six quarters in a machine and, amazingly, hit for 900 quarters. That was $225! Wow! It was time to quit. We went back to the room and retired early, because we had a tournament to bowl early the following morning.

We had to go to another hotel for our tournament. We arrived early, and as we were waiting, Juanita was putting a few quarters in a "Wheel of Fortune" slot machine. Suddenly she hit for 750 quarters. That was another $187.50. We just couldn't believe our luck.

We bowled in many tournaments that week, placing in some of them, but nothing big. Unfortunately, Juanita didn't do well in the "Tournament of Champions", but that's OK. She won a championship; something I could never do, and no one could take that away from her.

We had a very enjoyable week, visiting most of the casinos along "The Strip", but most of all we loved the great entertainment that was going on every night. Among others, we enjoyed concerts by Wayne Newton, Glen Campbell, and Lori Morgan.

It was 1998. I approached Juanita one day with a proposal. I said, "Why don't we sell the property in Virginia, and use that money to get out of debt. We're not going to ever live up there, and all we're doing is paying taxes on it." She reluctantly agreed, and we sold the property for $50,000. We got out of debt except for the home mortgage, but it didn't last. Soon we were going deeper in debt again. Bad luck continued. One weekend I decided to go to a little town north of Charlotte to bowl in a tournament. I stopped for a few minutes to visit a coin dealer friend in Albemarle, then continued on my way. I had not been to this location before, and I wasn't familiar with the roads. As I left

Kannapolis, I knew I had to make a left turn somewhere but wasn't sure exactly where. I was looking for the road sign when suddenly I looked ahead. To my horror, a car was stopped in front of me, no more than 50 feet away. At 55 mph, maybe 60, there was no way to stop, and I was too close to try to go around him. I barely had time to hit the brakes. The front of the Lincoln dipped down and apparently went under the bumper of the Toyota ahead. There was a deafening, grinding noise, and everything went dark. I realized my air bag had deployed. When it finally stopped, I heard the back end of the Toyota crashing down beside my door. I had lifted that car up on its nose. The first thing I noticed was that my glasses were missing. I felt around on the floorboard and found them between my feet. My mind was in a state of confusion. I didn't know if I was hurt or not. I didn't feel any pain. Then I remembered I had a concealed weapon in my car. I always carried a .38 Special in a secret compartment beneath the armrest. I didn't want the law to find my concealed weapon, so I took it out, unloaded it, and placed it on the seat. It seemed like several minutes passed before someone came to the passenger door and asked if I was OK. I said, "I think so", then climbed out of the car. The man started asking me questions like, "Do you know what day it is?" and "Do you know where you are?" I gave him the correct answers, and he said, "I just wanted to make sure you didn't have a concussion." As far as I could tell, my only injury was a hematoma on my right forearm where the air bag cover had hit me. The N.C. State Trooper was on the scene within minutes. There were three vehicles involved. I had pushed the Toyota into another car. I had hit the Toyota with such force that it broke the back of the driver's seat and laid him flat of his back on the floor. He was alone in the car. Thank goodness no one was seriously injured. The trooper asked the three of us to get in the back seat of his car. He gave us a pad and told us to write in our own words exactly what happened. Then he noticed that I had my .38 Special in my lap. He said, "Go put that in your car." I told him it was not loaded. He said, "I'd still feel better if you didn't have it." I put the pistol in the trunk of the Lincoln.

My car was a total loss. The hood was crumpled all the way to the windshield, and the windshield was broken. The engine was destroyed.

A wrecker came and towed me back to his home. I then called

Juanita and told her what had happened and asked her to come and get me. While I was waiting, the driver of the wrecker invited me to have lunch with him and his wife, a very hospitable family.

My insurance company acted promptly and paid me $6,500 for my car. I took that money and made a down payment on a 1992 Corvette, something I had been wanting for a while. I drove that car for five or six years, but it was expensive to maintain, so I eventually sold it.

After my car was broken into, I dreaded carrying all my coins to shows every weekend, so I purchased a Gateway computer, set up an eBay account, and began selling my coins at auction. That was much better. It was no more expensive, much safer, and I didn't have to be away every weekend.

Wayne Turner was one of my most interesting clients. He walked into my office one day and handed me a check for $15,000. He said, "I want you to get me some coins." I said, "You don't even know me. Why would you pay me $15,000 in advance?" He introduced himself and told me he had done his homework. He said, "I've checked you out thoroughly, and I know you can be trusted." That was nice to know. He wanted me to get him a 12-piece gold type set in mint condition, graded by PCGS (Professional Coin Grading Service). That set would consist of two $20 gold pieces, two $10 gold pieces, two $5 gold pieces, two $2 1/2 gold pieces, a $3 gold piece, and three $1 gold pieces. I told him that I would be going to a major show in Orlando, FL in a few days and should be able to find all his coins there.

He was pleased with the coins I bought for him, and he told me he would like to begin working on a complete set of $2 1/2 Indian gold pieces in mint condition. That would also require a few thousand dollars.

Wayne bought many coins from me over the years, and we also became good friends. In addition to collecting coins, he also collected guns, and he loved to fish. He had his own boat, and he and I went on many fishing trips, mainly to Lake Jordan and Lake Sharon Harris, both within an hours' drive from home. He loved to fish for crappie, and that pleased me because I had never fished for crappie before. I don't ever recall having a bad fishing trip with him.

Earlier in his life, Wayne had been in some kind of accident and had fractured a vertebrae in his neck. He had constant pain that seemed to be getting worse. A doctor prescribed a drug that apparently was altering his mind. His wife complained to the doctor that he might be becoming suicidal. The doctor did not change his medication. His wife, fearing what might happen, hid all the guns.

One day Wayne found a shotgun that she had overlooked. He sat on the floor, put the barrel in his mouth and pulled the trigger. What a great tragedy. That was not Wayne. He and I had so often talked about how to prepare for the future.

I was sitting at my desk one afternoon working with my eBay account. Juanita, for some reason I don't remember, was not working at the donor center that afternoon and was sitting in the office with me. Suddenly, I had a feeling that I can't describe, but it wasn't right. I sat back in my chair, staring straight ahead. Juanita looked at me and said, "Are you OK?" I was not OK, and I tried to tell her, but I couldn't talk. I knew exactly what I wanted to say, but it wouldn't come out. It was just an inaudible noise. She said, "Oh my God! He's having a stroke." I already knew that, and it was going through my mind that I would never be able to do the things again that I enjoyed doing. She grabbed the phone and dialed 911, telling them that I had a stroke. By now, one of my hands was numb, and I couldn't move my fingers. One side of my body was becoming paralyzed. The paramedics came and carried me out to the ambulance and took me to nearby Cape Fear Hospital, where I had worked for so many years. By the time I reached the emergency room, I was becoming able to speak again, and I could move my fingers. I was gradually recovering. I knew then that I had not had the "big one", but rather a TIA, or mini-stroke. The emergency room doctor began ordering all kinds of tests, all of which checked out OK, and I was finally released at 3 AM. By now, I felt fine but was apprehensive about it re-occurring.

The next day Kelly graduated from Fayetteville State University with her master's degree. I reluctantly went to the graduation. I had to share that moment with my daughter.

I believe the TIA was due to my blood pressure being too high. I had had a problem with high blood pressure for some time and had refused to take medication. I could no longer refuse it, because I didn't want to risk another TIA or worse. That was 21 years ago, and I have not had another mini-stroke.

I had been a longtime fan of auto racing, especially drag racing as I talked about in earlier chapters, but I was also a NASCAR fan. Over the years, I had been to several races including the Southern 500 at Darlington, SC and the World 600 in Charlotte, NC. My son-in-law, David Sears, managed to come up with two box seat tickets to the Charlotte Motor Speedway for the World 600 in 1998. For some reason, he was unable to attend, so his wife Kelly ended up with the tickets and asked me to go with her. I was excited about going, because I hadn't been to a big race in several years.

On race day, we got an early start, knowing the traffic would be very heavy, especially around Concord where the speedway was located. It was worse than we could have ever imagined. When we got to within two miles of the track, it was at a complete standstill. It was still two hours until race-time, and two hours later we were just getting to the parking lot. We heard the start of the race as we got out of the car. We were about a quarter mile from the gate, and Kelly was really moving out. I almost had to run to keep pace with her, and I wasn't going to be outdone. When we got to the box seats, it was packed. There were two seats left, but not together, so we were separated until some of the fans began leaving. During my hasty walk, I had begun to notice some little pains in my chest. They did not go away. I didn't tell Kelly, because I didn't want to spoil her day.

All during the race, there was some girl standing on a flatbed truck in the infield who kept flashing her bare breasts. I think she got more applause that the race did.

After the race was over, we went down to the infield and gathered around the car of one of our favorite drivers, Mark Martin. One of the crew members was throwing lug nuts to the fans, and we were lucky enough to catch one.

I never mentioned my chest pains which were still there the next day. That afternoon I decided to go to the emergency room and have it checked out. Juanita, who was working in the donor center, came rushing to me when she learned that I was possibly having a heart attack. I was admitted to the chest pain center overnight and scheduled for a stress test with radio-isotopes the following morning.

Overnight, I wore a heart monitor and a nitroglycerin patch on my chest. I actually felt pretty good the next morning and had no problem with the stress test. The results showed no significant abnormalities, and I was sent home.

Juanita had now been working in the donor center for two years and had been a very good employee and got along with everyone. Then one day while she was out working on the bloodmobile, the supervisor refused to let her have a lunch break. This did not sit well with Juanita, and she let him know it. Well, from that point on he began to look for an excuse to fire her. He never got that chance though, because Juanita resigned a short time later.

Shortly after that, she was going to work with me one morning, and as I started up the stairs to my office, suddenly I could barely walk. I was exhausted, had no energy at all, and my chest was hurting slightly. I asked Juanita to drive me to the doctor. I was really concerned that I might not make it, and I began saying things to my wife that I normally wouldn't have said. I walked into the doctor's office and told them I thought I was having a heart attack. I was taken to the hospital where I was once again admitted. All kind of tests were run again, with no serious abnormalities found.

Heart disease ran in my family. My father had a massive heart attack at age 50, and most of his brothers had suffered heart attacks, some fatal. I did not like my odds. Then one day I happened to read about two doctors who were doing research on the effects of zinc in treating the common cold. They had accidently discovered a way to prevent and cure angina, which was caused by the build-up of plaque in the coronary arteries. It was virtually 100% effective. I immediately began to employ their findings as a preventive measure against the build-up of plaque. I believe it has worked because I have had no further problems. During the same period of time, two of my brothers had quadruple bi-pass surgery, and the other brother had stents inserted. I have seen estimates showing that perhaps 90% of heart attacks could be prevented if everyone used this simple preventive measure. I'm not a doctor, so I can't tell you what to do, but there are numerous articles online discussing the use of zinc in curing and preventing angina. Unfortunately, the American Medical Association does not recognize this treatment, because it would devastate the cardiology business. Makes you wonder who is more important.

In 1999, we made our second and final trip to Las Vegas. We would be bowling again in the National NABI Bowling Championships, and it would also be a vacation. This time, our daughter Kelly would be going with us, and her husband David, would fly out to join us later in the week. In addition to playing the slots, we planned to visit the sites and casinos along the "Strip" as well as taking in as many concerts and shows as possible. We also planned to visit the nearby Hoover Dam. One day was set aside for a visit to Death Valley and another for a trip to the Grand Canyon.

On the day of the Death Valley trip, Juanita did not feel well and decided not to go. Kelly and I left early that morning in the new Buick we had rented, and we left unknowingly, totally unprepared for such a trip. The month was August, the month when the fewest number of tourists visit the park.

As we neared the entrance, we came to a little rest area and decided to stop. There was one car already parked there. The only thing there was a large board with a map of Death Valley and a port-o-let type toilet. Kelly stayed in the car while I was going to the toilet, but before going I began to study the map. Suddenly, Kelly appeared beside me saying, "Daddy, I don't like the way those two guys are looking at us." Out of the corner of my eye I saw two sleazy looking young men, who had gotten out of their car, staring at us. I said, "Go get in the car, now." She began walking and so did I. Our car was close by, maybe 20 or so feet away, and they were probably 60 feet away. We got in the car, started it up, and drove away. They jumped in their car and began tailgating us. They were right on our bumper. I was afraid they might try to run us off the road, so I kept my speed at 50 mph and kept an eye on them for any moves they might try to make. We were in a desolate place. We had not seen another car since we entered the park, and there was no cell phone service in the area. It was a perfect place for someone to commit a crime. I know Kelly thought we were going to die, and I was also concerned about our safety. Kelly told me later that she had videoed their car in the outside rear view mirror, showing the front license plate.

She said that if something happened to us that maybe her video would be found, and it would help solve the crime.

The car followed us for probably two miles, but it seemed like an eternity. Suddenly, it sped around us and was out of sight within seconds. We were now in the midst of Death Valley, and after a few miles we came to a motel, and there was also a gift shop and a restaurant. It was about noontime, so we decided to have lunch. I've made the comment many times that I had the best cheese-steak hoagie I had ever had.

Millions of years ago Death Valley was a large lake. Due to climate change, the lake dried up and left a bed of salt deposits. There was also a borax mine there. At the lower end of the valley was Bad Water. That was the deepest part of the lake and there still remained a small lake of shallow water which was very salty. It is also the lowest point in the United States at 288.7 feet below sea level. I find it interesting that the highest point in the lower 48 states is Mt. Whitney at 14,495 feet, and it is only about a hundred miles away. Kelly and I toured almost all of Death Valley that afternoon. It was extremely hot with the temperature as high as 121 degrees. It's a good thing our car didn't break down, or we would have been in real trouble. We had not taken any water with us, and we couldn't have survived long in that kind of heat, and the park was almost deserted.

Late in the afternoon, we began our ride back to Vegas by a different route. Shortly after leaving the valley, we came to a little town. I don't remember the name, but it was deserted. We saw only one car in the entire town, and it was backed into an alley, and we saw no people whatsoever. It gave us an eerie feeling. Driving for what seemed like hours with darkness already setting in, we began to see the lights of a city ahead. Back to civilization at last! We were entering the city of Pahrump, Nevada. We stopped at a fast food restaurant and got a burger to go. It was still a long way to Vegas. As we approached the city from the northwest, we were at a much higher elevation, and we got a breathtaking view of Las Vegas at night, from a good 10 to 15 miles away. It was 10 PM when we got back to our room. It had been quite a day and certainly one we would never forget.

We met Kelly's husband, David, at the airport the next day, and then on Friday we headed to the Grand Canyon. Our route took us into Utah and through beautiful Zion National Park. As we headed into Arizona, we began to gain a lot of elevation, and there was a noticeable drop in temperature. I was amazed to see so much wildlife along the way, especially mule deer. When we reached the north rim of the Grand Canyon, we were at an elevation of 8,000 feet, and the temperature was 65 degrees. Quite a change from the 109 degrees back in Vegas. We walked the trail along the north rim of the canyon. The enormous size, the rock formations, and the colors were fascinating. It was another unforgettable visit.

Since I had moved into my office in the bank building, my landlord had raised my rent by ten percent each year. It was getting to the point where I couldn't afford to stay there. I had a decision to make. Since I wasn't setting up at coin shows anymore, why not move my coin business home and sell on eBay. That's exactly what I did. I would probably be able to take on another job also.

There was a job fair going on at one of the hotels that weekend, and I decided to go. I talked to several merchants, but the one that impressed me most was a new car dealership. They would train me for a month and pay me $1000 while I was training. Then I would work on commission. I decided to give it a try.

CHAPTER **19**

Trying Something New

THE YOUNG SALES manager that I met at the job fair had done a great job at inspiring me to try my hand at being a car salesman. Had he not been a good salesman, I would never have taken an interest. I was committed to giving it my best shot.

At 8 AM on Monday, I walked into the dealership showroom. John, the person I had spoken with at the job fair, recognized me right away and then introduced me to the other managers. After a tour of the dealership, I was assigned to Jack, a veteran salesperson who would be by trainer. Jack had been a salesman for many years and apparently had made a good living doing so.

First, I needed to familiarize myself with all the new vehicles we sold, and there were many different models. That would take some time. I followed Jack around as he spoke with potential buyers, and if he was fortunate enough to make a sell, I would follow him through the process of negotiating a price, filling out paperwork, running credit checks, and taking care of financing and insurance. The very minimum one could earn on a sale was $200 and it could be much higher, with an average commission of around $400 per sale. The average salesperson would generally sell two cars per week. That doesn't sound like many cars, but this dealership had 25 salesmen, split into three shifts. This dealership was selling between 200 and 250 cars per month.

I quickly learned that there was a lot more to this job that selling cars. Every shift started out with a sales meeting. Each salesperson would have to give his report for the previous day, and you had to give the names and phone numbers of at least two people you had spoken with.

This was October 2000. After leaving the donor center at the hospital, Juanita had taken a job working in the cosmetic department of Hecht's Department Store at Cross Creek Mall in Fayetteville. Now I was trying to sell cars during the day and sell coins on eBay at night. We rarely had a day off together. It was hard to believe that just ten years ago we had everything we wanted: fine cars, clothes, eating out at our favorite restaurants, no bills other than a small mortgage payment and utilities. We had money in the bank and money in our pockets to spend as we pleased. Now for the past ten years we had struggled just to make ends meet, and sometimes they didn't meet. I know we took some trips to Las Vegas and other parts of the country, and maybe we shouldn't have, but sometimes you just have to get away from the stress of struggling day after day. Why had this happened to us? I'm sure we hadn't managed things properly, but there had to be more. Were we being punished for something? I really didn't know.

I was now 61 years old, and here I was going to work at a car lot every morning and blowing up balloons to decorate the car lot. I couldn't see any hope that it would get any better.

The weather was getting cold, and I was standing outside with a bunch of other salesmen, acting like wild animals waiting to pounce on their prey when someone drove into the parking lot. If I was lucky enough to talk with a potential customer, I had better not let him leave without talking to at least one other person, or I would be reprimanded by the general manager. Sometimes we would be told to get a phone book and began calling people at random to try to sell a car. I don't recall having seen a single car sold that way.

The biggest thing people were talking about was the presidential election. It had been the tightest race in history, and we still didn't know who won and wouldn't for some time.

Juanita and I were still enjoying bowling in a league. Prior to taking this job, I had practiced my game almost every day, bowling about 25 games per week, and my average had greatly improved. In the summer league, I had finished with a 205 average and had bowled 279 on three occasions. That's 11 out of 12 strikes. In a NABI tournament in Raleigh,

I started a game with 10 strikes in a row and finished with a 288, my highest game ever. I was still dreaming of that perfect 300 game.

It was Thursday. I always looked forward to Thursday, because we would be bowling in our league that night. I was working third shift, which was 12 Noon till 8 PM. Our league started at 8:30, and I was only five minutes from Lafayette Lanes where we bowled. On that particular evening, I had a customer who came in late, and I was busy working with him. I wasn't sure if I would be finished in time to make it to the bowling alley for the start of the first game. I finally finished right at 8:30 and hurried to the bowling alley as fast as I could. When I arrived, they were already in the third frame. I could still catch up. If the third frame had been over, I would not have been allowed to bowl that game. Without any practice balls, I stepped up on the lanes and threw three quick strikes. I made the comment that I didn't need any practice. Well, I continued to throw strike after strike, and suddenly it was the 10th and final frame. At this point, I had nine in a row. As I stepped up for the 10th frame, I suddenly realized that everything was deathly quiet, no sound of pins falling, or balls being rolled down the lanes. I looked around and everyone in the bowling alley was standing behind me, watching to see what I would do in the final frame. My wife stood up and said, "Concentrate, and just keep doing what you've been doing." My first shot was a perfect pocket hit. Strike! The second shot was the same. One to go. Now I was nervous, excited, making it difficult to concentrate. When I sat the ball down, I missed my mark by two boards to the left. I thought, "Oh, no. It's coming in on the head pin and probably be a split." But it didn't. It went straight into the pocket for a strike. My perfect game! The crowd cheered. Juanita met me on the lane and gave me a big kiss.

For my achievement, I received a certificate from the National Bowling Museum and Hall of Fame and a 300 ring, which I have worn proudly every day since. The bowling alley gave me $100 and told me that at age 62, I was the oldest person to bowl a perfect game at Lafayette Lanes. My daughter Kelly, made a showcase for me with my certificate and all my awards, except my ring. I proudly display that showcase on the wall of our office.

In February 2001, I had been working as a car salesman for four months. It wasn't working out as well as I had hoped. In the first place, there were too many sales people. If was very difficult for a new sales-man like me to succeed with eight other salesmen out there competing for every customer that came on the lot. Many of them had been there for years and had built up their own clientele. Several new salesmen had come and gone since I had started, some quitting on their own and some being asked to leave. I had only sold 20 cars in four months, and that was well below average. I didn't know how much longer I could last.

I talked it over with Juanita and decided to apply for Social Security at age 62. I could continue to work and earn $10,500 without being pe-nalized. That month, I managed to sell eight cars which ended up being my best month. Sometime in April, I had earned my limit of $10,500, so I said goodbye to the car business. Although my sales had been below average, the General Sales Manager had been pleased with my perfor-mance and told me that if I ever wanted to come back, I would be wel-comed. That pleased me, but I knew that I'd never be back. However, it had been a good experience, and I'm glad I gave it a try.

I went home and began to step up my coin business, increasing the number of coins in my auctions. Juanita decided she wanted to get back into some type of medical work, so she took a job with Portamedic. Portamedic was a company that did paramedical exams on persons who were applying for life insurance policies. A typical exam included a medical history, vital signs, doing a urinalysis, and collecting a blood sample to be submitted to a laboratory. Sometimes an EKG would be required. Exams were done at the applicant's home or place of busi-ness and would take 30 to 45 minutes. Juanita's territory was the nearby county of Moore.

Kelly and David had given Juanita the 1990 Mustang GT which had belonged to Kelly. The car had been completely restored and was like new. Juanita loved that car and still has it today.

We were struggling to get by in 2001. I was selling lots of coins on eBay, but it still wasn't enough to pay the bills, and it took my entire so-cial security check to pay the high-interest mortgage on the house. One month I was late on my Corvette payment, and the bank sent someone out to re-possess it, but luckily, I wasn't home. By the time they came back, I had scraped up the $250 payment. Juanita was keeping us going with her job at Portamedic. In 2002, she could apply for her social security, and that would give us another boost.

I don't think anyone will ever forget September 11, 2001. I was in the kitchen preparing breakfast while Juanita was getting ready for work. She always had the TV on while making herself more beautiful. She came in the kitchen and told me a plane had hit the World Trade Center. I turned on the little TV in the kitchen and watched in awe as the second plane hit the other tower on live TV. The events that unfolded were beyond belief. I was glued to the TV the entire day. It was truly a sad day for America.

My niece Diane and her husband Danny managed a large hunting reserve in Southwest Georgia. Every year we would visit them at the beginning and at the end of hunting season. We would have a big party on both occasions at the hunting lodge with all the hunting club members and many family members present. We always played music. The band consisted of me, my son Harvey, brother Jimmy, and my great-nephew, Doug, Diane's son. A good time was always had by all with music, dancing, and great food.

In 2001, I killed my first deer ever and would bag another each year for the next three years. In 2005, my vision was beginning to fail me, and I stopped hunting.

In January 2002, I had to get a job, otherwise, we weren't going to survive much longer. There was another paramedical company in town that did insurance exams. I was well acquainted with the owner, and after an interview, I took the job. It even paid a little better than the company Juanita worked for. All my life, I had strived to give my very best, no matter what it was, and this job was no exception. However, this woman was a real bitch to work for. She was never satisfied. I tried my best to please her, sometimes doing exams at night or before sun-up. I even drove 50 miles one way to do exams that no one else would do. There were so many picky things that bothered me: her refusing to let me weigh a piece of mail on her scales, refusing to give me an envelope, making me turn in my key to the office by telling me no employees could have a key. Then I found out that only I had to turn in his key. She also wanted a copy of my driver's license and liability policy. Heck, you don't drive in NC without those. I quickly realized I had made a mistake taking a job with this woman and didn't know how long it would last.

There were some funny things that happened too. One night I agreed to do an exam on a pro-football player who lived in a gated community. He was to meet me at the gate and lead me to his home. When I got to the gate, I saw this car parked by the road. It pulled away, and I began to follow. Then it began to go faster and faster, and soon we were running 50 to 60 mph in this gated community. Suddenly, I noticed a car in my rear-view mirror that was rapidly gaining on me. He began flashing his lights. I knew exactly what the problem was, so I stopped and got out of the car. He said, "Hey, you're following the wrong car." That was a little embarrassing.

The boss lady was very particular about mistakes on the exams, and she would dock your pay for it. I couldn't afford that, because I wasn't making that much to begin with. Therefore, I was very careful not to make an error. Sometimes errors occur anyway, and it happened to me one day. I turned in some exams at the office one morning, and the boss called to let me know I had made a small mistake. I said, "OK, I'll come back and correct it." She said. "No, you won't. I'm turning it in like that." I said, "This is crazy. I'm offering to drive 50 miles to correct a mistake that you could correct for me. You had better not dock my pay." She said, "I will if they dock mine." I said, "If you do, it will be the last time." I was threatening to quit the job, but she told everyone that I made a threat against her. She didn't send me any more work, and about a week later she called to say she had a replacement for me. She said I could come and pick up my check. I guess she thought I was going to attack her, because when I went for my check, she had a small army of people around her. Without a doubt, she was by far the worse boss I ever had.

Portamedic had been asking me to come to work for them. I called the next day, and they were thrilled to have me as a new employee. Katrina was my new boss. She was young, but well educated and very smart. No doubt, she was my best boss ever. Now Juanita and I were working together again. Once we were awarded "Employees of the month", working as a team, Juanita and I continued working for

Portamedic for the next six years. During that time, we had some very interesting experiences which I would like to share.

We were doing an exam on a very wealthy lady in Pinehurst, NC. Upon entering her home, she asked us to remove our shoes, which we did. Her carpet was beautiful, snow white, and very shaggy. As part of the exam, I told her we needed a urine sample. I gave her a container and asked her to leave it in the bathroom, and I would test it there. She said, "You're not going in my bathroom!". I said, "No problem. Juanita will go." This woman had been downright hateful all through the exam. I think her husband was a little embarrassed by her behavior. While she was out of the room, he asked, "Have you ever witnessed a murder?" I thought, "Oh my God! He's going to kill the "Old Lady." I said, "No sir, I can't say that I have." He said, "Well, you're about to." There was a beautiful Persian cat beside his chair. He said, "See that cat. He just took a shit on my carpet. I'm going to kill him!" I was a bit relieved to say the least.

On another occasion, I was doing an exam on a lady who was applying for a $500,000 policy. As I began to take her medical history, her husband walked in and said, "Are you da man what bring da check?" It caught me by surprise, so I said, "Pardon me?" He said, "When she die are you da man dat bring my money?" I said, "No sir. I don't bring any checks." He said, "Well, when she die, how long do it take to get my money?" I said, "Sir, I really don't know." Then he said, " Do there be an investigation when she die?" I said, "I feel sure there will be." His wife never spoke a word. It sure sounded suspicious to me. When I got home, I told my family about it. Kelly said, "Daddy, you should call the law." I told her as far as I knew, he hadn't committed any crime, yet.

On this next case, I had to send a written report to the regional office in Raleigh. The manager said she had never seen anything like this in her more than 20 years with Portamedic. It started when I called an applicant to set up an appointment. I told him that I would need a blood sample, and that he should fast for 12 hours. He informed me that 12 hours was not a fast, that a fast was 72 hours. I said, "The insurance company only requires 12 hours, but you can fast longer if you like." This guy was an air traffic controller and lived in a gated community. When we arrived at his home, he had been out working in the hot sun, and he said he had fasted for 72 hours. First off, he wanted to see our ID from Portamedic. I began to take his medical history, and Juanita was doing his blood pressure. His BP was 134/86. He jumped up and shouted, "My BP has never been that high!" He grabbed his own BP cuff with a digital read-out and as Juanita watched over his shoulder, it read 136/86. Then he asked, "Are you an RN?" She said, "No, I'm a med tech." "Then you don't know what the hell you're doing", he said. Juanita said, "I think I have a pretty good idea what I'm doing. I've been doing it for 50 years." He said, "If you open your mouth again, I'll slap your teeth down your throat!" I told him. "You'd better not lay a hand on her." Then he said, "Get the hell out of my house!" I had already told Juanita that this exam was over, and we were already packing up. "Get out!", he repeated. I said, "We're going." He followed us and watched from the door as we were walking to the car. Juanita said to me, "Can you believe this guy?" Apparently, he heard her and said, "I'm coming out there and punch you out right now!" Juanita is the type you only push so far, then she pushes back, and she wasn't taking any more. She said, "Why don't you just come on and try it!" He ran down the steps with his fist drawn back, but he thought better and stopped short. After my report, no one else would attempt to do his exam, not even from the Raleigh or Charlotte offices.

There were many more good stories and we even talked about writing a book on the life and times of a paramedical examiner.

Juanita and I really enjoyed working together. After all, that's the way we met. Not only did we work together, we loved and played together. We loved to play games, especially word games like scrabble and boggle. We also played chess, dominos, and many different card games. We were very competitive, but on the word games, I would have to give her a slight edge. There were a few online video games we played; one in particular was a game called "Strike a Match", where you had to match either two or three words that had common bonds. There would be eight to ten people in a game, all competing against each other. We had two computers in our office. We would each get on a computer and try to get in the same game. We would pretend we didn't know each other, except as random players, then we would chat. This was one of my favorite conversations. In the game I was JW, and she was Jan. JW said, "Hi Jan." Jan said, "Hi JW." JW said, "Nice to see you on Strike a Match again." Jan said, "Thank you." JW said, "Nice to play with you again." Jan said, "I'll beg your pardon!" JW said, "I'm sorry Jan. I meant compete against you, but anyway, you're a lot of fun." Jan said, "You just don't know how much!" A gentleman said, "Marry her!" JW said, "Not a bad idea." Then a lady said, "Can I be the brides-maid?" A lot of lols. JW said, "Win or lose, this has certainly been a fun game. Almost all agreed. That's the kind of stuff we did. No one ever knew we were husband and wife.

I was diagnosed with glaucoma in 1974 at the age of 35. My doc-tor put me on various glaucoma drops over the years, and I was able to keep it under control. At times, I struggled to afford my medication, but always managed to find a way to get it, even if I had to beg for sam-ples. All was fine until late fall of 2003. I was due for an appointment with my ophthalmologist but didn't keep my appointment. I thought I'd just wait until February, because I'd be on Medicare then. Well, in the meantime I ran out of my glaucoma drops and went for a while without them. Around the first of February, I noticed I was losing vision in the lower part of my visual field. When I looked at people's faces, I couldn't see their legs. When I finally went for my check up, the pres-sure in my eyes was dangerously high. I got a new prescription for my drops, but the doctor said I needed glaucoma surgery on my right eye. Not knowing any better, I agreed, and surgery was done. Big mistake. It did nothing to relieve the pressure. Instead, it left my vision greatly impaired. I'm almost completely blind in that eye, with only a little vi-sion in the extreme right portion of my visual field. Thank God I didn't let him operate on my left eye as he wanted to do, otherwise, I'd be completely blind. I also had cataract surgery which was also a mistake. It did nothing to help me see better. Over the past 15 years, my vision has gotten progressively worse, and I am almost legally blind. The only way I can use the computer is by reversing the contrast, that is, using a black background. I can no longer see color on the TV. Everything is in black and white. I'm thankful that I can see at all.

Duncan's Creek flows north to south through the center of our prop-erty. Wildcat Branch flows from the west and runs into Duncan's Creek near the center of the property. There are many colonies of beavers along the creek, and beavers like to do two things: cut down trees and build dams. Back in the '60s, there was a gentleman who came every winter to trap them for their pelts, but this ceased long ago. During the '70s, they built a dam down a fence row along the property line, forming a nice little pond. I purchased a flat-bottom boat to explore the pond. One day I decided to try fishing in it, not expecting to catch anything, but to my surprise, I caught several chain pickerel, commonly called jack, as well as some catfish. I put a trot line in the pond with about 20 hooks, and I would bait it in the late afternoon, then check it after dinner and then again in the morning. We always had plenty of catfish. One night, Juanita and I went to check the line. As we paddled the boat to the first hook, it was jumping like crazy. We said, "We've got a big one here." When we pulled it up, it was big alright, but not a fish. It was one of the biggest cottonmouth moccasins I had ever seen. We backed the boat away and went back to the house, not even thinking about the other hooks. The next afternoon I went back with my pistol and took care of the snake.

The largest beaver pond I have ever seen is located on the property joining us. We obtained permission from the owner to use it for fishing. That pond covers about ten acres and is ten feet deep at the dam. A beaver lodge sets near the dam. In the early 2000s, my son-in-law David, cleared a trail to the pond so we could reach it easily. It is completely isolated with no houses in sight or no other easy access. There's also an abundance of Canadian geese and wild ducks that stay there all year. I put a trot line in that pond also, and fished it regularly from around 2002 to 2007, catching some really nice fish. I had to finally stop using the pond because of my failing eyesight. I didn't feel comfortable taking the boat onto it with all the hazards, like stumps, not to mention the snakes. The trail is almost overgrown with bushes now, and someone recently purchased the property and have, for some reason, broken the dam.

Despite my eyesight being impaired, I was still able to do my exams in 2004. I had to re-new my driver's license that year, and I was concerned about that. I hesitated a few times on the eye exam but was able to pass.

Financially, Juanita and I were better off now than we had been in

15 years. We were both working for Portamedic, both drawing social security, I was selling coins, and I was on Medicare. Juanita would be on Medicare next year. We were able to keep up with all the bills, but we couldn't get ahead, because of the high interest rate credit cards and charge accounts, not to mention the high interest rate on the mortgage.

I don't recall the exact date, but I believe it was sometime in 2005 that I got word that Brenda, my ex-wife, had passed away. She was only 63. She had been fighting lung cancer for several years. She had been a smoker since about age 18, and although I begged and tried so many times to get her to stop, it never happened. I can't say for certain that smoking caused her cancer, but it's very likely it did. I attended her funeral in Cusseta, GA. It was a very sad day for Harvey and Wendy, because they had always been so close to their mother. I told them that day that even though our divorce had been a bitter one in some respect, that I was glad that we had put our differences aside and had had a friendly relationship for the past several years.

Two years earlier, a longtime friend of Juanita called to let us know her ex-husband had passed away at age 65. This news came well after the fact, so there was never any consideration for her attending his funeral.

Our 1992 Cadillac had been a good car and served us well for many years, but it finally gave out. We went car shopping for the first time in what seemed like ages. We knew we couldn't afford a new car, so we were shopping for a nice pre-owned one. We found a 2004 Chevrolet Monte Carlo that we really liked. Although it was two years old, it was clean and only had 43,000 on the odometer. We were able to finance it for five years at a payment we could afford, and we drove it away. That car turned out to be the best car we ever owned. We drove it for 11 years and never had any major problems. We finally sold it in 2017. It had more than 200,000 miles on it.

In the fall of 2007 our daughter, Kelly announced that she was pregnant. At age 35 she was about to run out of time. There were no complications, and on April 22, 2008 she gave birth to a healthy baby boy, Blake David Sears, at Cape Fear Valley Hospital, the same place she was born. We couldn't ask for a nicer grandson and even though Kelly and David are now divorced, they are both very loving parents, and

Blake shares his time with both.

When our good friends Edna and C.W. Johnson lived across the road from us, we visited often. We always enjoyed a good card game, and many times I would play my guitar. After Edna's job took them to Germany, I all but stopped picking the guitar. However, before they left, C.W. took me to meet an acquaintance of his by the name of Ralph Mangum. I had not met Ralph before, but I knew his father Brooks reasonably well. He was the one who would till my garden each year or let me use his tractor. Ralph enjoyed playing the guitar and singing country music just as I did. We sat on his front porch that afternoon and played and sang for a couple of hours. It was about 20 years before I saw Ralph again. One evening I received a phone call, and the voice said, "This is Ralph Mangum. Are you the Mr. Wills that plays the guitar?" I said, "I am." He told me that a group of guys got together every Thursday to play country music and that one of the guys in the group, a Mr. Hardin, was looking for a lead guitar player. I hadn't played more than a half dozen times over that 20-year period, but I agreed to go. Elbert Hardin had been our mail carrier at one time, and I also learned that he was the father of the world-famous wrestlers, the "Hardin Boys". Even though I hadn't played in years, I suppose Elbert was impressed enough that he asked me to begin playing in his group, "The Back-Porch Boys". That was around 2007. I worked with Elbert for a few years and still play with the group on a regular basis, about twice per week on average.

Dr. Stuart Davis was my personal physician. I first met Stuart when he was in medical school back in the '70s when he took a summer job working in the lab at Cape Fear Hospital. He had also become a good customer of mine in the coin business. When I went for my annual exam in 2006, he informed me that my PSA (Prostate Specific Antigen) was slightly elevated, around 6.4, and that he was concerned. He had me see a urologist, who repeated the test with about the same results. He informed me that there was a 1 in 3 chance that I had prostate cancer, and that he wanted to do a biopsy. I refused the biopsy, thinking that if cancer cells were present, the bleeding could spread them to other parts of my body. I also knew that the PSA was not a specific test for prostate cancer, that it could be elevated for other reasons, such as an enlarged prostate, which was common in men my age.

Over the years, we were able to visit our friends in Kentucky, Edna and C.W. Johnson, on several occasions, including the weddings of both their daughters. One thing that was so unique about Ammia's wedding was that the couple left the church in a hot air balloon. The crowd stood and waved to them as they slowly drifted out of sight. It was so cool. Ammia and her husband now have four children and live in Seneca, SC. Jamie's marriage, unfortunately, didn't last. Juanita and I don't see Jamie as often as we would like, but we both play video games with her almost daily. She is such a sweet person, and we love her very much. On two occasions while visiting Edna and C.W., we took a dinner cruise on the Ohio River. River cruises are so much fun, and we've been on many, including the Mississippi, Savannah, and Cape Fear Rivers.

From the beginning of our marriage and even before, Juanita's family has been an important part of my life. I have always loved them as they have me. Clyde, her oldest brother was very close to Juanita when they were growing up, always watching out for her when they were in school. During most of our marriage, Clyde lived in Texas. While managing the VFW in Ft Stockton, Clyde ended up killing a man who was trying to get him to deal in illegal drugs and also saying bad things about his wife. He spent five years in Huntsville Prison. After being released, he married a Mexican lady and lived in Mexico where he died of a heart attack in 2000. He is buried there.

Jewell, who was four years younger than Juanita, had a hard life. Her first husband, Jerry, was killed in Vietnam just a few days before he was due to return home, leaving her with two young boys. Jewell also had two children by her second husband, Lloyd Melton. In my opinion, he was never a good husband nor a good father. They were married for several years. One day he left, never to have contact with his children again. Jewell spent lots of time with us over the years, even living with us for a while in the early years of our marriage. We went on many trips together and always enjoyed her company. Jewell died unexpectedly in her sleep in 2016. We still see her children quite often as well as her grandchildren. Her youngest son "Little" Lloyd is almost like a son; if fact, we sometimes refer to him as our adopted son. We have always been very close. He and our daughter Kelly are best of friends.

Lloyd married Misty Fowler of Hillsville, VA. They now make their home in Dublin, VA. Misty is a high-school English teacher, and Lloyd is a manager at a Buffalo Wild Wings restaurant. They have one daughter, Haley, who is about the same age as our grandson, Blake. Blake and Haley have become very good friends.

We see Lloyd and Misty more than any of Jewell's children. We always enjoy going out to eat, then returning home for a great card game of Spades. On one of their visits, Lloyd mentioned that he would like to purchase a shotgun. I had an extra single-shot 12 gauge, and I sold it to him at a favorable price. We took a walk down one of our nature trails, and as we were crossing Wildcat Branch, I almost stepped on a large water moccasin. The snake swam across the branch and began crawling out the other side. I said, "Shoot him Lloyd." He fired, and the recoil kicked him back a couple of feet. He wasn't expecting that. He said, "He's still moving!" I said, "Shoot him again Lloyd!" He fired again, but the snake continued to move. I said, "Shoot him once more!" Lloyd didn't want to be kicked any more by the shotgun, so he said, "No! You shoot him." However, Lloyd had made his first kill with his new gun. We still laugh about that incident.

Juanita's other brother Robert is six years younger than her. Earlier in my story, I mentioned how he had lived with us for a while before getting into some trouble and moving to Arkansas. While there, he married for the second time and was there for many years before getting a divorce and moving back to North Carolina, where he re-married his first wife, Geneva. Robert and Geneva had four children, one of which is deceased. They are now separated, and he has moved to Virginia. His health has declined rapidly over the past few years, and he is now suffering from emphysema and COPD. He is currently on oxygen 24 hours a day.

Lois Kay, Juanita's sister who is younger by 10 years, married at a very young age and had one child, Cheryl. She was divorced and married for a second time on the same day as Juanita and me, but unfortunately, theirs didn't last. She has done well for herself and now owns her own home near Hillsville, Virginia, where she works as a CNA (Certified Nurse's Assistant).

Before being married, Lois's daughter Cheryl, spent a lot of time with us and traveled with me to many coin shows. Cheryl has four children.

Joyce Anne, Juanita's other sister spent most of her life in a home for the retarded. She passed away while in her 50s.

My son-in-law, David Sears was a big fan of auto racing. In the late '90s, he had a Chevy Nova that he ran on a quarter mile oval track in Garner, NC every weekend. That came to an end one night when he was rear-ended, and his car was totaled. He purchased a 1974 Corvette which we took to the Fayetteville Drag Strip one night. This was his first time to try his hand at drag racing. I gave him all the pointers I could, and he caught on quickly.

Sometime around 2008 or 2009 he bought a Jeep Grand Cherokee. It had the SRT (street racing technology) package, which came with a 6.1-liter Hemi engine rated at 425 horsepower and also had an all-wheel drive. It was an awesome vehicle. Included in the purchase price was a full one-day clinic in high performance events, including drag racing. Chrysler Corporation would be providing all the cars for the events, and that would include all the vehicles they offered with the SRT package. David invited me to go with Kelly and him to the event which took place at Charlotte Motor Speedway. There were many participants, and we were broken down into small groups. Our instructor was a young lady who went by the name of "Psychette". She acquired that name because she had been an actress who had done a stabbing scene in some horror movie. I struck up a conversation with her about my previous experience in drag racing. Apparently, she took a liking to me, and let me participate in the drag racing event along with the car owners. In addition to driving the Grand Cherokee, I raced the Dodge Charger, Dodge Magnum, and the Chrysler 300. I was having a blast! At the end of the day she said, "Come on Johnny, I'll take you for a spin in the Dodge Viper". That car had a V-10 engine rated at 600 horsepower. That girl could drive! We went around the track sideways at full throttle with the tires smoking! Afterwards, she gave me a ticket valued at $110 which was good for three laps around the Charlotte Motor Speedway in one of the NASCAR cars. I climbed through the window into a Dodge Chargers, although the regular driver was not under the wheel. We cruised around the track three times at 170 miler per hour. David and Kelly also took their turn at cruising around the speedway in one on the NASCAR cars. I think I had more fun that day than anyone. "Psychette" was a fun person and I thoroughly enjoyed her friendship and hospitality that day.

Returning to Fayetteville, David and I took his Grand Cherokee to the strip for a few runs. It was the most awesome car I ever drove on the strip. My best run in the quarter mile was 12.87 seconds at 103 mph, my all-time best run.

On my 60th birthday in 1999, Juanita was taking me to dinner at Sandpiper Seafood, one of my favorite restaurants. What I didn't know was that she and Kelly had planned a surprise party for me. When we walked in, there were about 20 people shouting, "Happy Birthday"! The guests were family members from Georgia and Virginia and friends from the coin club. It was a great party and it definitely caught me by surprise. I didn't think I could ever be surprised like that again, but when I turned 70 in 2009 it was even a bigger surprise. Juanita and Kelly pulled it off again, this time at Kelly and David's home. They lived just 200 yards across the field from us, and Juanita had gone over to their house that morning for some reason I don't recall. Anyway, they called me to come over, that we were going out for lunch. When I walked over, I saw nothing suspicious, like cars in the yard. They had told me to come in the garage door, and when I opened it, it was decorated and packed with people. My son Harvey and family were there, along with my daughter Wendy, and they brought barbeque to be served for our meal. Juanita's family was there from Virginia, and many of my family members were there also. After we ate, Harvey, along with a couple of my music friends provided entertainment for us. Great party!

It was hard to believe I was 70 years old. Where did all those years go? Juanita wasn't too far behind. Kelly and I would be giving her a 70th birthday party in a little more than a year.

We had been struggling financially for almost 20 years, and even though we were now keeping up with the bills, we came to realize we could never pay them off because of the high interest rates. We also knew I couldn't keep working forever. We were already well past retirement age, and I was beginning to have health problems. It was decision time.

Shortly after my birthday, we decided to file for bankruptcy. It was the only way we would ever get out from under all that debt. We had several credit cards and charge accounts that totaled around $21,000. Bankruptcy would allow us to eliminate those payments immediately, and the creditors would not be able to harass us. That's exactly what we did. We met with an attorney in Raleigh, and it was arranged so we would make a single monthly payment of somewhere in the vicinity of $200 per month for a period of 40 months. Our home and car were not included in the bankruptcy. We would continue making payments on those. The attorney told us that only 23% of those filing for bankruptcy would follow through and complete it. I was determined to be in that 23% and although it was difficult due to the fact that both of us would soon be unable to work, it was finally completed in the summer of 2012.

In August 2009, Juanita began complaining of an uncomfortable feeling in her lower abdomen. She set up an appointment with her personal care provider, Cheryl Rachels, FNP. Upon examination, Mrs. Rachels found what appeared to be a mass in her lower abdomen and immediately made her an appointment with a gynecologist. Apparently, Mrs. Rachels feared the worst, because later that afternoon she called Juanita at home and said, "Juanita, I just want you to know I'm praying for you."

I didn't like the way that sounded, but it made me start thinking. Did she say praying? When was the last time we prayed?

During the early years of our marriage, and up until the time we went into business with Bill Page in 1978, we had gone to church regularly and even though we didn't have much, we thanked God for what we did have. Then we got so caught up in trying to get our business started and working seven days a week, we had gotten away from going to church. Maybe it was time to start praying.

I went with Juanita to the Pinehurst Surgical Clinic for her appointment with the gynecologist. As we took our seat in the waiting area, I couldn't believe what I was hearing on their sound system. They began playing the song "Honey", a story about a man who loved his wife so much, and they enjoyed life together. Then, she unexpectedly dies, and her husband talks about how much he misses her. I loved the song, but it was the last thing I needed to hear that day.

After the doctor examined her, I was called into the examining room, and he told me to feel her abdomen. I said, "It feels like a ball, the size of an orange." He said, "It's more the size of a grapefruit. We have to get her to an oncologist-gynecologist as soon as possible, and we don't have one here. I'll make her an appointment at North Carolina Memorial Hospital in Chapel Hill."

After seeing the doctor in Chapel Hill and having some tests done, she was diagnosed as having ovarian cancer. She needed surgery as soon as possible. We were sent to an office to have the surgery scheduled, but they were unable to put us on the schedule and said they would have to call us. A couple of days later, I answered the phone, and it was Dr. Ko, a young resident oncologist-gynecologist who had been one of the doctors examining Juanita. She told me the surgery was scheduled, but it was three weeks away. I said, "Dr. Ko, I don't think she can wait that long. Don't you think we need to move that up a little sooner?" She said, "Yes, I agree. Let me see what I can do." She called back the following day to let us know that it was scheduled for the following week. The surgeon would be Dr. Victoria Bae-Jump.

Juanita had already resigned from her job with Portamedic, but I was still working. I was so worried about my lovely wife, that I cried for her every day. I had been told that the survival rate for ovarian cancer was only 30 per cent, and I couldn't bear the thought of losing her. Neither could our daughter, Kelly. She was so afraid that her son, Blake, who was one year old, would never know his grandmother.

It was time to start praying. I asked God to spare her life, and we even went to church. The church added her to their prayer list and many of our friends had her added to a prayer list at other churches.

I had recently read an article about a new medication that was being used routinely to treat all cancer patients in Japan. It was a prescription drug called AHCC (Activated Hexose Correlated Compound). During a study of the substance, 67% of the persons using it became cancer free and all the other were in remission. Not a single person in the study had died. To me, that was most impressive. I also learned that it was now available in the United Stated through one company, The Harmony Company, and though it was somewhat expensive, it did not require a prescription in the United States, because it was a natural substance

305

derived from a specific type of mushroom that was only found in Japan. It was said to be the most powerful, natural, immune system booster ever discovered. It was sold under the name of Immpower. I placed an order for some, and Juanita began taking it immediately and would continue taking it until after the completion of her chemotherapy in January 2010. It apparently works by strengthening the immune system so that it could destroy any cancer cells left after surgery or chemotherapy.

On the morning of Juanita's surgery, we waited patiently for hours. Dr. Bae-Jump finally came out to speak with us. She was a young woman, late 30s and very petite, less than five feet tall. She said that the surgery went well, although the tumor, now the size of a cantaloupe, had ruptured during surgery; and Juanita received two pints of blood. She classified the cancer as stage-3, meaning it had begun spreading, but was still localized. It was attached to the intestine, and she said she scraped it off as much as possible. She would need to begin chemotherapy soon.

During her stay at the hospital, she was visited regularly by Dr. Bae-Jump. Sometimes she would sit on the bed and talk for half an hour. She was never in a hurry. I have never seen a more caring doctor. Juanita recovered rapidly from her surgery, and I was soon able to take her home. In a couple of weeks, she would begin her chemotherapy. Juanita maintained a positive attitude and just assumed that after her treatment was over, all would be fine. I went with her for all her treatments, except one. I went to Georgia one Friday for the beginning of hunting season and would be playing music for the big party.

On Saturday morning, Kelly called me to say that her mom was very depressed, and that I should call her. When I called, she said that while she was receiving her chemo the previous day, all the other women who were receiving chemo were there because their cancer had returned. Now she wasn't so sure anymore that all would be OK following chemo. I tried to assure her that she would be fine, although I knew the odds were against us.

She finished her chemo in January and would return for a checkup in July. Dr. Bae-Jump would examine her, and a CA-125 would be done. That would tell us if the cancer had returned. The normal for the CA-125 is 30 or less. When Dr. Bae-Jump called on the evening of her first check-up and told us the CA-125 was 11, we were overjoyed. She would have a check-up every six months for the next five years and afterwards, once a year. As I write this more than eight years later, her CA-125 has always been in the 10-12 range. Juanita has been one of those lucky 30 percent. Did God hear and answer our prayers? Did the Immpower help? I don't know the answers to those questions, but I thank the Lord that she is still cancer free. Dr. Bae-Jump calls Juanita her miracle patient. Her personal physician, Mrs. Rachels admitted that she thought Juanita was going to die. As of now, she is very much alive and we're all so very thankful for that.

CHAPTER **20**

Retirement, Life's Final Chapter

FEBRUARY 1, 2010 was my last day of work as a paramedical examiner for Portamedic. Age had taken its toll on my health. In just ten days, I would be 71. Glaucoma had robbed me of much of my vision, and my PSA was elevated. That could mean trouble down the road, but at present, I had no symptoms. Juanita had been forced to resign her job with Portamedic due to having ovarian cancer. Her treatment had gone well, and she was recovering nicely, but it was unlikely she would ever take another job.

Kelly was already planning Juanita's 70th birthday party, which was coming up on May 1. During Juanita's first marriage, she had lived in Hawaii for three years, and she loved it there. Kelly really wanted to send the two of us there as Juanita's birthday present, but unfortunately, it was going to be a little above her means. Instead, she decided to send us to Niagara Falls for a few days. The party would be at Kelly and David's home, which was next door to us. We would have someone cook a whole hog for the party. Although Juanita had not bowled since the previous season, I decided to invite our best friends from the league as well as other friends and of course, all the family members on both sides. I would invite all my musician friends to come and entertain, and as a special guest, I would invite Kelly's old school principal, Linda Smith, whom I had teamed up with as a duet. We had been performing as Ebony and Ivory for several years. We would also rent one of those bouncy houses for the kids. All total we were inviting between 50 and 75 people. As a teacher, Kelly had had lots of experience, and she was an excellent organizer and planner. Everything was set.

On the day of the party, I was up early and began setting up the tables and chairs in Kelly and David's backyard. The bouncy house was picked up at Ft. Bragg, and we got it ready. The hog was cooked the night before the party, and it would be delivered on the cooker around mid-morning. Some family members were arriving early, but most of the guests would be there at 11 AM.

The hog was delivered around 10 AM, and I began chopping up the meat and preparing barbecue. Many of the family members were very helpful in getting everything ready. Kelly had made a large display board of pictures illustrating Juanita's life. That was most impressive. The band members were setting up their equipment and preparing to entertain.

Somewhere between noon and 1:00 PM, we were ready to eat. The band members were the first to go through the line, so they could start playing. After everyone had eaten, I joined in with the band to sing a song. As I began singing "Hula Love", my partner, Linda Smith, walked out in her grass hula skirt, to join me. The crowd cheered. The two of us sang several songs together.

After singing "Happy Birthday" to Juanita and cutting the cake, it was time to open presents. Kelly had suggested to the guests that monetary gifts would be appropriate to help on the trip to Niagara Falls. Juanita received more than $1,000. By 3 PM, the party was about over, and most of the guests were leaving.

After the party, we all went inside. Some family members were still there as were our good friends from Kentucky, Edna and C.W. Johnson and daughter Jamie. However, there was one person from the bowling alley that I had invited who was not a bowler. Every time we would bowl, this guy, and I don't recall his name, would sit behind us and watch. People began to think he was a relative of ours, but, heck, we didn't know him. I finally learned his name and began talking to him. He seemed innocent enough, so I invited him to the party. He seemed to fit in OK, that is, until it was time to leave. He came in the house and made himself at home, just like he was family. Finally, I made an announcement, "The party is over. It's time to leave." I was looking at him when I said that. He hesitantly got up and slowly made his way out. With a funny look on his face, C.W. got up as if to leave. I said, "Sit down C.W.! I wasn't talking to you. I was trying to get that weirdo out of here." He started laughing and said, "Oh, I thought you meant us." I said, "No, you guys are spending the night with us."

It was beginning to get dark, and I was totally exhausted from the long, busy day. For some reason that I don't recall, I got in the car to drive home, which was just next door. I met a car as I approached our driveway and waited for him to pass. Then, as I turned in, I missed the driveway and ran the car into the ditch with the right front wheel. The left rear wheel was two feet off the ground. This was more than embarrassing. At that time, my vision wasn't the greatest, but it wasn't that bad. I blamed part of it on the fact that I was so exhausted. I walked back and announced that I had run the car in the ditch and asked David if he would bring his truck and pull me out. I walked back and got a heavy chain from the barn. By now, Juanita had walked up there. When she saw the car, she said, "Oh, my God. I didn't know it was that bad. I thought you just drove off the road into the ditch." David got his truck in place, and as I began to crawl under the car to tie the chain around the axle, Jamie said, "Let me do that Mr. Johnny." I said, "Yeah, sure." After all, you don't argue with a girl who carries a gun in one pocket and a knife in the other, as she had previously shown us." She carried those items for protection. C.W. was stopping traffic, so David could pull me out. A car stopped, and a man got out saying, "Ain't no way that pick-up is gonna pull that car out." The 4-wheel drive GMC didn't even strain. I untied the chain and drove into the driveway. Then the man asked C.W., "Has he been drinking?" C.W. said, no, he hasn't drunk anything." The man insisted that I had been drinking, and C.W. was beginning to get upset with him. C.W. was right. I hadn't drunk anything.

It had been a long day for Juanita also. The party had been overwhelming for her. She said it was almost like her mind was in a daze. When I would ask her about something specific that happened, she would say, "I barely remember that." It had been a great party and certainly one we'd always remember. Now it would be time to start thinking about our trip.

Traveling to Canada required a passport, so we went to the post office in Sanford to put in our application. In about a week or ten days, we had our passports and began preparing for our trip. Kelly had already gotten our airline tickets and made our hotel reservations, so all we had to do now was pack our bags.

We flew out of Raleigh-Durham Airport with a stop in Washington, DC before proceeding to Buffalo, NY. On the way to Buffalo, we experienced some brief turbulence, probably the worst I had ever experienced. It was a little scary for a moment. Short of renting a car, there was no good way to get to Niagara, which was a little surprising. We ended up having to take a taxi. It was about an hour's drive, and we took the back roads, which was good, because there was no back-up of traffic at the border. The only thing the border agent was interested in was how much money we were bringing into Canada. We told him and were on our way. Upon arriving at Niagara, we told the driver we wanted to exchange some money into Canadian Dollars. He said the best and quickest way was at the casino. They charged us a small fee, but that was expected. Our hotel was marvelous. We had a room with an excellent view of the American Falls. We could also see the top of the Horseshoe Falls on the Canadian side. After researching some of the possibilities for sightseeing in the area, we purchased a ticket to take a bus tour of the area the following day. One thing that amazed me during our bus trip was the squirrels in the area. I didn't know squirrels came in so many colors. There were black, white, red, and gray. It was extremely expensive to eat at the hotel, so we decided to walk a couple of blocks to find a restaurant that would fit our budget a little better. There were plenty of restaurants, and they were filled with tourists who were also apparently getting away from those high prices at the hotels. On subsequent days, we visited the falls, taking the walk on the trail that led you behind the Horseshoe Falls. Then we took the boat ride, "Maiden of the Mist" which took us right inside the horseshoe. A disposable raincoat was issued to everyone to keep us from getting wet from the mist. We spent a limited time in the casino, did a little shopping, and dined at a well-known restaurant.

The taxi driver who brought us from Buffalo to Niagara Falls said he would call us to see if we wanted him to take us back to Buffalo, but we decided we could take a bus much cheaper, so on the morning we were to leave, we exchanged what Canadian money we had back to

U.S. Dollars, checked out of the room, and took a cab to the bus station. We had to wait a couple of hours for the next bus going to Buffalo. When we got to the border, busses were lined up all the way across the Niagara River Bridge and into Canada. The line was not moving, and we knew that at that rate we'd never make it back to Buffalo in time for our flight. Finally, after we sat there for what seemed an eternity, the bus driver got permission for us to move to the head of the line, by telling them he had passengers that had a flight to make in Buffalo. The U.S. border agents made everyone get off the bus, and one by one we were interrogated. By now, we were wishing we had taken the cab back to Buffalo. When we finally got back to the airport, we had maybe 10 to 15 minutes to spare before our flight departed. It was a wonderful vacation, and we were very grateful to have a daughter who loved us so much as to send us on that vacation.

Despite the fact I was using three different eye drops to control my glaucoma, my vision appeared to be getting progressively worse. I was also beginning to have some difficulty urinating. I had every symptom of an enlarged prostate. To make matters worse, I began to notice that I was having difficulty understanding voices, especially when trying to watch a movie on TV. When people asked how I was doing, I would say fine, except for the fact that I can't hear, see, or pee. I got a lot of laughs from that.

When I had my annual check-up in 2011, at age 72 my PSA was 46. I was sent to see a urologist who told me I might have prostate cancer and that I should have a biopsy. I refused, and he got very upset with me and told me what a painful death prostate cancer caused. As I left, he said, "If you change your mind, let me know." At that time, I had no intentions of ever seeing him again.

2011 was a tough year financially. Our only source of income was our social security payments and from the sale of rare coins and precious metals, which netted us around $200 per month, however, we would occasionally have a transaction that would net $1000 or more. In December of that year, we made the final payment on the Monte Carlo, which gave us an extra $250 per month.

Our grandson Blake was now in pre-K at St. Luke's in Sanford. Juanita took him to school on Monday, Wednesday, and Friday. On the way to school, he listened to the early Johnny Cash songs, as well as some of the early rock and roll songs from Elvis and others. It wasn't long until he knew every word to many of them. He began going to Anderson Creek where I played on Friday nights, and he would sing a song. People loved him. Unfortunately, that eventually faded away.

Blake's mother was the first to introduce him to music, playing songs from the Johnny Cash sound track, "Walk the Line". Later she would introduce him to other genres, so that he could enjoy all types of music, as opposed to only one.

Juanita had recovered nicely from her bout with ovarian cancer. We felt so blessed that God had seen fit to spare her life, and we were now going to church again. In the early days of our marriage, we had only attended churches of the Primitive Baptist faith, but now we realized we could praise God in other churches as well. After all, she had been put on the prayer lists in churches of many denominations. We had chosen to attend the Crossroads Community Church near Carthage, NC. I had been watching their services on TV each Sunday morning and liked what I heard. Crossroads was a non-denominational church that simply preached what the Bible said. It was good to be praising God again after 30 years. Good things were about to start happening again.

One day we noticed that the woodwork around the eaves of our house were in desperate need of repair. I called Ralph Mangum, one of my musician friends, who was also a handy-man. He said, "You need to take care of that right away." He told me he could begin working on it in a couple of days. I had no idea how I could pay for it, but the following day, one of my coin customers called and asked me to sell some gold for him and asked what I would charge. I said, "Ten percent." He said, "Let's do it." I picked up the gold, took it to a buyer that I dealt with, and my commission came to $1300. Ralph was there the next day to begin work. He did a fantastic job, and his fee was $1250. Was it a co-incidence that I got that gold deal, or was God working in some mysterious way?

Later that year, my urinary symptom had gotten to the point that I had to have something done. I made an appointment with the same urologist that I had vowed never to see again. He recommended a TURP (trans-urethral resection procedure). That procedure had to be done at the hospital outpatient surgical clinic, and I would have to pay the hospital $1000 up front. He also told me that he could do a TUMP (transurethral microwave procedure) in his office. He said it was an effective procedure but would take a few weeks for me to see any improvement. I chose that procedure.

The TUMP procedure involved a process by which an electrode would be placed within the prostate gland and utilizing a microwave, heat the electrode to 122 degrees F. It would last for a duration of 30 minutes. This would cause the tissue surrounding the electrode to die, decompose, and eventually be flushed away, therefore, creating a larger opening for urine to pass. By contrast, the TURP, sometimes called the "roto-rooter" job involved surgically snipping away the tissue to create a larger opening and offering relief sooner. Both procedures would require having a catheter in place for about a week.

I was scheduled to come in a few days later for my work-up which would include a cystoscopy and an MRI. During the cystoscopy, I could see everything the doctor was seeing except I didn't know what I was looking at. I asked if he saw anything that looked like cancer. He replied, "No cancer." The MRI was used to determine the size of the prostate to find the right electrode to use. During that procedure, the doctor said, "You've got a big one alright." I said, "Pardon me?" He said, "I'm talking about your prostate." It was embarrassing, especially with the nurse standing there watching everything.

I was back a couple of days later for the procedure. They gave me a sedative to make me drowsy and inserted the electrode. The microwave was turned on, and the timer was set for 30 minutes. It was a lot worse than I had expected. I don't think they performed the procedure properly. When I had read about the procedure, it stated that water would be circulated within the rectum to keep the surrounding tissue from getting too hot. They did not do that. The pain was almost unbearable and that 30 minutes seemed an eternity. A catheter was inserted with a collection bag tied to my leg, and I was sent home.

For the next few days, I was in agony. My rectum was severely burned, and large blisters formed. Unable to sleep at night, I usually sat on a heating pad to help relieve the pain. I went back a week later, and they removed the catheter and filled my bladder with water to see if it would pass out on its own. It did, and I went home. That's when things got really bad. Later that day, I had the urge to pee, and I couldn't. No matter how hard I strained, it wouldn't come out. Meanwhile, my bladder was getting fuller and fuller, and I was in misery. I went to my wife and said, "Honey, I need to go to the emergency room, now. We began the 35-minute drive to Moore Regional Hospital in Pinehurst. By now, I was really hurting. I thought my bladder would burst at any time. I told the ER receptionist, "I need help now. I can't pee." I was taken into an examining room where it seemed like it took forever before a nurse finally catharized me. What a relief! They put in a new catheter and told me to see my urologist as soon as possible. I believe I wore that catheter for another week before it was removed. I was so relieved when I could pee a little this time. It continued to get better, though slowly, until it reached a point I felt I could live with. I think the biggest benefit I got from that microwave procedure was that it burned out a large internal hemorrhoid that I had had for years. One thing is for certain. I will never have that procedure done again, nor would I recommend it to anyone.

In the summer of 2012 we made the final payment to the bankruptcy trustee. That was a happy day. It had been a long struggle, but now it was over, and it gave us a great financial boost.

One day when I was taking a shower, the drain plug broke loose from the tub, because of rusting, and fell to the ground beneath the house. We couldn't be without a bathtub, but I didn't have the money for a new one. Would a miracle happen again? Amazingly, it did. That evening I overheard my daughter talking about some of the teachers at her school wanting to sell their gold jewelry, because the price of gold was so high. They were planning to sell to a pawn shop. I interrupted her and said, "Tell them to let me sell it. I can get them almost double what a pawn shop will pay." Within the next three days, I had sold over $10,000 in gold for several of the teachers, and I had charged them 10%. I had more than enough to have a new bathtub installed. Again, I believe it was a blessing from God.

My grandson Blake, was now six years old and beginning to participate in sports. His mother wanted him to get involved just as I had wanted her to do. Juanita and I went to all his games just as we had gone to Kelly's games. Blake tried basketball, football, baseball, and soccer. Basketball would be his favorite, followed by baseball. He did not care for football or soccer.

Blake loves nature, and we live at a place where he can enjoy it. We have woods, streams, ponds, and a variety of animals. Our woods have many trails, and we have walked those trails many times. One day I decided to teach him the different kind of trees, by studying the leaves. It wasn't long until he could identify many varieties such as the maple, sweet gum, water oak, walnut, pecan, poplar, and wild cherry. He also loves domestic pets, especially cats, and he also has had, or currently has: fish, frogs, hermit crab, and has temporarily captured many different insects. His father is also an outdoorsman, and he is teaching Blake to hunt and fish. So far, Blake has caught a 10-pound channel catfish and has killed a 20-pound wild turkey. A deer will likely be coming soon. As I write this, Blake is 10 years old.

When I purchased our original 19-acres of land in 1966, it was covered in young loblolly pines, approximately 11-years old. In 2013, at 58 years of age the trees were very large, and we decided to harvest about six acres. The timber company who harvested the trees told us that they had never seen that much timber cut from six acres. We re-planted with an improved variety of loblolly pine that is supposed to grow much faster than the native trees. After four years, they are coming along nicely, with an average diameter of four inches and a height of 15 feet.

In early 2015, I began to occasionally have some moderate pain in my lower abdomen, that over-the-counter pain medication had no effect on. I had my annual checkup in April of that year, and my PSA was 200. My urologist was notified, but I got no response from him. With the symptom continuing to get worse, and by now I had begun to have some pain in my legs and hips, I finally made an appointment with the urologist in October. At that time my PSA was 552, so the urologist ordered a bone scan and an MRI. I was told that they would call me with the results in about a week, but they didn't call. So, I began calling, but still couldn't get any results. Finally, I got an appointment on November 24, the day before Thanksgiving. The doctor told me that I had cancer in every bone in my body, and he diagnosed me as having stage-4 prostate cancer. My first question was, "How long do I have?" He said, "Without treatment, less than a year, but with treatment, you could live for years." I said, "OK, let's start the treatment." He explained the cancer fed on the hormone, testosterone, and that he wanted to treat it with a Lupron injection, which would stop the production of testosterone, but he couldn't start it until he could confirm that it was in fact prostate cancer, and that could only be determined by biopsy. In the meantime, he prescribed a pill which he said would help.

Shortly after returning home that afternoon, my children Harvey and Wendy, along with their families, arrived to spend Thanksgiving with us. It was a shock when I greeted them with the news that I had Stage-4 prostate cancer. I wanted to get my prescription filled as soon as possible, so I could begin my treatment. I couldn't believe it when I learned that the cost was somewhere around $600 to $800 for a month's supply. Wendy said, "Daddy, give me that prescription, and let me see what I can do." She returned later with my medication. I don't know how she did it, but she was able to get my medication for well under $100. I was so grateful to her for doing that.

The following week, I went back to my urologist for the biopsy. Twelve samples were taken, and all were positive for cancer. Within a week, I had received my first Lupron injection. Within days, I could tell it was working because I was no longer having pain, and to my surprise, my urinary symptoms also disappeared. On my next checkup, my PSA had dropped from 552 to 52. Three months later it was 26. I felt great, with no pain whatsoever. The only side effect I had was hot flashes, and I could live with those.

Blake was getting ready to play baseball, so I began working with him on his batting skills. He developed great power and began hitting line drives when I would pitch to him. With my poor vision, it was difficult for me to avoid being hit. One day after our batting session, he came in and announced, "I hit Granddaddy three times. I hit him in the head, in the leg, and I hit him in the wee-wee." Everyone got a big laugh out of that. Kelly was afraid I would get hit in the face, so one day she ordered me a catcher's mask. I'm probably the only pitcher in history to wear a catcher's mask.

Kelly had been separated from her husband David since 2010. Her divorce became final in 2017. Shortly after her separation, she became friends with Scott DeBoer, which would turn into a romantic relationship.

They had attended high school together at the Fayetteville Academy, where they both played on the varsity basketball teams. Scott was point guard for the Eagles and led his team to a State Championship. He was also Kelly's escort at the homecoming game during her senior year. Both Kelly and Scott graduated from the University of North Carolina at Chapel Hill, although they did not see each other during their college days.

Kelly and Scott are engaged, but I don't think a date has been set. They now live in beautiful Carolina Lakes and are considering purchasing the home they are now renting. Like Kelly, Scott is the victim of a failed marriage. He has two lovely teenage daughters, Abby and Grace. They seem to get along well with Kelly, and they love Blake like a little brother. Blake even calls them his "sisters". Scott is a hard-working, fun-loving. conservative, patriotic American who loves family and country. The only bad thing about Scott is that he's a "Yankee", being from Pennsylvania, but I don't hold that against him. Just joking. We have come to love and respect him as he does us. He has done so much for us the past few years. Scott is the regional manager for a flooring company, and he has installed new carpet in both of our bath rooms and new floors in our kitchen and dining room, as well as painting the kitchen, including the cabinets. He and Kelly also replaced the sliding glass door in the dining room.

Scott's father is a retired physician, and his mother is a nurse. They reside in Fayetteville. He has one brother, Todd, in San Diego, CA, who has a young teenage daughter, Allie, a very sweet girl.

We Live about 100 miles from the Carolina coast, and although it is a prime target for hurricanes, we rarely get hurricane force winds in our area, but it does occasionally happen. In 2016, strong winds from hurricane Matthew blew down a very large pine tree in our back yard, which took out more than 50 feet of chain length fence on the back side of the swimming pool. We were very fortunate that it didn't hit the house. After that, maintenance problems began popping up everywhere. The sinks in both bathrooms became completely clogged because of the 50-year old plumbing. The drains on the bathtub and washing machine were also bad. Next our dryer broke down, and the ice-maker stopped working. After that, a power window on the Mustang stopped working, and we needed rear brakes on the Monte Carlo. We also had two places where the floor needed repair. It was never ending problems, and we had company coming for the weekend. Our long-time friend, Edna Johnson, along with daughter Jamie and a friend of Jamie, from Kentucky, would be spending a night with us. Edna's husband, C.W., had developed several serious medical problems over the past few years, including kidney failure. His daughter, Ammia, had donated a kidney to him, but later he began suffering from liver failure and in February 2017, he passed away.

After our company had left on Sunday afternoon, Juanita came to me and said, "You're not going to believe this." I said, "What is it?" She said, "Edna told me to get the plumbing in the bathrooms fixed, and she handed me this." I looked at the check. I was speechless. Nobody would think enough of us to give us that kind of money. Another miracle had happened. This was truly a blessing from a wonderful friend who had been inspired by God. When I expressed my gratitude to her, I asked why she did it. She said she just wanted to help us, and when one does a good deed, it comes back two-fold.

By shopping around and getting Juanita's nephew, a plumber and also a minister, from Winston-Salem, we not only got the plumbing done, but everything I mentioned above, was also taken care of.

Juanita's sister, Jewell, who passed away in 2016 left her car, a 2005 Monte Carlo to her son, Lloyd. Lloyd offered the car to us at a price we couldn't pass up, and we purchased it from him. That car had about 60,000 fewer miles on it than did our 2004. Not needing three cars, we parked the '04 in the front yard with a "For Sale" sign on it, and within a week it was gone. The '04 had much nicer wheels, so we switched wheels on the two cars and we kept the cargo net from the '04.

After being diagnosed with stage-4 prostate cancer, I responded well to the treatment for two years. Then I began to experience some pain in my legs and hips. My check-up in December of 2017 showed that my PSA was 150. My Lupron injection was no longer doing the job. My oncologist explained that my adrenal gland was beginning to take over and was producing testosterone. We needed to find a new treatment. A powerful new drug called Zytiga had been found to be highly effective for prostate cancer in most patients. There were two problems with Zytiga. It could cause some serious side effects, and it was also very expensive. A month's supply could cost $11,000. I applied for the medication through the patient assistance program and fortunately, was approved at no charge. After three weeks on Zytiga, my PSA was 18 and after three months, it was 2.6. That was the first time it had been normal in 12-years. Three months later it was only 0.73. Side effects have been minimal. The most noticeable thing is that I don't seem to have the strength I once had, but that I can handle. I feel great and stay as active as possible.

On my next birthday, I will be 80 years old. Despite the fact that I have stage-4 prostate cancer, going blind with advanced glaucoma and poor hearing, I am continuing to enjoy life to the fullest. I am so blessed that my mind is still in good working condition, because Alzheimer's seems to run on my mother's side of the family. It hurts not being able to drive anymore, but I have the most wonderful wife in the world that drives me wherever I need to go and to do all the little things I can't see how to do.

My typical day starts out by my arising at 6 AM, sometimes earlier. The first thing I do is take my cancer medication, Zytiga. Then I clean up any dirty dishes from the evening before, and I make a pot of coffee. During the school year, Kelly drops Blake off around 7 AM each day. I always have breakfast prepared for him and make sure that he brushes his teeth and has his hair combed. Since he goes to a Christian school, he had many Bible verses to memorize, and I try to help with that as much as I can. On Monday, Wednesday, and Friday, Juanita is up at 6:30 and making herself more beautiful. At 7:30 she and Blake are on the way to school. Blake's other grandmother comes over on Tuesday and Thursday to take him to school. Sometimes I have breakfast with Blake, or I might wait until he leaves. I clean up the kitchen again, hook up the dishwasher if need be, take out the trash, and make the bed. Juanita is usually back home by 8:30. Then it's time to do the outside chores. During the summer, I care for the pool by adding the chemicals, cleaning out the skimmer, and vacuuming out leaves whenever necessary. We most always have domestic ducks on the pond, and we also have some wild Canadian geese that stay here, so I put out corn or scratch feed for them. I also feed the fish. It's amazing how they can see me as I approach the pond, even from a long distance. You can see waves coming across the water as they swim toward me. I usually try to take a little walk each morning for exercise. It seems that we have to make a trip almost every day, whether it be a medical appointment, or just pick up something from the store. Sometimes Juanita will pick up Blake at school in the afternoon, if his father is unable to do so.

During the day, we watch some TV and play video games. Juanita usually prepares dinner for us, which is about the only time we sit down for a meal together. We watch the news every evening, and maybe a few more programs before retiring around 9:30 or 10 o'clock. About two evenings per week, I will be playing music somewhere. Sometimes Juanita will take me to the place I am playing, but many times I will ride with Tim Marks, one of my best friends.

David Sears, my ex-son-in-law lives in the large house next door, a home that he and Kelly built. Although we do not approve of some of his activities which resulted in their break-up, we have remained good friends. David once told me that he looks up to me like a father. I don't think there's anything he wouldn't do for us. Among other things he keeps the grass cut and trimmed in our large yard and hauls the garbage away on a regular basis. He has two dogs, and I usually stop by each day to take them a milk bone treat. They look forward to that.

In May 2018, I rode with Juanita to Chapel Hill for her annual check-up by her oncologist-gynecologist. As we drove along, I heard a new and strange noise, that appeared to be coming from somewhere at the front of the car. The noise reminded me of the sound made by a model airplane. I thought it might be coming from the front differential, but I wasn't sure. I said to Juanita, "I don't like that sound. I hope the car doesn't fall apart." The noise stayed consistent throughout our trip and upon returning home, I suggested we stop by our local mechanic, Chuck Hines, at Auto Business. Upon describing the noise, he said, "That sounds like a wheel bearing. Does the sound change when you turn either left or right?" I thought I had noticed a slight change but wasn't sure. He had one of his mechanics drive the car, and we definitely noticed a change in the sound. He put the car on the rack and checked it out. He said, "Sir, you are fortunate that the wheel didn't fall off the car, and not only that, the wheel was leaning to one side so badly, that the tire was worn down to the steel belt. It could have blown out at any moment." To repair the car and get a new tire would be $400.00. I said, "Chuck, I don't have the money to repair it today." He said, "When can you pay me?" I told him I could pay him in about 10 days. He said that would be fine. I had been a customer with them since they opened the shop nearly 23 years earlier, and I had given them lots of business, including buying two cars, otherwise, I don't think he would have extended me the credit. Later that afternoon the car was ready. We were so thankful that we had made it home that day. The good Lord was definitely watching over us. When I went back to pay him a few days later, Chuck said, "It's already been paid." "By whom?", I asked. His answer, "By someone who really cares for you." Another blessing had come our way.

Tim Marks is my best musician friend. He lives on a small farm about 14 miles from me. His first love is horses. At age 75, Tim doesn't do much riding anymore, but he keeps two horses in the pasture and is dedicated to caring for them. I met him about 10 years ago, at about the same time he began playing the guitar and singing. He has a great voice, and I believe he would go out and play every night if he had a place to play.

Since I don't drive anymore, Tim is always there to offer me a ride to wherever we happen to be playing, if Juanita doesn't take me. We entertain once a month at two different rest homes in Sanford. Every Thursday night, we try to go to Fayetteville and play with some of our musician friends. Our audience is almost entirely made up of seniors, and we have an open mic, meaning that anyone from the audience can sing if they choose. Our home base is Anderson Creek, a community near Spring Lake, NC. We play at the home of Charles and Nellie Griffin, who have converted a free-standing, two-car garage into the "Gathering Place." We play there on the 1st and 3rd Friday of each month. The guests bring food, and we start the evening with a prayer, then enjoy a great meal and play music for a couple of hours. A dance floor is available for those who care to dance. We have made some very nice friends there. No alcohol is allowed at any of the places we play, just old-fashioned fun.

I mentioned earlier how Juanita and I enjoy playing games. One of our favorites is a video game called "Ruzzle", a game where you have a block of 16 letters. The object of the game is to make as many words as possible in two minutes by connecting the letters. Not only do we play each other, but we play people from all over the country, many of them on a regular basis. These are on our list of Ruzzle friends. You can also chat with your opponent while playing, although most players don't chat, they just want to play. This past Christmas, I wished all my "friends" a "Merry Christmas from North Carolina." I had responses from friends in New York, Pennsylvania, Michigan, and Tennessee. I had never chatted with anyone on line, so one day, for some strange reason, I decided to see if anyone would like to chat with me. With almost all my friends being female, I first got permission from Juanita, to make sure she didn't mind. She said it was OK as long as I didn't flirt.

Since I had never chatted with a stranger online, I didn't know exactly how to "break the ice". March madness, the NCAA basketball tournament, was just getting underway, so I chose three ladies who were from states with teams playing in the tournament, and I asked if they were fans of those teams. The lady from Tennessee was the first to respond, saying she was a huge fan of the Tennessee Vols. She introduced herself as Sherrie. I told her I was Johnny, but she could call me John. The lady from Michigan said she pulled for both Michigan and Michigan State, but she wasn't really a fan, and she also wasn't interested in chatting. I asked the lady from Pennsylvania about Villanova, one of the favorites in the tournament. She responded by saying she was not a fan of Villanova, but rather pulled for Penn State. I told her my name, and she introduced herself as Lori, and she was more than willing to chat. During our early chats, she told me she had once lived in Georgia, my home state, and to my surprise, she said she might possibly move to North Carolina when her 14-year old son graduated from high school. She was surprised to learn that she had also been playing Ruzzle on a regular basis with my wife. Lori Piekanski is an elementary school teacher. She is a fun-loving person with a great sense of humor. We have a great time competing against each other in Ruzzle. I hope our friendship can be a lasting one.

Sherrie Farmer impressed me as being one of the most amazing people I have ever met. She is obviously a highly educated person and very well-off. She is a Latin teacher and is mother to seven children, and she home schooled all of them. She is also a born-again Christian. Sherrie lives with her husband, Ken, in Johnson City, TN. I don't know why, but one day I told her briefly about myself and the business I had been in. She responded by telling me that my life sounded like a movie or a good book. I couldn't get that thought off my mind. A few days later, it hit me. I had a very strong feeling I was being told to write a book! In my 79 years, writing a book had never crossed my mind. But that day, in April 2018, I sat down at the computer and began writing. I did not miss a single day of writing, and four months later my story was completed.

With my age and medical condition, I have no idea how long I have on this earth, but my dream is to get my book published. If that happens, I feel like my work here is done. Oh, by the way, Sherrie has invited Juanita and me to come to Johnson City, and she and Ken will take us to dinner. I look forward to meeting them, and I promised to take Sherrie an autographed copy of my book. As my life comes to a close, I have never been happier or felt more blessed.

CHAPTER **21**

Looking Back

AS I LOOK back on my life, I have many questions about things that happened, how they happened, and why they happened. I have a lot more questions than answers. At a very young age, I remember my Grandpa Gordon Chambers saying, "The Lord works in mysterious ways." That's the only answer I can come up with on so many of my questions.

The very first incident that comes to mind, was the first night I was back from my first tour of duty in Germany. My mother-in-law sent me out to their store for drinks. I didn't know which door the key fit, and by the time I found the right one and turned on the light, I was looking down the barrel of my father-in-law's shotgun. Knowing his reputation, I would have to say the odds were, he would have pulled the trigger before I switched on the light. Did the hand of God stop him?

I have looked death in the face on several other occasions, like the time I went fishing in the Gulf of Mexico with my dad and brother, Jimmy. We got caught in that storm, and foolishly, didn't put on our life preservers. Had the boat capsized, and it easily could have, no doubt we would have all drowned. Not only that, but another boat nearly crashed into us. Someone was certainly looking out for us that day.

Then, there was the night I did the foolish thing by visiting Gloria, a married woman whose husband was one bad dude. He got pleasure from killing Viet-Cong soldiers and cutting off their private parts. He could have easily come home and caught me that night. Someone protected me.

This one is the worst of all. I don't even like to talk about it, but at one time in my life a hit man was approached, and a request was made to take me out. I was saved only because the person requesting the hit could not come up with the money the assassin wanted up front. No doubt my life was spared for some reason.

The most recent one occurred a few short years ago when I was attending a basketball game to see Blake play. I walked up on a four-foot high stage to sit and watch the game. With my poor vision, I was just one step away from stepping off the stage, and I was contemplating taking that step, and I couldn't see the stage's edge. Had I fallen from that distance and my head hit the hard-wood floor, I could have been killed, or certainly, seriously injured. That incident preyed on my mind for a long time. Without a doubt, the hand of God reached out and kept me from taking that step.

I've made some terrible mistakes along the way, but the first to come to mind was the affair I had with Elizabeth, the German girl. That was wrong, but why did I have to tell my wife? That was also not only wrong, but stupid. I think I know the answer to that one. It was because I had a terrible feeling of guilt, and it was preying heavily on my mind. By telling her, I thought it would make me feel better. I didn't consider what it would do to our marriage. That was likely a decision that changed the course of our marriage and my life.

Then in Germany, when I neglected my family by putting my music first. Then my wife leaves, saying she doesn't love or want to be with me anymore. Then Vera, the Swiss lady and I fall head-over-heels in love and start talking about someday being married. Should I have taken my wife back after she changed her mind? Was dumping Vera, and breaking her heart the right thing to do? I probably did the right thing for the sake of the kids. After all, they were innocent, and they loved and needed their parents. Would a marriage to Vera have worked out? That's a tough one. She had been cautioned to not get involved with me because of her superior education and coming from a very well-to-do family. Vera couldn't see that, probably because she was blinded by love. We were totally different, except that we were both lab technicians, and we both needed lots of love and attention. I truly have my doubts that a marriage could have been a happy one for either of us. Finally, did our break-up have any bearing on her committing suicide? Probably not, because of the time lapse, although I was deeply concerned about that happening immediately after our break-up.

Sometimes a small decision will make a huge change in the direction of one's life. When I was coming home from my second tour of duty in Germany, I suddenly made a last-minute decision to stop off at Fayetteville to visit my good friend Bobby Melton. That decision ended up getting me assigned to the Special Forces at Ft. Bragg, as opposed to being assigned to the hospital lab at Ft. Ord, CA.

Why did I break my leg in jump school? Technically, I know the answer to that one, but was there another reason? That injury kept me at Ft. Bragg instead of having to go to Vietnam. Staying at Bragg allowed me to get that job at Cape Fear Valley Hospital Laboratory, and ultimately the decision to leave the military after 10 years.

The Bible says, "The Lord giveth and the Lord taketh away." It also tells us that we will reap what we sow. I believe that both of those applied to me after I left the military in 1967. I was fortunate to get that job as supervisor of the hospital blood bank. Then a few years later, along came the woman of my dreams, Juanita. I have said many times that she was a gift from God. Was she? That I can't answer. I only know that she has been my best friend and has made me happy for almost 50 years. I hope God will see fit for us to reach that milestone in 2022. Our marriage has also resulted in the most beautiful, and wonderful daughter and grandson we could ever dream for. This happened despite the fact that Juanita had tried to become pregnant during her 14-year marriage to her first husband, and it could not happen.

We struggled during our early years of marriage, but we went to church and we thanked God for what we had. Then we were rewarded by finding a way to the American Dream with those rare blood group antibodies. Several miracles occurred during our path to success. Every time it looked like we were destined to fail, something miraculous happened. Did we simply get lucky or was there a power out there watching over us? I believe there was.

Then after we succeeded in our business, we forgot about God. Instead of going to church, we went to parties and began enjoying the worldly things we could enjoy with our money. Plainly, we were living a life that was not pleasing to God. Then after nearly 10 years, we lost everything. Did we really lose it or was it taken away? That's another question I can't answer with any certainty. Now we would struggle for 20 years, until Juanita was on death's doorsteps. That's when we finally saw the light, and her life was miraculously spared, when no one thought she would live.

Since that day in 2009, we have lived a different life. Even though we don't go to church as often as we should, we thank God for our blessings every day, and each Sunday morning, I listen to preaching on TV. I currently listen to a well-known pastor and Bible teacher from Dallas, Texas.

Blessings are once again flowing. I still can't get over the means and timely manner by which we received the funds to take care of all those major repair jobs that I described in chapter 20. Were those simple co-incidences? No way! Coincidences just don't occur that timely and that frequently.

Sometimes I wonder why we are still here. My ex-wife and Juanita's ex-husband both died 15 years ago. Obviously, God still has plans for us. Our work is not yet done.

One more thought that I think about frequently; something my dear old mother said to me many years ago. She said, "Johnny, if you are a child of God and you live a sinful life, you will pay for those sins, before you leave this earth." Maybe she was right. Just maybe that's why I'm afflicted with blindness from glaucoma and stage-4 prostate cancer. I've assumed it was stubbornness and stupidity on my part, but there just may be more to it than that.

I truly believe God wanted me to tell my story. I now understand why I had such a strong desire to talk with Sherrie. Talk about working in mysterious ways, I could never have imagined that God would have conveyed His message to me through a born-again Christian in Tennessee, someone I had never met, in a video game!

The End

CPSIA information can be obtained
at www.ICGtesting.com
Printed in the USA
BVHW040438040419
544536BV00002B/2/P